The Negotiator
Freeing Gilad Schalit from Hamas

Toby

Gershon Baskin

THE NEGOTIATOR

FREEING GILAD SCHALIT FROM HAMAS

WITH

Ilene Prusher

The Toby Press

The Negotiator
Freeing Gilad Schalit from Hamas

First Edition © 2013

The Toby Press LLC

POB 8531, New Milford, CT 06776–8531, USA
& POB 2455, London W1A 5WY, England
& POB 4044, Jerusalem 91040, Israel
www.tobypress.com

Gershon Baskin © 2013

Back Cover Photo: Edna Baskin

ISBN 978 159 264 349 3, *hardcover*

A CIP catalogue record for this title is
available from the British Library

Printed and bound in the United States

I dedicate this book –

to Edna, my wife,
who continues to demonstrate remarkable
patience, understanding, encouragement, and love;

to my three children, Elisha, Ben, and Amit,
who will hopefully soon live in peace;

to David Meidan,
with whom great achievements were made,
and hopefully will continue to be made, in the future;

and finally, to Gilad Schalit,
may you cherish every day of freedom.

Contents

Prologue

This book goes behind the scenes during the five years and four months of work to bring Gilad Schalit home, examining the many circumstances and factors that combined to clinch the final deal. At the same time, this book is also the personal story of how I, an Israeli who had spent thirty years working for peace between Israelis and Palestinians, felt empowered and determined to bridge gaps and build trust where none existed.

Only the prime minister of Israel and the leadership of the Hamas Islamic Resistance Movement were responsible for reaching an agreement. I was never in a position to make decisions and had neither the responsibility nor the authority to broker any understandings between officials. Nonetheless, I used my experience, knowledge, and ideas to develop contacts and convince officials that a deal was possible.

The deal could have been made years before. Gilad Schalit should not have languished all that time in Gaza. This book reveals the many lost opportunities over the years. David Meidan, the senior Mossad[1] officer appointed by Prime Minister Benjamin Netanyahu in April 2011

---

1. Israel's intelligence agency.

to bring Schalit home, had the courage, confidence, and experience to recognize the opportunity I presented to him. He trusted me, and used my ideas and connections to get to Schalit's captors. As promised, I kept our contacts and back channel top secret. Once Netanyahu understood that this channel was real and that I could be trusted to leak nothing to the press, he gave Meidan the green light. It was Meidan who convinced him that a deal could be made with risks that were acceptable for Israel's security. That assessment was based on the work I conducted with my counterpart in Hamas, Ghazi Hamad, which produced the declaration of principles that guided the final negotiations and brought Gilad home.

Aspects of the story still remain secret. Perhaps one day they will be disclosed. Meanwhile, the account presented here is based on over seven hundred pages of documentation, e-mails, text messages, faxes, and notes following more than five years of continuous activity. There were periods of frustration, anger, and despair. But this tale is also full of hope and intrigue, of passionate dedication to a mission, and of the naïve, wildly optimistic belief that one citizen can make a difference.

Gershon Baskin
August, 2013
Jerusalem

Chapter 1

The Abduction

The Palestinians entered before dawn, hoping the Israelis would be asleep. The militants descended from Gaza through an underground tunnel dug near the Kerem Shalom border crossing between the coastal strip and Israel. When they emerged, they were inside Israel, having infiltrated the powerful state that they – members of Hamas' Ezzedin al Qassam Brigades, the Popular Resistance Committees, and the Army of Islam – viewed as their sworn enemy. They ambushed an Israeli army post from behind, hitting a tank with rocket-propelled grenades and semi-automatic Kalashnikov rifles. In the ensuing fight, Israeli soldiers killed two of the eight Palestinians, while the Palestinians had felled two Israelis and injured three.

Cpl. Gilad Schalit

What would change history was the wounded young soldier the Palestinians managed to capture and then spirit back to Gaza. They had kidnapped Corporal Gilad Schalit, a nineteen-year-old from Mitzpe Hila, in northern Israel. Hardly anyone had ever heard of it, but the international media would soon descend on the small

3

community – and people the world over would come to know Gilad's name. Presidents and prime ministers would spend hours working for his release. Prayers would be composed and read across the globe, posters would be hung, demonstrations held – all expressing the hope that the soldier who'd abruptly lost his childhood would come home to his family.

On that very Sunday morning, June 25, 2006, I was attending the last day of a conference of the Israeli-Palestinian Peace NGO Forum at the Dead Sea in Jordan. We had just finished breakfast and were gathering in the lobby with our luggage for checkout. There were about one hundred Israeli and Palestinian participants, some from Gaza. The hotel's Israeli cell phone reception was limited. I wanted to hear the news and check my messages, so I went out behind the hotel, looking for a signal from Israel. I dialed *11 and heard the news on the Voice of Israel's Channel 1 radio broadcast, which reported an attack on the Kerem Shalom base of the Israel Defense Forces (IDF) near Gaza, including casualties. That didn't sound like big news. But I was experienced enough, particularly after the Second Intifada and almost daily reports of attacks against Israelis, to detect the tension in the reporters' voices.

Something terrible had happened.

I came back into the hotel and told my colleagues what I'd heard. The Palestinian delegates were concerned about how they'd get home that day – would the border be closed? Our Palestinian colleagues tuned into Palestinian radio and other Arab sources and immediately reported that an Israeli soldier had been abducted and taken to Gaza. But there were no such reports on the Israeli news. Whom were we to believe?

I had been in this situation many times – being in the midst of a meeting of Israeli and Palestinian peace activists when something bad happened back home. During the worst years of the Second Intifada, we could not convene such meetings in Israel or in Palestine. If there was a Palestinian attack in Israel or an Israeli attack in Palestine, the meeting would immediately end. People wanted to hurry home, where they felt more secure surrounded by family. Holding meetings abroad, however, meant that when attacks took place at home, the gatherings would continue, but the participants would be forced to confront the most horrendous aspects of our conflict. Sometimes those meetings would be extremely tense and difficult. Sometimes we would need to take a break. Sometimes the Israelis had to sit in one room and the Palestinians in another in order to talk among themselves.

A meeting of the Peace NGO Forum was somewhat different. The delegates were used to being with people from the other side when terror struck. Nonetheless, looking around the hotel lobby, it was quite obvious that the Israelis were sitting together and the Palestinians were huddled among themselves, all trying to gather information and determine the gravity of the situation. This audacious attack had taken place just five months after Hamas' victory in the Palestinian parliamentary elections. If an Israeli soldier had indeed been abducted, we were now entering a new era.

An image of Nachshon Wachsman flashed through my mind. This young Israeli soldier had been kidnapped by Hamas in the West Bank in October 1994, and killed not a week later, when an Israeli commando raid failed to secure his release. If another soldier had now been abducted, it would be much more difficult to work for peace.

I had no idea how the capture of Gilad Schalit would change my life and how, over the next five years and four months, his life and mine would intersect. On that June morning, sitting on the shores of the Dead Sea in Jordan, looking westward toward Israel, all I could think of was how tragic our situation was. How many innocent Israelis and Palestinians would be killed as a result of this attack?

But I'd been involved in Israeli-Palestinian peacemaking groups for thirty years. This wasn't the first act of violence to yank the rug out from under us, eclipsing our attempts at dialogue and reconciliation. Rather than sink into despair, I usually ended up feeling more determined than ever to work toward ending the conflict.

So I went home and got on the phone. And started sending e-mails. As it happened, two months earlier I'd forged a connection with some important figures in Hamas.

Naturally, the fact that I had contacts in Hamas raised eyebrows. Hamas, which means "enthusiasm" in Arabic and is also an acronym for the Islamic Resistance Movement, is classified as a terrorist organization by many countries – including the US, where I grew up, and Israel, where I've been a citizen since 1978. But Hamas also has a political wing, which has been governing Gaza since a coup deposed its Fatah rivals in

June 2007. True, the organization's charter calls for the destruction of Israel, my chosen home. But after three decades of work on resolving the Israeli-Arab conflict, I understood the complexities of Palestinian politics well. I had seen sworn enemies communicate, if not necessarily agree. I knew that if I could get the right people talking, we could bring Gilad home.

Oddly enough, I'd recently confronted the reality of another Israeli hostage. In this small country where the tragedy of conflict has touched every family, he was one of my own relatives.

Chapter 2

Making Contact

In September 2005, I was in Switzerland at an Israeli-Palestinian conference on the future of Jerusalem. My wife, Edna, called me, her voice trembling. Her cousin Sasson Nuriel had disappeared. He had gone to his workplace – a factory in a settlement outside Jerusalem. He'd told his wife he was going to Ramallah with a coworker to look at some equipment. He hadn't come home.

The family asked me to use my Palestinian connections to see if anyone knew what had happened to him. It had been illegal for Israelis to enter Palestinian cities such as Ramallah since the beginning of the Second Intifada in October 2000. The Israeli army forbade it, considering it too dangerous.

Sasson had met many Palestinians through his work, befriending several. (Sasson was of Iraqi descent and spoke fluent Arabic.) A few months earlier, I had spoken with him at a family gathering. He'd told me about his Palestinian friends and his belief in peace. Abdallah Arrar, a former employee of Sasson's, had an older brother who was a senior member of Ezzedin al Qassam, Hamas' military wing. The Israel Security

Agency (ISA)[1] had asked Sasson to organize a meeting with Arrar in an attempt to recruit him to work for Israel. The meeting had taken place and Arrar had rejected the offer. The ISA then instructed Sasson to fire him, and Arrar was forbidden to reenter Israeli industrial zones in the West Bank and Israel.

Some five years later, Sasson met Arrar in an industrial zone and understood that he had been allowed to return to work in Israel. Sasson rehired him. Arrar convinced Sasson to go with him to Ramallah to see a machine he could purchase and resell in Israel in order to supplement his factory wages. Arrar was accompanied by Ali Kati, who had been working in the factory only a few days. Sasson was reluctant to go, but he had known Arrar for a decade, so he felt safe wandering into enemy territory with his employee.

I asked Hanna Siniora, my co-director at the Israel Palestine Center for Research and Information (IPCRI)[2] in Jerusalem, to go to Ramallah and see whether anyone knew anything about Sasson. Siniora went all over the city. He visited the headquarters of the Palestinian security forces and even met with Ramallah's chief of police, Mohammed Salah. But no luck.

On September 27, six days after Sasson's disappearance, Hamas released a videotape of him handcuffed, blindfolded, and bleeding. The video had been recorded, it later became apparent, several hours before Sasson was brutally murdered with a butcher knife. He left behind a wife and three children.

Sasson was my wife's age; they had grown up together in the same town. His family had asked me to help find him, to save him, but I'd failed. I later learned that one of Sasson's murderers, the head of the Hamas cell responsible for his abduction, was Yasser Mohammed Salah, son of the Ramallah police chief. The latter was arrested by Israel but released after it was found that he'd had no knowledge of his son joining Hamas.

1. The Israeli equivalent of the CIA, the ISA was formerly called the General Security Service and is also known by the Hebrew acronym Shin Bet.
2. An Israeli-Palestinian public-policy think tank I founded in March 1988, co-directing it until December 2011.

Hours after Sasson was murdered, Said Siyam, one of the leaders of Hamas in Gaza, promised more kidnappings of Israelis in order to free Palestinian prisoners from Israeli jails.

I attended Sasson's funeral late at night in Jerusalem. There were hundreds of people there, family members as well as many who had not even known him. I vividly remember standing over his grave, feeling horrible and sad. I had worked with Palestinians for decades, but all of my contacts had done nothing to save Sasson. I swore on his grave that if ever again asked to help save a life, I would do everything humanly possible to accomplish that mission. I would not rest until I'd succeeded.

Seven months later, and two months before Gilad Schalit was abducted, I was in Cairo attending the United Nations Seminar on Assistance to the Palestinian People. It was late April 2006. While there, my friend Professor Mohammed Samhouri of Gaza's al-Azhar University introduced me to Dr. Mohammed Migdad of the Islamic University of Gaza, who had been his student. Migdad had traveled from Gaza to Cairo just to meet an Israeli. Migdad was a member of Hamas. We were both treading on new territory.

Migdad had never met an Israeli or a Jew. Despite all my years of working with Palestinians, I had never met anyone from Hamas. He wanted to speak with me and I was equally interested in speaking with him. We left the conference and spent the next two days together discussing politics, philosophy, theology, and history.

Back in 1976, as a student at New York University, I'd met with the Palestine Liberation Organization (PLO) ambassador to the United Nations, Zuhdi Labib Terzi. Several other young Zionists and I had urged the ambassador to recognize the State of Israel and support a two-state solution to the Israeli-Palestinian conflict. Terzi was a real gentleman and an astute diplomat, but his response was far from diplomatic. "Over my dead body," he said. "The Palestinian people will never recognize the legitimacy of Israel's existence. You Jews should go back to where you came from and allow us to live in our land, Palestine."

Since 1976, a lot of water had passed under the proverbial bridge. In 1988, the PLO had adopted the two-state solution, and in 1993, the official leadership of the Palestinian people had entered into a peace process with Israel based on mutual recognition. Yet my conversation with Migdad was like a time warp. Having never had any contact with Israelis or Jews, he was filled with misconceptions about who we are. He couldn't imagine that there were Israelis, like myself, who wanted peace with Palestinians and had devoted their lives to working for it. He thought we were all colonialist invaders who wanted to dispossess all Palestinians of their land and their rights. Migdad simply could not envision himself supporting peace based on two states for two peoples. But that didn't stop me from entering into a dialogue with him. I have always been willing to speak with anyone willing to speak with me.

Professor Migdad and I decided to continue meeting and talking, and to try creating a forum for discreet dialogue, which would include additional Israeli and Hamas academics. Those meetings couldn't take place in Gaza, which Israelis would rightfully be frightened to visit. Neither could they be held in Israel, from which Hamas members were barred. The sessions had to be held in a third country, one that neither boycotted Hamas nor deemed it a terrorist organization. Arab states aside, and since we didn't want to travel too far, only four possibilities existed: Russia, Switzerland, Norway, and Turkey. I approached officials in each country. All were willing to provide safe, discreet facilities for dialogue between Hamas and Israelis.

Encouraged by this response, on May 23, 2006, I sent Professor Migdad the following e-mail:

Dear Dr. Mohammed,

I hope you are well. I would like to follow up the discussion we began in Cairo. We have an invitation from the International Center for Strategic and Political Studies in Moscow to bring together a small group of Palestinians affiliated with Hamas and a parallel group of Israelis in order to begin a dialogue on the future of Palestinian-Israeli relations. There are no preconditions for this meeting. We thought we might focus the discussion on the issue of hudna,[3] but we have not

---

3. *Hudna* is an Arabic term meaning truce or cease-fire based on Islamic law.

made any decisions. The participants will ultimately have to agree on the subjects for discussions. The invitation will be issued by our Russian friends.

I want to make sure you are still willing to participate and to check if you could recommend additional participants from the Palestinian side. We would like about five people from each side. Hanna Siniora and I will also attend the meetings. We are talking about sometime in mid-July for the first meeting. Please let me know your thoughts. I look forward to speaking with you again.

Best wishes,
Gershon Baskin

Migdad wrote back to me the same day:

Dear Dr. Gershon,

First of all, thanks for the follow-up. It is good to start a discussion between us on different issues, including the hudna. I'll share your e-mail with others and suggest some additional participants. I think some Hamas figures will agree to participate, and I hope a member of the Legislative Council[4] will accept as well.

Dr. M. I. Migdad

I was very encouraged by Migdad's positive response. I notified our Russian hosts that we would accept their invitation. The Russians requested that I send them photocopies of the Hamas participants' passports so that visas could be arranged. I called Migdad, and he told me he would send them the following day.

I waited a day, two days, one week, and two weeks, but the passports didn't arrive. I understood from Migdad that there were political problems. I told him I would come to Gaza to discuss how to overcome these difficulties.

---

4. The Palestinian Parliament.

A few days later, Hanna Siniora and I traveled to Gaza. We both had Israeli-government-issued press cards. Hanna had been the editor and publisher of the Fatah-connected *Al Fajr* daily. More recently, he was producing an Internet version of a Palestinian daily, the *Jerusalem Times*. I'd started writing a weekly column in this publication, called "This Week in Israel: Behind the News with Gershon Baskin," along with my weekly "Encountering Peace" column in the *Jerusalem Post*. My two columns earned me a press card, which permitted me to venture into the Palestinian areas. However, Israeli citizens who enter these territories must sign papers releasing the government of Israel from any responsibility should anything happen to them. I signed without hesitation.

We went from the Erez crossing between Israel and Gaza directly to the Islamic University. We met Migdad in his office and then several of his colleagues. Migdad explained that they were afraid to participate in dialogue with Israelis unless they had "the green light" from the Hamas political leadership. This fear was understandable considering Hamas' non-recognition of Israel and prohibition of contact with Israelis. Migdad suggested that we try speaking to someone from the Hamas leadership.

We drove in Migdad's car to the office of Hamas Prime Minister Ismail Haniyeh. There we were directed to the office of Dr. Ahmed Yousef, Haniyeh's political adviser. Yousef is considered a leading moderate in Hamas as well as one of its main ideologues. He lived for years in Fairfax, Virginia, where he was a professor and directed the United Association for Studies and Research (UASR), an Islamic political think tank. Yousef was deported from the United States for being a Hamas member and fundraiser.

Dr. Ahmed Yousef

After a long, probing discussion with Yousef, he agreed to join the group. Migdad and I left Yousef's office satisfied that he could give his colleagues the green light and that we could proceed. So I went back to Jerusalem and once again waited for the photocopies of the Palestinian passports. And once again, I waited a day, two days, a week, two weeks. And then I understood that the Hamas political leadership had vetoed our dialogue.

Just over two weeks later, on June 9, 2006, a bomb exploded on a north Gaza beach, killing eight family members, three of them children. Hamas accused Israel of attacking the Ghaliya family intentionally and responded with rocket fire for the first time since its truce sixteen months earlier. The Israeli army said it regretted the deaths, saying that the explosives on the beach were likely from artillery shells that had landed there when Israel fired into the Gaza Strip in response to the launching of hundreds of Palestinian rockets into the country.

The following day, Hamas officially withdrew from the ceasefire and unleashed barrages of rockets and mortars on Israel's civilian population.

On June 12, I wrote to Professor Migdad:

Dear Dr. Migdad,

I would like to express my sincere condolences on the killing of so many innocent civilians. This senseless violence must end. My heart weeps for those who were killed, and I extend my deepest sympathy to their families.

I hope that the decision of Ezzedin al Qassam[5] to renew fighting is only a temporary release of anger, and that this will not lead us to even further violence and suffering. People of reason must do everything to end this madness. Please accept my condolences and share my prayers that we have the wisdom to get back on the track of peace.

Sincerely,
Gershon

5. Ezzedin al Qassam is the military wing of Hamas, which would later be responsible for the abduction of Gilad Schalit.

Migdad replied:

> *Dear Gershon,*
>
> *Thanks a lot for your letter. The killing of innocent civilians on Friday and the continuous killing is not reasonable, and it is too difficult to understand. In my opinion, and based on knowing the Hamas fighters, I consider their decision non-final and only a release of anger. But if the hudna is important to the Israeli government, Israel has to help in this matter, stop killing Palestinians, and start making their lives easier. The alternative is too terrible for all of us.*
>
> *I hope we can do something. I feel that we need to think of a mediator to help start a discussion between Hamas and the Israeli government as soon as possible, to keep civilians safe on both sides.*
>
> *Dr. M. I. Migdad*

Less than two weeks later, on the morning of June 25, Palestinian fighters ambushed the Israeli army base at Kerem Shalom. In the process, they killed two Israeli soldiers, Hanan Barak and Pavel Slutzker. But it was Gilad Schalit whose name was fated to be in international headlines for the next five years. In the course of the attack, he was wounded from shrapnel from a hand grenade and then abducted. It was at least an hour before Israel discovered he was missing. Soon afterward, Israel closed the Gaza Strip and sent forces there to find him.

Three days later, on June 28, Israeli forces launched a major ground operation, code-named "Summer Rains," aimed at locating the abducted soldier or at least preventing the scenario of his being smuggled out of Gaza. The stated aims of the operation, however, were to prevent the continued firing of Qassam rockets[6] into Israel, and to secure Schalit's release.

---

6. Home-made by the Ezzedin al Qassam Brigades.

On the first day of the operation, Israel bombed the Gaza electricity plant, plunging 65 percent of the Gaza Strip into darkness. Israeli forces also struck roads, bridges, and Hamas military installations. Gaza International Airport, which had long been closed, was placed under Israeli control, and attacks were made on political and civilian targets.

Early on Saturday July 1, Professor Migdad called me at home.

"Gershon," he pleaded, "we are being bombed! We have no electricity, our water has been cut, my children are screaming every time they hear an Israeli plane above our house. People are afraid to go outside. We must do something!"

Prime Minister Ismail Haniyeh

Migdad suggested that we open a line of communication between Israel and Hamas. Perhaps we could figure out a way to resolve the situation and return to the cease-fire. Half an hour after speaking with Migdad, I received a call from Dr. Mohammed Madhoun, the director of the office of Hamas Prime Minister Ismail Haniyeh. Madhoun told me Migdad was there, and asked to open a channel of communication to discuss Schalit's release. He also informed me that someone else from Haniyeh's office would be calling me; he would be my liaison to Hamas.

Dr. Ghazi Hamad called about an hour later. To my surprise, I immediately connected with Ghazi, a Hamas spokesperson and adviser to the prime minister. Ghazi's insistence on speaking Hebrew also took me by surprise.

After discussing the need to open a channel of communication to the Israeli government, Ghazi asked if it was possible to arrange a call between Haniyeh and Noam Schalit, Gilad's father. He suggested that I speak to Schalit and gauge his reaction. As a father with children around Gilad's age, I could not think of a more humanitarian gesture. Ghazi promised to check with Haniyeh and get back to me later that day.

Noam and Aviva Schalit

I phoned Noam Schalit, introduced myself, and said that I had been approached by Hamas with an offer to open a line of communication. I asked Noam if he would be willing to speak with someone from Hamas. "Of course," he responded without hesitation. "I want to know if my son is alive. I want to know his condition. I want to know what they want for his release."

I spent hours that day, and on many occasions in the future, waiting for Ghazi Hamad to call. Throughout the more than five years that we were partners in trying to reach an agreement between Israel and Hamas, Ghazi never disappointed me. Sometimes it took a lot longer than I would have liked to get a response, but in the end, Ghazi always called.

Dr. Ghazi Hamad

Finally, Ghazi got back to me. He said that Haniyeh could not speak with Noam Schalit. As prime minister, he needed to distance himself from the kidnapping, because the attack had been conducted by the military wing of Hamas, which does not consult the political branch. But Ghazi said that he himself would be pleased to speak with Noam Schalit. He made the call.

Ghazi phoned Schalit that afternoon – six days after Gilad's abduction. His main message was that Gilad was alive and well and being treated in accordance with Islamic law, which strictly governs the treatment of prisoners. Ghazi encouraged Noam to lobby the Israeli government to negotiate a prisoner exchange; there were more than ten thousand Palestinians in Israeli prisons at the time.

With thoughts of Sasson Nuriel and how I had failed to save my wife's cousin, I resolved to do everything possible to help bring Gilad Schalit home. I vowed to spare no effort, and to use my experience working for peace, mediating and facilitating dialogue between Israelis and Palestinians. The Schalit imbroglio would be the ultimate test of my ability to build trust and confront one of Israel's most unyielding foes, whose commitment to the state's destruction is based on a religious fervor that is completely foreign to my own secular, rational worldview.

First we had to establish that Schalit was still alive. A sign of life would provide evidence of a channel of communication leading to his captors. It would also ensure that I got through to Israeli Prime Minister Ehud Olmert, who I knew would refuse not only to negotiate with Hamas, a terrorist organization, but to work with a well-known peace activist.

I called Ghazi Hamad and told him that if Hamas wanted a prisoner exchange, as stated in the media and in speeches made by Hamas leaders, it had to provide a credible sign of life. Recalling the videotape Hamas had produced after abducting Sasson Nuriel, I suggested that a video of Schalit be sent to me or to a news agency, or posted on a webpage. Ghazi promised to relay the message to "certain people" able to respond.

The following day, Ghazi informed me that the captors had agreed to deliver a videotape of Schalit – in exchange for the release of all 350 Palestinian women and minors in Israeli prisons. I told him that the government of Israel would likely refuse, but that I would pass the message on to the highest levels.

Matty Stern

Prime Minister Ehud Olmert

The Israeli government was clearly not interested in a negotiated endgame for the release of Schalit. Prime Minister Olmert vociferously maintained, in and out of the Knesset, that Israel would not negotiate with terrorists or release Palestinian prisoners. This position was reiterated by cabinet ministers and military personnel. Olmert declared that Hamas was responsible for Schalit's well-being and would pay dearly for the Kerem Shalom attack, an assault on Israel's sovereignty within its own borders.

I believed that had a successful military rescue of Schalit been possible, it would likely have been the best course. But I had vivid memories of October 1994, when Corporal Nachshon Wachsman was abducted by Hamas. Palestinian President Yasser Arafat asked Prime Minister Yitzhak Rabin to give him time to find Wachsman and bring him home safely. I personally pleaded with Rabin's people to give Arafat the opportunity to find him. I trusted Arafat; Israel didn't.

On October 14, five days after Wachsman's abduction, the ISA located the building where he was being held and sent in a group of Israeli commandos to rescue him. The operation was a colossal failure: Wachsman was killed by his captors as soon as they came under attack. Three Hamas militants and Israeli commander Nir Poraz were also killed in the process; another ten Israeli soldiers were wounded. I did not want Gilad Schalit to be another Nachshon Wachsman.

If Hamas claimed Schalit was alive and the Israeli government believed this to be true, then everything had to be done to bring him home. The State of Israel has an "unwritten covenant" with its citizenry: Israel will leave no soldier behind. It is this doctrine that enables Israel to have a people's army with conscription for most citizens. Our boys are drafted at age eighteen and are expected to serve a minimum of three years, while girls serve two.

I needed to contact Prime Minister Olmert. He knew me, and – as stated above – I understood that he held peace activists like me in low regard. If I wrote to him that I had contacts with the Hamas terrorists holding Schalit, my message would never end up on the prime minister's desk. Phoning wouldn't work either. I had to reach him directly, circumventing the secretaries and other aides whose job it is to intercept people and messages before they reach the prime minister.

An unconventional conduit came to mind: the prime minister's daughter.

Dana Olmert

On June 11, 2005, Dana Olmert had participated in a demonstration against the new IDF Chief of Staff Dan Halutz. Prior to his appointment, Halutz had been the commander of the Israeli Air Force. In July 2002, the air force dropped a one-ton bomb on the home of Salah Shehadeh, head of Hamas' military wing. Fifteen people were killed, in addition to Shehadeh and his wife and daughter, including seven members of the family next door. Between 50 and 150 were injured. When Halutz was asked in an interview about the feelings of a pilot when he drops a bomb that kills so many innocent people, he answered: "I feel a light bump to the plane as a result of the bomb's release. A second later it's gone, and that's all. That's what I feel."

After the anti-Halutz demonstration, Dana Olmert was attacked in the media by politicians from most of the parties in the Knesset. I sent her an e-mail commending her bold act and encouraging her to stand by her principles and not be intimidated, even by her own father. She sent me a thank-you note.

We had never met, but I felt her to be a kindred spirit. I admired her courage. So I decided to ask whether she might be willing to pass messages between her father and Hamas, with me serving as conduit. Dana replied to me on July 8, 2006:

Dear Gershon,

I have no problem trying to help, but I know my limits in this situation.

It has been made absolutely clear to me that on the Israeli side there is no doubt that Gilad Schalit is alive. [The Israelis] know this for sure and, consequently, the prospect of getting a sign of life is not terribly exciting for them. Furthermore, any attempt to speak to Hamas is simply out of the question for them. This is an impenetrable, insurmountable wall.

My impression is that there must be a third-party mediator. There is great doubt regarding the seriousness of the other side. This is a paralyzing trap – just as Hamas fears that Israel will humiliate it, the Israelis are convinced that the other side is all talk, unable to commit to anything real. As I said, I am happy to help, but we have to think about how to do this, as my impression at the moment is that initiatives like yours won't be taken seriously.

If Noam Schalit would give his personal backing and ask [representatives of] the Prime Minister's Office to meet with you, I would be pleased to assist. That could really smooth the progress of this initiative, because the prime minister is very apprehensive about any Israeli who

has contacts with Palestinians. He suspects their real intentions. That's
the situation, I am sorry to say. Speak to me.

Best and hopeful wishes,
Dana

Based on Dana Olmert's advice, I contacted Ezzedin Choukri, a friend
in the Egyptian foreign minister's inner cabinet of advisers. One of the
most experienced Egyptian diplomats I have ever met, Choukri worked
for the United Nations secretary general and in the Egyptian Embassy
in Tel Aviv.

July 10, 2006

Dear Ezzedin,

*I am sure Egypt is working hard behind the scenes to end the Gaza
crisis. Now is the time to work on a cease-fire. There must be a bilateral,
enforceable cease-fire, composed of the following elements:*

Palestinians:
- *Release of Gilad Schalit – I suggest that he be released to the Egyptian representative in Gaza;*
- *An end to Qassam rocket attacks against Israel;*
- *An end to all attacks from Gaza, including suicide bombings and attacks against Israeli bases along the border.*

Israel:
- *An end to Israeli shelling and Israeli incursions into Gaza;*
- *An end to targeted killings in Gaza and the West Bank;*
- *An end to Israel's massive arrest campaigns in the West Bank.*

*Israel will release all Hamas members of Parliament and ministers
with the release of the soldier.*[7]

---

7. After the abduction of Schalit, Israel arrested almost all Hamas' elected members of

One week following the implementation of the cease-fire, Israel will release all Palestinian minors from prison. One week later, Israel will release all Palestinian women prisoners who have no blood on their hands.

One month following the cease-fire, Israel will release a certain number – between one hundred and two hundred – veteran prisoners.

Egypt will establish a mechanism for dealing with real-time intelligence information from Israel regarding time bombs.

Egypt, the US, and France will set up a monitoring committee (like the one in southern Lebanon in July 1993) to deal with complaints and violations.

The cease-fire agreement will be in place for six months, after which it can be renewed.

There is no one better than Egypt to work out the details of this agreement. Everyone wants a ladder, and Egypt is the best partner to put it in place.

I am personally willing to do anything to make this work. I can get directly to Olmert, and I am sure Hamas would agree to Egyptian mediation. Can Egypt make this happen?

Dr. Gershon Baskin

Ezzedin told me Egypt was working on a cease-fire and had begun speaking to the relevant parties, but he was pessimistic. He felt that neither side was interested in talking.

Two days later, on July 12, 2006, a Hezbollah force attacked an Israeli military vehicle on the Israeli border with Lebanon. Two Israeli soldiers, Eldad Regev and Udi Goldwasser, were abducted and dragged into Lebanon. Israel responded with a military operation deep into Lebanese territory, and the government of Israel soon authorized its second war in Lebanon. This was in addition to the ongoing military campaign in Gaza, with Palestinians firing rockets at Israel's civilian population in the south.

the Palestinian Legislative Council (known as the Palestinian Parliament) and the ministers in the Hamas-led government in the West Bank.

Hezbollah launched hundreds of Katyusha rockets into northern Israel, reaching all the way to Haifa. Fatalities were rising and hundreds of thousands of Israelis evacuated their homes. In the south, Hamas, Islamic Jihad, and other groups in Gaza were shooting hundreds of rockets into Israeli communities along the Gazan border. Most local and international attention focused on Lebanon, but Israel was waging war on two fronts, both sides. More than one million Israelis were under fire.

With Israel politically and militarily preoccupied with the conflict in the north, I tried to launch an initiative vis-à-vis Hamas that might help to refocus attention on Gaza. On July 15, after speaking with Ghazi Hamad by phone, I sent him the following proposal:

Dear Ghazi,

This is the proposed deal and how I think it would work:

1. *Gilad Schalit will be allowed to call home this evening – this will prove to his family that he is alive and well.*
2. *The Schalits will notify Olmert that they spoke to their son and are convinced that he is alive and well, and will ask the prime minister to agree to the following:*
   a. *Tomorrow Gilad Schalit will be released to one of the international representatives in Gaza – the Egyptians, the UN, or anyone else.*
   b. *President Mahmoud Abbas (Abu Mazen)[8] will announce a complete cease-fire – no more Qassams, no attacks of any kind. Abu Mazen will announce an understanding with the government of Israel that the cease-fire will be bilateral. Olmert will publicly confirm that as long as there are no attacks from Gaza and the West Bank, Israel will stop all targeted killings, the shelling of Gaza, and the arrest campaign in the West Bank.*
3. *Three days after the release of Schalit, Israel will release all Palestinian minors and women from prison.*

---

8. President Mahmoud Abbas, chairman of the Executive Committee of the Palestine Liberation Organization (PLO), is the elected president of the Palestinian Authority. As such, he presides over the West Bank and Gaza. Abbas is also known as Abu Mazen.

4. *I am personally willing to be a "guest" of the kidnappers or of Prime Minister Haniyeh until the women and minors are released. Israel could give President [Hosni] Mubarak a guarantee that the prisoners would be freed.*

5. *One week after the release of Schalit, if the cease-fire is upheld, Israel will release all Hamas members of Parliament and ministers from prison.*

6. *Egypt, France, and the United States would be requested to monitor the cease-fire. You could, if you wish, announce how long the cease-fire would be for – three months, six months, a year, etc.*

I believe this is how it could work. If this is acceptable, I am willing to get to Olmert with it. The most important thing is the phone call tonight from Gilad Schalit to his family.

Gershon Baskin

President
Mahmoud Abbas

The phone call never came, but Hamas did stop shooting. Ghazi said that security reasons precluded the call, but he was checking whether we could get a video from the soldier.

Prime Minister Olmert rejected the proposed cease-fire. Dana Olmert relayed to me that he had no faith in Hamas or in its ability to enforce a cease-fire. It was senseless, therefore, for Israel to even make the offer.

Regarding the fate of Schalit, Israel refused to negotiate with Hamas. Contact had been established with Palestinian President Abbas, who was held responsible for the welfare of the kidnapped soldier. The following day, July 16, I wrote to Dana Olmert:

Dear Dana,

With the new situation in the northern arena, it seems to me that the crisis in Gaza has been somewhat forgotten, and with it, the fate of Gilad Schalit. I initiated something yesterday that I hope will lead to positive results, though I have no illusions about the matter. I arranged another phone call between Ghazi Hamad – the spokesperson for the Hamas government – and Noam Schalit. They had a long and positive conversation. I spoke with Hamad many times yesterday and today. In my assessment, Hamas wants to find a way out of the situation. Hamad said that the Hamas government is not in physical possession of Schalit but does have influence over those who are holding him.

I emphasized that the first step must be a demonstration that Schalit is alive and well. Hamad told me he is. I told him they must bring a videotape or a live witness via a third party, or even a phone call to his parents. I believe they are trying to arrange something. In any case, the ball is in their court.

I proposed that after they show a sign of life, we could begin to roll out a plan that would lead to his release. [I described my proposed plan to Dana.]

Hamas accepts that Abbas is in charge of the negotiations. Hamas would accept a cease-fire for all organizations and factions in Gaza. They say they are searching for a way to end the crisis.

If they take the first step and show a sign of life from the soldier, I would like to bring this proposal to your father. We have to help both sides come down from their ladders, and above all, we must save lives on both sides.

I hope you can help advance this proposal – if it ripens in the coming days.

Best wishes,
Gershon

Dana replied the same day:

Gershon,

This looks quite serious – do you want me to pass it on to the prime minister? Tell me what to do.

Ahmed Jaabri

I responded to her immediately: Once we get the sign of life, it will be time to act.

I knew that without a sign of life from Gilad, no one would take my efforts seriously. I had to get Olmert to listen to me. Even if the Israeli security service really did believe Gilad was alive, which I wasn't sure about, I had to prove that the channel I'd opened to Hamas led to Ahmed Jaabri, commander of the Ezzedin al Qassam Brigades, which were holding Gilad. Ghazi Hamad seemed to be a serious person who sincerely wanted to help. He had spent five years in Israeli prisons – charged with membership in Hamas and activities such as participating in demonstrations, writing slogans, distribution of leaflets, and punishment of drug dealers and collaborators with Israel – and learned to speak fluent Hebrew. He was now the spokesperson for the Hamas government and, despite the refusal of Hamas to recognize Israel, Ghazi's voice was heard on Israeli radio, in Hebrew, speaking to Israeli citizens.

July 19, 2006

Dear Ghazi,

When I couldn't reach you today, I was worried about you. Another eighteen Palestinians were killed last night, and more than twenty the night before. This madness has to end. I am saddened by every person killed and by every home destroyed.

We began our conversations on Saturday. I was very glad you took the initiative to speak with the father of the soldier, which was a very good thing to do. I know you're very interested in continuing this initiative we have begun, which will hopefully result in a mutual cease-fire, the release of the soldier, and a significant Palestinian prisoner release.

I know you're encountering problems on your side. My understanding is that Khaled Mashal[9] has direct control over Gilad

9. Leader of Hamas' political bureau.

Schalit's captors, but that Prime Minister Haniyeh has significant influence as well. Because you're based in Gaza and Mr. Haniyeh is the recognized prime minister in Palestine, his influence could be even stronger than Mashal's – if he makes the decision and is courageous enough to take that step. There seems to be tension between the internal leadership and the external one. But you people in Gaza are the ones who bear the consequences of decisions made by your leaders. You are the ones whose lives are on the line; with all due respect to Mr. Mashal, he is far away in Damascus and cannot begin to imagine the reality of your lives in Gaza.

I am probably out of place in writing these things to you, but because the lives of every single Israeli and every single Palestinian have equal value in my eyes, I believe that everything possible must be said and done to protect the lives of so many innocent people who are at risk. I believe we can find a way to end this crisis without more people being killed.

Time is the one element in short supply. Every passing day without a resolution of the current crisis puts more people at risk. I am convinced that if Israel determines the location of the soldier, it will immediately proceed with a military raid aimed at freeing him by force. In that scenario, the soldier could be killed in the crossfire. If that happens, the Israeli response will be even harsher than what you have seen until now. No one wants this to happen.

It is time for the leaders in Gaza to demonstrate their leadership. Everything rises or falls on proof that the soldier is alive and well. Please share my letter with Mr. Haniyeh; please implore him to be courageous. I believe you can influence the captors to prove that the soldier is alive and well. I believe in your ability, and I hope and pray that you will take this step so we can work together to end the crisis. Then we can begin working toward agreement on a long-term hudna that would ensure security for both of our peoples.

Sincerely yours,
Gershon Baskin

Meanwhile, Hamas rocket fire into Israel intensified, and Israeli Air Force bombardment kept targeting Hamas and other Palestinian targets

Khaled Mashal

in Gaza. Still no word from Gilad Schalit. No negotiations, no demands issued, no success in locating the abducted soldier. Every path seemed to lead to a dead end. But Ghazi and I continued speaking several times a day, trying to think of some way to progress. Most of the time, I called him. On occasion he would initiate the call or return mine. He never sounded angry. He was always calm, even optimistic, beyond the traditional *Inshallah* (God willing).

I came up with an idea that I thought could break the stalemate: Olmert would announce a twenty-four-hour cease-fire, and during those twenty-four hours Hamas would provide a sign that Gilad was alive.

I thought that if I produced results – such as the sign of life from Schalit – I could prove that I had an effective channel of communication. In addition, Olmert could see that enough trust had developed between key Hamas members and me for it to be relatively safe to proceed. I informed Noam Schalit of all my moves. Soon, I knew I had at least two direct channels to Olmert – his daughter Dana and Noam Schalit. I knew Dana was sharing all our conversations and proposals with her father, and she reported back to me. I was also quite certain that Noam Schalit was sharing with the prime minister the most essential messages exchanged by us.

Various Hamas sources indicated that Hamas was indeed interested in a cease-fire and called on Israel to halt its attacks. Some Hamas spokespeople said they had already declared a cease-fire. I called Dana and told her about the reports coming from Gaza. Then I wrote to Ghazi:

July 23, 2006

Dear Ghazi,

Olmert has rejected the idea of issuing a formal statement on an Israeli cease-fire. It seems that because there was no official announcement from Haniyeh and Abu Mazen, he is not taking the announcements from various factions seriously. He says that even after the so-called official announcement, various people from Hamas told the media there was no agreement. The fact that there were more Qassam rockets this morning also didn't help convince Olmert that Hamas was serious about a cease-fire.

I think there may still be a chance of getting Olmert to agree. I am trying to enlist Noam Schalit to speak to Olmert and request it from his side. It would be much easier to do anything on the Israeli side if there were already a sign of life from the soldier.

Sincerely yours,
Gershon

Chapter 3

A Sign of Life

The War in Lebanon was raging. The tragedy developing in Gaza was being ignored. The UN was working on proposals for a cease-fire in the north. The war was not going well from Israel's perspective. I was speaking day and night with friends in both Gaza and Lebanon. A good friend, Professor Mkhaimer Abusada, lives in Beit Lahia, in northern Gaza, from which many rockets were being fired into Israel. Israeli troops had surrounded the town. Mkhaimer had moved with his family to a small flat in Gaza City, which seemed safer. Nevertheless, his brother's home was hit with Israeli artillery fire, and wounded children needed to get to the hospital. Mkhaimer called me after 11:30 p.m. to say the ambulance driver was afraid to approach the house, lest Israeli soldiers in the area shoot him. The Israelis were accusing Hamas of using ambulances to transport combatants in order to ambush Israeli troops.

I phoned the defense minister's office and was transferred to the command center. With Mkhaimer on one line – he was also on the phone with his brother – and me on another with the Israeli army command center, we directed the ambulance driver to pick up the wounded children and bring them to the hospital.

My friends in Lebanon, who had not supported Hezbollah before the war and even talked about peace with Israel, were now saying Israel had gone too far. Civilian infrastructure all over Lebanon was being targeted by the Israeli Air Force in retaliation for the constant rocket fire into Israel. Both in Lebanon and in Israel, people were furious. Hezbollah leader Hassan Nasrallah appeared on television every night, threatening to strike new targets in the center of Israel. Israelis throughout the north felt the pain of rockets, as did Lebanese citizens and every single Gazan who had no place to hide. Hundreds of thousands evacuated their homes to wait out the deadly rain of rockets in safer locations. The Israeli public called on Olmert to hit back even harder. That was the feeling in the north as well as the south. Olmert was in no mood to negotiate with terrorists in Gaza or in Lebanon. Both sides had abducted Israeli soldiers within sovereign Israeli territory. He was also not inclined to accept any cease-fire. He and his government wanted to hit back hard, so the enemy would think twice before striking again. There were similar sentiments in Lebanon and in Gaza.

August 6, 2006

Dear Ghazi,

I understand that the Egyptians have been working on a cease-fire, but that all progress including the release of the soldier and the prisoners is frozen. I understand that Abu Mazen is abroad until August 11, and that nothing is expected to happen at least until after his return.

This situation is unacceptable, and we should do everything possible to renew the initiative of getting a cease-fire and a sign of life from the soldier. Israeli attacks on Gaza will continue almost completely unnoticed by the local and international media as long as the disaster in Lebanon continues. It is amazing that no one seems to care about Gaza.

I've mentioned that if you want to get international attention back on the Palestinian issue, the easiest way is to show a sign of life from the soldier. With that I would be able to speak to Olmert about making an immediate gesture in return.

Why should we wait another week while so many people continue to suffer? I know your direct influence on the captors is limited. It is very important to hear Prime Minister Haniyeh and other Hamas leaders in Gaza publicly call on the captors to show a sign of life. It will help renew movement toward improving the situation. Every day that passes without a resolution of the immediate crisis means that more innocent people will die.

I want to thank you for speaking with Noam Schalit again – that is very important. I would welcome the opportunity to speak with Prime Minister Haniyeh, and it would be great if he spoke with Noam Schalit. I would also like to speak to the Hamas leaders in Damascus. Please assist me. I don't know if it would help, but I am willing to do anything that has even the slightest chance of helping.

If we can come up with some kind of concrete proposal for a cease-fire that could be honored on the Hamas side, I am willing to take it directly to Olmert. Abu Mazen would also support it, I believe. The Egyptians are doing everything they can to help. I am in contact with General Nader El-A'aser from Egyptian intelligence in the Egyptian Embassy in Tel Aviv,[1] who is willing to help as well.

We must to find a way to move forward. You know that in Israel/Palestine, if we don't move forward, we move backward. When that happens, innocent people get killed. Ghazi, I know that you really want to help and that you personally believe in resolving this problem. Please don't give up – we need your dedication and we must move forward.

Best wishes,
Gershon

---

1. El-A'aser was the consul and chief intelligence officer in the embassy, reporting directly to Omar Suleiman, head of the Egyptian General Intelligence Service (EGIS) and believed to be the most powerful man in Egypt after President Mubarak. Upon returning to Egypt, Nader headed the Israel and Palestine desk of the EGIS and in this capacity led the Egyptian mediation team that finalized the prisoner exchange leading to Schalit's release.

My messages to the Hamas people were becoming repetitive. Through-out my more than five years of contact with them, I sensed the need to keep reiterating what I wanted. Constant persistence was imperative in order to take measured steps, such as gaining the sign of life. In general, over the years, Hamas tended to speak of large steps – "free a thousand prisoners and Schalit will be released." Its members seemed to have little awareness of how decisions are made in Israel, and the limits of the Israeli political system. Hamas didn't understand why the life of one little soldier meant so much to us. Dr. Ahmed Yousef, Haniyeh's political adviser, once said to me, "We have ten thousand Gilad Schalits in Israeli prisons – why is this one soldier so important?"

But the analogy was skewed. An abducted soldier who is denied contact with the outside world and whose family has no information about his welfare – indeed, does not even know whether he is dead or alive – cannot be compared to prisoners who receive visits from the International Red Cross, mail from loved ones, consultations with lawyers, and, in most cases, even family visits. Captivity is captivity, but to my mind, there were differences between the two situations.

I contacted Dana Olmert again. It was crucial that I get through to her father. The Egyptian representatives in Gaza, headed by General Mohammed Ibrahim, had begun talks with the military wing of Hamas in an attempt to achieve a cease-fire and a resolution of the Schalit crisis – but without success.

August 8, 2006

Good morning Dana,

I hope you can assist me once again, as it is a matter of life and death. Negotiations conducted by Egypt have been frozen. Due to the escalation in the north, the captors have retracted their offers for a cease-fire and prisoner exchange, and even the Egyptians have said we must wait until the north is quiet. I speak with Noam Schalit almost every day and cannot sleep at night, thinking about what the Schalit family is going through.

With every passing day, Palestinians are also paying a very heavy price. We must make another effort to advance the release of the soldier, reach a cease-fire, work out a prisoner exchange, and return to the peace process.

Late last night I received a phone call from Haniyeh's office. They want to re-examine my proposal that a sign of life from Gilad could move the process forward. They would like to know what to expect if they give a sign of life.

It seems to me that both sides need to take measured steps in order to build a little trust. The Palestinian leaders do not believe there will be a significant prisoner release after they free Gilad. They believe Israel will not fulfill their demand, and they will be humiliated in the eyes of their own people. They feel Israel is setting them up. I believe the phone call to me last night was a signal of their seriousness.

I told them I would try to clarify what they can expect from Israel if they provide a sign of life. Dana, I hope you will once again deliver this message to your father. I told them I would try to get them an answer today. I am waiting to hear from you.

Gershon

Dana spoke with her father. Her reply to me is contained in my next letter to Ghazi Hamad:

August 8, 2006

Dear Ghazi,

Olmert says the Israelis are already 100 percent convinced that the soldier is alive, so the step of showing a sign of life is not sufficient. What could be compelling enough to get the process moving? A phone conversation between the soldier and his father is what I think. We must be practical and consider what would influence Olmert.

What steps would you like to see Olmert take that are practical and reasonable to expect? You expressed concern that Olmert would not actually release prisoners. What kind of guarantee would suffice to convince your side that he would release them?

Olmert is very skeptical about your ability to deliver anything. He believes everything is controlled by Mashal and by the Hamas leadership in Damascus. He has no confidence in your side, or even in Abu Mazen.

I had a crazy idea. We must keep it top secret, since Olmert believes nobody (myself included) concerning the Palestinian issue. What if we transform this into a "women's initiative," using Olmert's daughter and Abu Mazen's daughter-in-law Nisreen Haj Ahmad Abbas? Perhaps Olmert would be more willing to listen to them. I believe Olmert's daughter is willing to help. She doesn't want her name mentioned officially, as it would damage her ability to influence her father. We have to respect her wish and her willingness to help.

I think I could also get Nisreen to help. She is a very smart lawyer, and she works in the President's Office as an adviser. Please let me know what you think.

Gershon

I then wrote to Dana Olmert:

August 8, 2006

Dear Dana,

Thank you for your willingness to continue working for Gilad's release. My feeling is that the central problem is the total lack of trust between the sides. I believe it is possible to alleviate this in one of two ways:

1. *I have a crazy idea that depends on your direct involvement. One of the people closest to Abu Mazen is his daughter-in-law, Nisreen Haj Ahmed Abbas, a lawyer who works in the President's Office. I believe that an initiative involving the two of you could create the trust necessary to advance the deal for Schalit. I have not yet spoken with Nisreen, but I believe that if you agree, so will she. The whole process would remain top secret until implemented.*
2. *I understand your father's reservations about the involvement of*

Israelis who have contacts with Palestinians. My contacts with Palestinians all come from my Zionist motivations, but I am prepared to replace myself with someone your father trusts.

What do you think could create the momentum necessary to convince your father of the real intentions of the Palestinians to reach a deal? This is the question to which Haniyeh's office wants an answer.

Gershon

Dana replied:

August 8, 2006

Dear Gershon,

I think the key to launching the process is in the hands of the Schalit family. If the Schalits were to discreetly ask the prime minister – or perhaps a senior aide such as Yoram Turbowicz[2] or the director general of the office, Raanan Dinur – and they would include you in the meeting, presenting you as someone they have confidence in, it would be possible to begin the process of your working together with the decision makers.

     Your idea about Abu Mazen's daughter-in-law is indeed crazy, but I won't say no to anything. It seems very unrealistic that our side would agree to two women being messengers of peace and reconciliation, one of them being me. I am sober enough to know that this kind of cooperation is still far away. But as I said, I am willing to cautiously check out the possibility, provided that the proper atmosphere is created. First, we have to convince someone serious on the Israeli side that there is something real in your initiative, and for that we need the backing of the Schalit family.

Dana Olmert

---

2. Chief of staff in the Prime Minister's Office.

The next day, August 9, I continued pushing Ghazi that if the terrorists wouldn't allow anyone to visit Gilad Schalit, they should send a videotape of him. Ghazi and I had a long phone conversation that evening. He suggested three stages: (1) Hamas would release a videotape. (2) Israel would release all the women and minors in its prisons (about 350). (3) Both sides would agree to a full cease-fire. After that, a prisoner exchange would be negotiated.

I told him I would pass the suggestion on to Olmert via his daughter. More than once, Ghazi had asked who was receiving my messages. I told him they were being sent directly to Prime Minister Olmert, without specifying how. He then told me he'd been instructed to verify that Olmert was in fact receiving the messages, so I told him about Dana Olmert. Sometime after that, Dana called me, deeply concerned. The head of the ISA had informed her that her name had been heard in a conversation that was listened to and that he had to inform her father, the prime minister. Later that evening, I received a call from Shalom Turjeman, Olmert's foreign policy adviser, summoning me to his office the following morning.

I showed up at the designated time. Red in the face, Turjeman told me the prime minister had yelled at him for the past twenty minutes. "Tell Baskin to take my daughter out of this!" Olmert had bellowed. I said nothing, but thought to myself that the prime minister himself could have taken Dana out of the story from the start.

August 10, 2006

Dear Ghazi,

We still don't have a final answer from Olmert. I'll follow up this morning. Olmert has a problem releasing prisoners in exchange for the video of the soldier. General Nader El-A'aser from Egyptian intelligence (in the Egyptian Embassy in Tel Aviv) and I spoke last night about an idea I had: After the video is released, President Mubarak will ask Olmert to release a certain number of minor and women prisoners to Abu Mazen – they'll be brought to the muqataa[3]

---

3. Presidential quarters.

in Ramallah. Nader spoke last night with Minister Omar Suleiman,[4] *who said that in order for President Mubarak to make that request, he has to receive it from the Israelis through the official channels.*

We should also think about what should happen after the release of the soldier and the prisoners. We should be thinking in terms of a bilateral and comprehensive cease-fire. This is vital to calm the area in order to renew the possibility of some kind of political process.

When this situation calms down, I would like to come to Gaza to discuss how we can push the political process forward. I will speak to you later once I have news.

Gershon

Friday morning, August 11, I went to Ramallah with my Palestinian partner, Hanna Siniora, to meet with Abu Hisham, a senior political adviser to President Abbas. Hanna was one of the few people who knew of my involvement in the negotiations. My idea was to get Abbas to take responsibility for negotiating with Hamas for the release of Schalit. I explained to Abu Hisham that the first step had to be getting a sign of life from Schalit. Though the Israeli officials claimed they knew Schalit was alive, we needed this sign to prove we had an effective channel of communication. We called Ghazi Hamad from Abu Hisham's office. I explained to the latter that Olmert had refused to pay anything for information on the welfare of Schalit, and that Hamas was demanding 350 women and minor prisoners for a videotape of him. This was a non-starter. After two hours of phone negotiations, Abu Hisham convinced Hamad and others in Hamas that if Israel released one busload, fifty women and minors, they would provide a video of Schalit. Hamas even agreed to have the bus come to Abbas in Ramallah, as Abu Hisham demanded.

On the way back from Ramallah, I called Olmert's office. Chief of

4. Suleiman held firm control over Egypt's military and security apparatuses and was a staunch advocate of close military relations with the United States and Israel. He was highly respected both in the West and within the Arab world, including within Egypt itself. Hamas regarded him with extreme caution, because he also held sway over its allies, the Muslim Brotherhood in Egypt.

Staff Yoram Turbowicz answered via his cell phone but was on another call. For some reason, he put the phone down while he continued on the other line. I overheard him speaking with Elliott Abrams, deputy national security adviser in George W. Bush's White House. They were working out the details of the UN Security Council resolution for a cease-fire in Lebanon, adopted later that day. When Turbowicz realized I was still on the line, he picked up the phone and told me to call Ovad Yehezkel, another senior adviser to Olmert. I reached Yehezkel, and he told me to speak with Shalom Turjeman.

Turjeman repeated the Olmert mantras – no negotiations with terrorists, no release of prisoners for Schalit, and no payment for information. I also understood from him that the Prime Minister's Office was in direct contact with Saeb Erekat, the chief negotiator from the PLO, and refused to communicate directly with Hamas. This might have been disheartening, but I knew we were dealing with a bitter enemy that was in clear violation of international law by holding a prisoner of war without any rights, including the right of visitation by the International Red Cross. And I knew I had managed to open some doors that could help bring Schalit home, as soon as the prime minister was willing to listen and negotiate.

Sometimes I would lie awake at night, then go to the computer to jot down some ideas or send a message to someone. On August 14, shortly after lying down, I got out of bed at 12:23 a.m. and wrote to Noam Schalit.

Dear Noam,

I had a long conversation with Dana Olmert this evening. She told me that in the Prime Minister's Office, objection to any agreement with Hamas is very strong. Both Dana and I believe that if you don't pressure Olmert, we will miss the opportunity to see if the Hamas people are serious. Ghazi Hamad says they are and want to advance a deal. Now is a critical moment. I am meeting Olmert's foreign policy adviser at 2 p.m. We'll speak after that.

Gershon

I spoke with Noam later that day. He was very frustrated. There was no progress, and no one in the Prime Minister's Office could give him any encouraging news. His anger was growing, yet he was very reserved. I explained that he should be cautious and not believe everything the prime minister's people tell him, because while we all wanted Gilad home, his interests clearly diverged from theirs. It seemed to me that first the Israeli government had to explore every possibility of a military operation to rescue Schalit. Negotiating with Hamas would violate all the government's principles. Israel had demanded that the entire international community boycott Hamas unless it recognized the Jewish state, renounced violence, and adhered to agreements between Israel and the PLO. Negotiating with Hamas would put the country in a difficult position vis-à-vis the rest of the world. Additionally, the Israeli government did not want to do anything that could be perceived as a victory for Hamas. Giving in to its demands would be a major setback in the war against terrorism and could easily lead to more abductions.

Ofer Dekel

Later that day, Prime Minister Olmert appointed Ofer Dekel, former deputy head of the ISA, to take charge of bringing the abducted soldiers home from Lebanon and Gaza. Dekel had been a candidate to head the ISA but was passed over and left the service. He was a jogging mate of Olmert, however, who now called him back. It had taken fifty days from Schalit's abduction until Olmert assigned someone to the case. This alone is quite shocking; most experts on hostage situations concur that the period right after the abduction is the most critical. I immediately contacted Dekel through Noam Schalit and told him of my involvement. We arranged to meet in four days. In the meantime, I was going to Gaza, hoping that by meeting some of my contacts in person, something would move.

Chapter 4

Knocking on Gaza's Door

Gaza in August is broiling hot, and the morning of August 16 was no exception. Eager to meet Ghazi Hamad, I arrived at the Erez crossing early in the morning. I had been to Gaza alone many times in past years, but the situation was different now. Where workers once bustled in lines to leave Gaza and enter Israel early each morning, now there was only a trickle of foot traffic – most of it international aid workers and a handful of Gazans with medical problems or other exceptional cases that earned them rare entry permits into Israel or the West Bank. The military presence on both sides of the unofficial border had been beefed up considerably.

Hanna Siniora came with me so I wouldn't be an Israeli alone in Gaza. We were spending the day with Hamas officials, so we didn't tell our Fatah associates we were coming. We retained a Palestinian taxi for the whole day.

Our first stop was the Prime Minister's Office. It felt bizarre going through Hamas security. Despite my Israeli ID card, I had been invited by the spokesperson of the Hamas government, so I received a warm welcome. I admit to some anxiety while waiting for clearance, however. I also knew I was walking right into the heart of an Israeli army target.

In fact, several months later the Israeli Air Force shelled the building; it no longer stands.

I met with Ghazi Hamad, and Hanna spoke with Ismail Haniyeh's adviser, Dr. Ahmed Yousef. This was my first face-to-face meeting with Ghazi, so we got to know each other, briefly discussing our families. Then we turned to the subject of Schalit. I spent a lot of time explaining to Ghazi the importance of getting a sign of life from the soldier. Though the Israeli authorities said they knew for sure Gilad was alive, it was important to ascertain that my link to Ghazi led to those who were holding him. Only then would the prime minister take this channel seriously and allow us to negotiate the soldier's release.

Ghazi kept saying that without some kind of prisoner release, it was unlikely that the captors would provide a sign of life. I replied that surely they wanted to begin negotiations; their intention was not to hold on to Schalit forever, only to use him to secure the release of Palestinians incarcerated in Israeli prisons. Since the abduction, Israel had already arrested several hundred more Palestinians, including almost all the Hamas members of Parliament living in the West Bank. I appealed to Ghazi to push for the release of a videotape without "payment," in order to start the process.

Ghazi countered that because Israel had already made that demand, surrendering to it would be too humiliating. I told him that Olmert had said – as conveyed to Noam Schalit – that if Hamas released the videotape, "Israel would know how to respond." That is, Israel would release some prisoners in response to the videotape, not as payment for it. Ghazi reiterated that it would be hard to convince both the captors and the Hamas political leadership to hand over a video without any guarantees.

So Olmert refused to pay for information, and Hamas would not release a videotape without payment. How to break the deadlock?

I had an idea. What if instead of a videotape, we got a handwritten letter from Gilad to his parents? It was easy, quick, and involved no technology. Hamas could deliver the letter without any payment, as a means of launching negotiations. Ghazi liked the idea. He told me to stay in Gaza until I heard from him. Leaving Gaza with a handwritten letter from Gilad Schalit…What a dream!

Hanna and I spent the next few hours discussing politics with

Dr. Yousef. This was my first such talk with a senior Hamas leader. (Ghazi and I never discussed politics, only Schalit.) The most interesting part of our conversation focused on Hamas' end goals, which were quite difficult for an Israeli to hear. From Hamas' perspective, I had no place in Palestine. Hamas had no problem with Jews, Yousef explained, only with Zionists and Israelis. According to Islam, Jews were to be protected as the "People of the Book." The Jewish prophets are considered prophets of Islam as well. Jews are not considered enemies of Islam, he said, but Zionists are a different story.

I told him Hamas would never have peace until it came to terms with Israel's right to exist.

Yousef wasn't motivated by hatred, but he played the victim card with flair. He emphasized the suffering of the Palestinian people, driven from their land by the Israelis and living in refugee camps in Gaza, the West Bank, Lebanon, and Syria in poverty and despair. Negotiations with Israel were not the answer; the failure of the Oslo process had proven that Israel would never allow a Palestinian state. Israelis understood only the language of force and power, he said. Justice had to be done, and that meant returning all Palestinians to their land, with the Zionists going back to wherever they'd come from.

"My wife and my children were born in Israel," I pointed out. "Where are they supposed to go?"

He replied that they were living here at the expense of the original Palestinian residents, who have the real right to the land.

"Look, Gershon," he concluded, "I will never recognize Israel or make peace with it. Neither will my son. What my grandson will do, I do not know."

At least the door might open in two generations.

Hanna and I went for lunch in a nearby restaurant. We waited there until about 3 p.m., when Ghazi arrived, hot and sweaty from running around. He informed me that the idea of the letter was good and he thought we would get it. He also told me he would be sending me a paper from Hamas with their demands for the release of Schalit. He told us to wait in Gaza until I heard from him again. Hanna and I waited until it began to get dark, then we decided to go back to Jerusalem. I called Ghazi but he didn't answer.

The next afternoon Ghazi e-mailed me Hamas' demands, in English. In exchange for the release of the Israeli soldier, Hamas wanted (1) a full and immediate cease-fire; (2) the opening of all passages to Gaza and the end of the closure of Gaza's borders, which had been imposed immediately after Schalit's abduction; and (3) the release of 1,500 Palestinian prisoners, including all women and minors, and all Hamas MPs arrested since Schalit's capture.

I called Ofer Dekel, who was on his way to visit the Schalit family in Mitzpe Hila, near the Lebanese border. Dekel told me to send him the demands. He called me that evening with several questions, which I e-mailed to Ghazi.

August 17, 2006

Dear Ghazi,

It was a pleasure to meet you. The statement you sent was immediately transferred to Ofer Dekel, the prime minister's appointee for dealing with abducted soldiers. He had some important questions:

1. *Who wrote the document?*
2. *Did you get information from the captors and then write the document?*
3. *Is the document the captors' position?*
4. *Was there an original document in Arabic? If so, can we receive that too?*

Noam Schalit and I believe it is very important to move forward quickly by having your side submit a list of Palestinian prisoners for release. I told Dekel this, and I believe there was a positive response from him as well. The best way for everyone to know both sides are serious is to take concrete steps. We must begin negotiating about the makeup of the list. The sooner you submit a list of names, the faster we can get the Israeli side to review it.

Again, a letter from the soldier to his family would be most helpful. I would give the letter to his family and to Olmert, but we would keep it out of the media. It would encourage Olmert to take your side more seriously.

I hope you can get me some good news today.

Gershon

Ghazi answered me immediately:

August 17, 2006

Dear Gershon,

Thank you very much for your letter. Regarding the questions, these are the answers:

1. Who wrote the document?
I can confirm that this document represents the official positions of the people holding the soldier, and they agree to every word of it.

2. Did you get the information from the captors and then write the document?
I think the answer to the first question is clear.

3. Is the document the captors' position?
Of course.

4. Was there an original?
Yes, but it was written in Arabic and then translated to English.

Regarding the letter, I am still waiting and hope to have a positive response.

Best wishes,
Ghazi

The next day, August 18, I met Ofer Dekel and a member of his team from the ISA in the Crowne Plaza Hotel in Jerusalem. I recapped all my efforts to date. I gave a rundown of all the people on the Palestinian side I had contacted in Ramallah and in Gaza, focusing on Ghazi and the positive role he was playing. I reported that Hamas was interested in more than a prisoner exchange; it wanted a cease-fire as well as the opening of all routes to Gaza, so life there could return to normal. And I explained that I was spending most of my efforts trying to get a sign of life from Gilad.

Both Dekel and his colleague told me there was no need for a sign of life. Israel had concrete information that Gilad was alive and well, and held Hamas responsible for his welfare. They repeated the same slogans I had heard from Olmert through his daughter since the attack on Kerem Shalom: We don't talk to terrorists. We won't negotiate with Hamas. We will not free prisoners for Schalit. We will not pay for information.

I told them that Israel might know for sure that Gilad was alive and well, but nobody had a channel of communication with the captors. "Do you want Gilad Schalit to become another Ron Arad?" I asked pointedly.

Ron Arad was an air force navigator shot down over Lebanon in 1982. Israel began negotiating his release but couldn't agree to the terms. Eventually, Arad was probably smuggled out of Lebanon to Iran and was never located again. The fate of Ron Arad is like a black stain on Israel's promise to bring every soldier home – if not alive, then to be buried by his family on Israeli soil.

Dekel instructed me to continue my efforts and report to him directly. His colleague added that I should carefully document all my contacts, phone calls, faxes, and e-mails – documentation that later enabled me to write this book.

On August 20, Ghazi told me a letter was on its way. I didn't hear anything all day. I called him repeatedly and asked where the letter was. He said it was going through many hands, so it could not be traced. He said I should be patient. I told him my patience was wearing thin.

August 21, 2006

Dear Ghazi,

It is now 4:30 p.m. and if you haven't heard from the captors by now, that seems like bad news. By not receiving the letter, I understand that they want something in return. They must understand that there can be no negotiations unless the Israelis are certain there is a channel for them. Until there is absolute proof of communication with someone who has access to the captors and even influence over them, there can be no negotiations. Israel says it would view the letter as a confidence-building measure and would "know how to respond appropriately."

Ghazi, there must be some way to convince the captors to release the letter. I know how committed you are. Please try once again to convince them. Each passing day brings more risks of terrible events.

Best wishes,
Gershon

I waited a day, two days, a whole week, but still no letter. I was calling Ghazi at least ten times a day. He was clearly frustrated himself. Eventually, Ghazi told me the political echelon had vetoed the letter. There was no agreement to release it without an Israeli "payment."

I decided to appeal to the political leadership. Someone in the Israeli intelligence community told me that Dr. Mousa Abu Marzouk, deputy of Hamas politburo chief Khaled Mashal, was the best person to contact. I got the e-mail address and fax and phone numbers of the Hamas office in Damascus from a Palestinian friend in Ramallah.

Dr. Mousa Abu Marzouk

August 27, 2006

Dear Dr. Abu Marzouk,

I am writing on behalf of the family of the abducted soldier Gilad Schalit. We are all anxious to see a positive resolution of this issue. I am in daily contact with the family and with Mr. Olmert's office, speaking directly with the person appointed to deal with the issue.

We must find a way to negotiate and to see the soldier returned to his family. Tomorrow is his twentieth birthday. Since his abduction more than six weeks ago, there has not even been a sign of life.

To establish a channel for negotiating his release, we must ascertain that there is someone to speak with who can deliver. We need to know that there is a direct link to the abductors of the soldier and that once a deal is negotiated, he will be released. It is most urgent that we receive a handwritten letter from the soldier, or anything else that will prove that the people we are dealing with have real contact with the abductors and influence over them.

We would like to move quickly. The soldier's family has received a commitment from the prime minister that a significant release of Palestinian prisoners will be made at the end of the negotiations. The prime minister, however, will not provide any "payment" for proof of the existence of a channel of communication.

I can personally travel to Gaza to receive the evidence. I can travel anywhere to meet anyone who can help negotiate the release of the soldier. This has already gone on too long. Too many people have already suffered. It is time to put it to an end.

I know you are interested in the release of Palestinian prisoners held in Israel. I cannot tell you how many prisoners Israel will release, but I can tell you that I, together with the Schalit family, will be an effective middleman. We will communicate in your name directly to the prime minister, quickly and persuasively, without any press or media.

I appeal to your good sense to help resolve this issue quickly.

Yours sincerely,
Dr. Gershon Baskin

Receiving no response, I tried speaking to Abu Marzouk. I got his personal assistant on the phone, but once I identified myself, he said that Abu Marzouk refused to speak to me and hung up. Hamas policy, based on its ideology, forbids direct contact with Israelis. In addition, there was likely fear that calls could be traced. Most Hamas leaders, most notably Mashal, have been targeted by Israel's security forces. Because of the extreme distrust between parties, it was quite clear to me that we needed a secret direct back channel to negotiate the prisoner exchange. Two days later, I tried again.

August 29, 2006

Dear Dr. Abu Marzouk,

I am very disappointed that you will not speak with me directly. I am trying to serve a humanitarian function: to get the soldier released and also to release a large number of Palestinian prisoners from Israeli prisons.

There is currently no effective negotiator between the sides. Neither is there any information about the soldier, or knowledge of who is willing to negotiate his release. If I am not an acceptable go-between, I would be more than willing to find someone who is.

We must move quickly. Every day brings more casualties and suffering. I am not asking you to recognize Israel or make peace with Israel or cross any of your "red lines." Two months have passed, and no one has stood up and said, "I am negotiating the release of the soldier."

Perhaps you are not in charge and have no influence over the soldier's captors. I think that if you did, you would be anxious to negotiate the release of Palestinian prisoners.

Please let me know how we can enter into negotiations and with whom.

Gershon Baskin

I also sent this message in Arabic by fax and e-mail. Khaled Duzdar, a Palestinian from my office, called to ensure that the letter was received. I followed up that phone call with another letter in Arabic to Abu Marzouk.

August 30, 2006

Dear Dr. Abu Marzouk,

Thank you for having your office clarify to my colleague Mr. Khaled Duzdar that you have not rejected my proposal to open a channel for negotiating the release of the soldier Schalit and Palestinian prisoners.

If I understand correctly, the problem is that you do not speak on the phone for security reasons. Please inform me of how you propose that we proceed. Israeli security is working around the clock to find the soldier. If his location is discovered, the security forces will most likely try to rescue him by force. In this scenario, there is a good chance that he will be killed and probably many others as well. This would be very bad for both sides. It is only a matter of time. I urge you not to take this issue lightly. I do not work for the Israeli government. I direct a non-government organization (NGO) and am working with the Schalit family.

I await your proposal regarding how we can continue.

Gershon Baskin

Dr. Azzam Tamimi

I also tried another channel. While working on Hamas-Israeli dialogue, I was introduced to Dr. Azzam Tamimi. Originally from Hebron, in the West Bank, Tamimi has been living in London for years, where he founded the Institute of Islamic Political Thought. Tamimi is thought to be a member of Hamas, although he denies it. Some have even suggested that he is a member of the Shura Council, the secret body appointed by Hamas founder Sheikh Ahmed Yassin, which governs all Hamas decision-making. Whether or not this is true, I do know that Tamimi is very close to the Hamas leadership in Damascus. He speaks and meets with these leaders frequently. I called Tamimi, then e-mailed Noam Schalit.

August 30, 2006

Dear Noam,

I just had a long conversation with Dr. Azzam Tamimi, who heads an Islamic institute in London. I asked whether we might use his services for talks with Hamas. He was with Khaled Mashal two weeks ago. He told me Mashal is receiving negative messages regarding the possibility of negotiations for the release of Palestinian prisoners, apparently through the Egyptians. The Hamas people in Syria understand that Israel refuses to conduct negotiations and demands the release of Gilad for free.

Tamimi said we have to send messages to Hamas that Israel is willing to negotiate for Gilad's release, not directly but through the Egyptians, or via Abu Mazen. I told him that first we had to have proof that the people we are talking to can bring about the release of Gilad.

Tamimi said Hamas is very suspicious of the Egyptians, and he suggested that we work through the Qataris. I told Tamimi that he should tell the Hamas people in Syria and in Gaza that Israel is willing to negotiate if they can prove that there is a channel that leads to Gilad.

I spoke once again with Mashal's office, and was told that the Hamas leaders would not speak to me by phone for security reasons, but that they would answer my letters via Tamimi.

I am also contacting a British MI6[1] man I know, Alastair Crooke, who was stationed in Israel/Palestine in the past and is now in London and Beirut. He has contacts in Hamas. He is now on his way to Jordan.

I'll let you know what I hear from them.

On August 31, 2006, Azzam Tamimi wrote me an e-mail:

Hi Gershon,

I've inquired for you; I've been told that the soldier is well and that your people know that for a fact. The problem is not the nonexistence

---

1. British military intelligence.

of a channel for negotiations but the Israeli government's lack of seri-
ousness regarding indirect negotiations to bring about an exchange
of prisoners. It would seem that the Israelis are still hoping for an
unconditional release of the soldier by means of keeping the pressure
on Hamas. Lately, there have been too many players – from Egypt
to Jesse Jackson – seeking a role in securing the release of the Israeli
soldier. None of these have proven to be commissioned by the Israeli
government to negotiate on its behalf.

Two things must be done:
1. *Israel must signal its willingness to resolve the problem through*
   negotiating a prisoner exchange.
2. *A single mediator must be commissioned to act on behalf of the*
   Israelis with a clear mandate.

Azzam

This is the letter I sent to Azzam Tamimi on August 31, 2006, following
a phone conversation:

Dear Azzam,

It was good speaking with you. As I told you, I am in contact with
someone in Haniyeh's office who claims to have a channel to those
who are holding the soldier. I have for the past two days also sent
faxes to Dr. Mousa Abu Marzouk in Damascus to see about open-
ing a channel there. I can assure you and you can assure them (in
Gaza and in Damascus) that Israel will negotiate the release of
the soldier for Palestinian prisoners. The way it will be done can
be decided – the most important thing now is to prove that there
is a channel.

   Two weeks ago, we proposed that they deliver a handwritten
letter from the soldier to his family. According to what I was told, the
people holding the soldier agreed, and the letter left them to make its
way to Haniyeh's office, to be delivered to me. I am being told every
day that the letter is on its way. Israel will not open negotiations

without knowing if the channel we are talking with can deliver; hence the importance of the letter. We assured them that the letter would not be disclosed to the press.

I told the people in Damascus that if they have influence over those who hold the soldier, they should propose how to open a channel.

Olmert has promised the soldier's father that he would make a generous prisoner release for the release of the soldier.

Azzam, if there is anything you can do to help, it would be most appreciated. We are dealing with a straightforward humanitarian issue, which will hopefully bring the soldier back to his family and a good number of Palestinian prisoners back to their families. Please do everything you can.

Best wishes,
Gershon

The next day I wrote to Khaled Mashal:

September 1, 2006

Dear Mr. Mashal,

From all the information I have gathered, it seems that you are in charge of the case of the abducted soldier, Gilad Schalit. It seems you have instructed the abductors not to allow a letter from Schalit to be delivered. On the basis of that letter, we believe Olmert will agree to open negotiations for an exchange of Palestinian prisoners for Schalit.

I am aware that you do not wish to negotiate directly with the government of Israel, so I propose that we conduct the negotiations through me. I assure you that this will be the fastest and most effective way of progressing.

We want to bring this story to an end. Too many Palestinians have already died, and too much destruction is taking place every day in Gaza. If the Israelis locate where the soldier is being held, they will not hold back – they will conduct a military operation to find him, and in the process he may be killed, and many others as well.

> *I can pick up the phone any moment to Ofer Dekel, the person Olmert has put in charge of this file. Together with the soldier's father, we can get directly to Olmert. I suggest that we begin the negotiations.*
>
> *I have read in the newspapers that Hamas is demanding one thousand prisoners when Schalit is released to the Egyptians and then five hundred when he is released to Israel. I don't know if this is really what you presented to the Egyptians. I don't think the Israeli side will agree. Please, I urge you, let's begin the process. Please make your demands.*
>
> *Gershon Baskin*

I verified through Azzam Tamimi in London that Mashal received my message. I also spoke with Noam Schalit, who told me that Ofer Dekel had assured him that Olmert was willing to negotiate and would make a "generous" release of Palestinian prisoners in exchange for Gilad's freedom. On September 3, I sent Khaled Mashal another e-mail:

> *Dear Mr. Mashal,*
>
> *I have received confirmation that there is a willingness to negotiate, but only after proof is delivered. I assume you know this as well, because Olmert's representative was in Cairo last week and spoke to the Egyptians about the terms Israel was willing to discuss.*
>
> *Gershon Baskin*

Feeling completely frustrated, and knowing we had to find the way to break the deadlock, I suggested that Noam Schalit write to Khaled Mashal, father to father. Noam said he would consult with an Arab friend of his, so he could perhaps take quotes from the Koran that would appeal to Mashal. I sent Noam's letter, translated into Arabic, to Mashal:

September 7, 2006

To Khaled Mashal, Damascus

As far as I understand, my son, soldier Gilad Schalit, has been held in captivity in the Gaza Strip since June 25 by military organizations under your authority. As you know, in addition to the suffering caused to my family, hundreds of thousands of your Palestinian brothers in the Gaza Strip have been suffering every day since the abduction of my son – because of the pressure, the blockade, the destruction, and continuous military actions by the Israeli army for more than seventy days.

From what I know, Islam and the Holy Koran, which you believe in and respect, commands you to treat prisoners with generosity, mercy, and morality, as commanded by God's prophet Mohammed, may peace be upon him, after victory in the battle of Badr el Medina … as it is written, "I command you to treat them with honor. And the guards obeyed as the prophet Mohammed commanded when they returned the prisoners from captivity; they praised and blessed the Prophet for his generosity and his moral values." And I call on you today and say that the generous and moral treatment of a prisoner includes the sending of a sign of life from the prisoner to his mother and father after seventy days of captivity.

Today we are three weeks before the Muslim holiday of Ramadan and the Jewish holiday of Rosh HaShana. This is an extraordinary opportunity for both sides, Palestinian and Israeli, to end this story that has brought so much suffering to my family and to hundreds of thousands of innocent Palestinians. This is a unique opportunity to allow several hundred Palestinian prisoners and my son to be free to spend the holidays at home with their families without the continued threat of blockade and military actions day and night. Moreover, ending this story will enable the ministers of your government and the members of Parliament being held by Israel to return to their official jobs and spend Ramadan in the closeness of their families.

I call on you today, as a father and the head of a family, to consider concluding this unfortunate chapter that has brought so much suffering to so many people. Send a sign of life from my son Gilad, something that will show the Israeli side that you want to advance toward a solution. Without a sign of life from Gilad, as the Prophet commands to act with generosity and mercy toward a prisoner, it will be impossible to advance toward the end of this story. After receiving the sign of life, it will be possible to continue toward a solution through the distinguished Egyptian mediators, the people working with Minister Omar Suleiman.

I am hopeful that during the coming holidays many prisoners will be peacefully in their homes and that peace and quiet will come to Gaza. Inshallah.

Best wishes,
Noam Schalit

Twenty-four more hours passed, and Ghazi still had no answer about the letter. I didn't know if he was lying. Why should I trust him? Why should he be different from anyone else in Hamas? So far, its behavior had shown not a bit of humanity. Hamas was in clear violation of international law. There was no sign of life. Despite the assurance of Israeli officials that Gilad was taken alive, maybe he wasn't alive anymore. They intended to hold Sasson Nuriel for ransom in exchange for the release of prisoners too, but then they butchered him.

I was also beginning to doubt what I read about the case in the media. I understood from the papers that Olmert was preparing to meet with Palestinian President Mahmoud Abbas, also known as Abu Mazen, so they could together announce a prisoner release. This would make it "appear" that Olmert wasn't dealing with Hamas. Abu Mazen would get the credit, if any was due. It sounded like a feasible scenario – a way to paint Hamas out of the picture and prevent its people from looking like heroes – but I'd learned from this case and many others not to believe everything I read or heard in the news.

I appealed to Ghazi by phone, in writing, in text messages – please get that letter! Finally, on Saturday morning, September 9, Ghazi called. He told me the Egyptian representatives in Gaza had received a handwritten letter from Gilad Schalit. He asked me to request that

Israel release two bodies of Hamas fighters killed in the attack on Kerem Shalom. I told him I would transmit the request.

I was amazed. The pressure had worked. Noam's letter to Mashal had made its impact. My persistence had paid off! I immediately called Noam and informed him that a letter had reached the Egyptian representatives in Gaza. I told Noam that I would call Ofer Dekel and inform him too.

Dekel thanked me and said he needed to verify the information. Soon afterward, Noam called and told me that Dekel had checked and there was no letter in the hands of the Egyptians. Angry and frustrated, I called Ghazi, who insisted that the letter had been delivered. He knew it for a fact – 100 percent, he said. I called Noam and relayed to him what Ghazi had said. It was all so surreal – was there a letter or wasn't there?

It took about another hour before Noam called and confirmed that there was in fact a letter. Soon afterward Dekel phoned me. He told me it was time for me to back out. Now that an official track for negotiations had been established through the Egyptians, they didn't want another one. The Egyptians insisted, he said, that there be only one track, run by them. He said that if I received more information I could continue to channel it to him, but I should cease my activities.

I was shocked. I had opened a channel of communication with Hamas. I had brought out a letter from Gilad Schalit, proving beyond a doubt that this channel led directly to the people holding him. Now I was being told to step aside? I sensed that, if empowered by Israeli officials, I could help bring Schalit home through a secret but direct back channel. But now Ofer Dekel had rejected my help.

Chapter 5

The Drive for a
Direct Channel

Noam Schalit asked me to come to the King David Hotel in Jerusalem the following day, September 10, 2006. He was meeting British Prime Minister Tony Blair there, and after that we would talk. I also called General Nader El-A'aser and proposed that we meet later that day. Having spent years in the Egyptian Embassy in Tel Aviv, Nader had a fine appreciation for Israel and its people.

Noam Schalit was focused, direct, and completely unemotional. It was difficult to know what he was truly feeling or thinking. He couldn't afford to alienate anybody. His wife, Aviva, was also there but remained mostly silent, fear and deep sadness in her eyes. I often said to myself that if I were in the Schalits' situation, I would be screaming my head off – going to Gaza, to Damascus, to anywhere in the world. I'd be on a hunger strike. I would be anything but cool, calm, and collected.

Many people believe that the Schalits gained so much public sympathy and support due to the composure they displayed throughout the five years and four months of their son's captivity. As a parent, I tried to put myself in their shoes. It's impossible to know what kind of behavior might have led to a speedier return of the kidnapped soldier. Noam later described the first two years of his son's captivity as "our naïve period." During that time, the family believed the government would do everything possible to bring Gilad home safely and quickly. The Schalits obeyed official requests not to make noise, lest it "increase the price" Hamas was demanding. If they remained quiet and didn't pressure the Israeli government, they were told, all pressure could be put on Hamas. If only they would sit tight and remain steadfast and calm, Israel's leaders would see to their son's return.

At the King David, Noam told me he was meeting Ofer Dekel later that day. He said that General Mohammed Ibrahim, who headed the Egyptian office in Gaza, was now in direct control of negotiations with the Hamas leaders. The Egyptians wanted nobody else involved in the process; without full control, Egypt would back out.

Noam wanted me to help determine whether it was possible to create public opinion in Palestine and the rest of the Arab world that would pressure Hamas to make a quick deal. He proposed that we organize a press conference for the Arab media. Noam asked whether my partner in IPCRI, Hanna Siniora, would agree to participate. Of course, Hanna did so immediately.

Nader and I met later that day. As a well-trained intelligence officer, Nader was better at listening than at disclosing information, and he chose his words carefully. He did share that he too was being left out of talks on Schalit; his colleagues in Gaza were in charge. But he had his own way of getting information, he said.

Two things Nader told me that afternoon stuck with me during the next five years. First, he advised me not to listen to Ofer Dekel.

"We need someone like you, a free agent who can communicate openly with both sides. It is important to have someone who is not part of the system and can work behind the scenes," he said.

Nader also told me that if he were in charge of the negotiations, Schalit would be home in six months.

Five years later, in September 2011, Nader became the chief negotiator on the Egyptian side. Schalit was released about ten weeks afterward.

I decided to take Nader's advice and ignore Ofer Dekel.

After meeting with Nader, I wrote an e-mail to Ghazi:

September 10, 2006, 5:21 p.m.

Ghazi,

The Israeli side is pleased with the first step of delivering the letter. Dekel says that all steps must now be taken through the Egyptians. He is meeting Omar Suleiman tomorrow to move things forward.

Dekel says that Israel will consider a goodwill gesture, such as releasing the bodies of the fighters killed in Kerem Shalom. If this is what you want, the official request should go through the Egyptians. The Egyptians say they must control the process. Any interference will slow or even end it. I think it is time for your side to make official demands.

I propose that Schalit be released to the Egyptians. A few days later, Palestinian prisoners will be released. Israeli guarantees will be given to the Egyptians to help overcome the lack of trust. The Egyptians are also willing to accept this.

It is important for your side to realize that there are political limitations to how far Olmert can go. Your demands must be reasonable, not so great that Olmert will not be able to accept them.

We want to finish by the end of Ramadan (October 22, 2006). I think the Palestinians have to submit formal demands – a list of prisoners or categories (women, minors, veterans, politicians – ministers, Parliament members, etc.). Let me know as well exactly what the demands are, so we can know how to influence the Israeli side to accept the deal, if it is reasonable.

I think we can make progress. It is important to keep me in the picture.

Gershon

On September 12, 2006, I awoke to good news: Israel announced that it would release eighteen senior Hamas officials. When Hamas released the letter from Gilad, I had repeated to Ghazi Hamad what Olmert's office had said to me: "Israel will know how to respond if a sign of life is given." I now sent Ghazi a text message saying that Olmert was honoring his commitment to provide confidence-building measures, which could lead to real negotiations for the release of Gilad.

But later that day, the Israeli military prosecutor protested the release of Hamas officials, and it was canceled. That was the end of any positive reinforcement for sending the letter from Gilad. It was also a blow to my own credibility vis-à-vis Ghazi Hamad and the Hamas leadership. I began doubting whether Ehud Olmert would ever make a deal. It seemed to me that if Olmert had wanted the Hamas leaders released, it would have happened.

On September 13, 2006, the press conference was held at the Ambassador Hotel in East Jerusalem. It was attended by dozens of journalists and representatives of news outlets all over the Arab world. Noam hoped his message would reach the Hamas leaders in Gaza and Damascus, wishing even that they might allow Gilad to see the broadcast. He received extensive coverage on Al Jazeera and Al Arabia, the two leading Arab satellite television stations. He called on the captors to put their demands on the table and advance the negotiations to bring Gilad home. He wanted to reach every single Palestinian with a loved one in Israeli prison, thereby putting pressure on Hamas to move quickly toward resolving this issue.

The next day, I again urged Khaled Mashal to begin negotiations. I was convinced that Israel, rather than taking the initiative to make an offer, would wait for Hamas to issue its demands. I still believed that if Israel did agree to negotiate, it was only a stalling tactic. It was quite clear to me that the intelligence community was busy trying to locate Gilad, so it could plan a heroic military rescue that would include the assassination of the captors and perhaps some Hamas leaders.

September 14, 2006

Dear Mr. Mashal,

Thank you for allowing the letter to be delivered. The next stage is crucial. There seems to be a kind of "dance" regarding who will begin. Perhaps it is time for you to issue your demands through the Egyptian mediators. I believe the process will drag on much longer than necessary if you don't begin it with your list of demands.

As Noam Schalit said in his letter to you, let's make this a happy Ramadan for a lot of Palestinian families. An agreement can be reached quickly, but first the negotiations must get into full gear.

Gershon Baskin

I met again with Noam and Aviva Schalit about a week later. Rosh HaShana was three days away. I suggested that we try to deliver a letter from them to Gilad. They wrote:

Our Dear Gilad,

Giladi, we – Mom and Dad – hope you're feeling well and are holding up despite the difficult conditions and the hard situation that you have already been in for three months.

We received the letter you wrote to us, and were happy to get a sign of life from you after so much time.

We want you to know that we, together with many different groups all over Israel, in the Palestinian Authority, and throughout the world are doing everything to secure your release as soon as possible, including the release of Palestinian prisoners that the government is prepared to carry out before Ramadan, which begins this Saturday.

We of course miss you very much and want very, very much to see you with us and to hug you. The same for Hadas and Yoel[1] and the whole family, friends from your battalion, and everyone in Mitzpe Hila. We hope we will see you very soon, perhaps for the upcoming holidays, even for Rosh HaShana in three more days.

We ask you, Gilad, to be strong and hold on. Don't break down before your release – soon! We are trying to make it as soon as possible.

We wish for you that this will be a good year and that we will begin the new year with you at home in Mitzpe Hila with family and friends. Hugs to you.

Mom and Dad

1. Gilad's sister and brother.

20/9/2006

Letter from Noam and Aviva Schalit to their son

Gilad didn't make it home for the Jewish New Year. I read the Schalits' letter at our family Rosh HaShana dinner. There wasn't a dry eye among us; I completely choked up. As I sat with my three children, picturing one of them in Gilad's place was more than I could bear. No doubt that the hearts and minds of every Israeli family were with the Schalits. Many households left an empty chair at their table for Gilad. This became customary over the next five years, not only in Israel but in Jewish homes around the world.

For the next five years, before every major Jewish and Muslim holiday, I made a special effort to push Hamas to advance the negotiations and allow the prisoners to be released. No one ever responded.

After Rosh HaShana, Noam Schalit, who had spoken to Ofer Dekel, told me nothing was happening. I received the same report from Ghazi Hamad. Throughout Gilad's captivity, I never understood why the Israeli side was so passive. Israel seemed reluctant to take control by putting a serious offer on the table.

According to the media, Israel feared that the price for Gilad's freedom would rise. I heard this from Israeli officials as well. They would say: If we make an offer, it becomes a starting point for negotiations, not the closing point. Actually, the very first price that Hamas demanded was the highest one. In subsequent years, the price only came down, first quantitatively, then in the "quality" of prisoners it demanded be released. With all the resources at the disposal of the Israeli security establishment, what was it doing all day, every day, to bring Gilad home?

It seemed to me that the Egyptians wanted to help – but they also wanted full ownership of the deal. If President Hosni Mubarak could snag all the credit for getting sworn enemies in Hamas and Israel to agree to trade Schalit for more than a thousand Palestinian prisoners, it would raise Egypt's profile as a regional player. Yet Mubarak clearly did not want to inflate Hamas' importance, both for internal reasons – lest he strengthen Hamas' parent movement, the Muslim Brotherhood – and also because Mubarak was the main patron of Hamas' nemesis inside Palestine, President Mahmoud Abbas. I told Ghazi as much in a phone call, then followed up with an e-mail urging him to push Hamas for what we needed next – a list of Palestinians to be released.

September 26, 2006. Noam called early in the morning to tell me that Dekel had said no negotiations were going on. He said Mashal was blocking them, probably because of internal political power struggles. Noam was very frustrated. He wanted to know if I'd heard anything about a trip to Damascus by Abu Ala, former prime minister of the Palestinian Authority, which Noam hoped might shed light on Mashal's position. I suggested another letter from Noam to Mashal. Later that day I wrote to Ghazi.

> *Dear Ghazi,*
>
> *It seems that the Egyptians really want full control, and they have threat-*
> *ened to pull out if there are any initiatives outside of their efforts. Dekel has*
> *suggested that if you have a way to speed things up by working through or*
> *with the Egyptians, that would be greatly appreciated. If you could pro-*
> *duce the list of names we talked about and discuss it with the Egyptians,*
> *that would be helpful. If you want to send me the list, I could also give it to*
> *Dekel, and then perhaps he could work faster through the Egyptians too.*
>
> *Gershon*

I found that writing Ghazi the same messages I passed on to him by phone
helped reinforce them. It also gave him a hard copy to use in conversations
on his side. Our relationship was still quite new. Although we had already
proven the effectiveness of this channel, we didn't really know each other
well, and I suppose we were still quite suspicious of each other. Speaking
on the phone often left me uncertain – I couldn't see his face or interpret
his body language. I was never sure whether or not he fully understood me.

Whenever we could, we also chatted on MSN Instant Messenger. I found this the most effective way to really understand what Ghazi
wanted to say. It allowed more time to think between words. We chatted
in English because Ghazi didn't have a Hebrew keyboard, and his written
English was better than his spoken Hebrew. When I didn't get an answer
to a question I had asked repeatedly, in different ways, I understood that
either he didn't have an answer, or he couldn't give an affirmative one. In
conversations with Palestinians, if the answer is negative, the response will
often be *"Inshallah"* – God willing. I came to understand that a firm "no"
was difficult for many Palestinians – just as it is elsewhere in the Middle
East and in Asia – because it can sound brutish and impolite.

That day, I also wrote to Khaled Mashal once again:

> *Dear Mr. Mashal,*
>
> *I understand from the Israeli negotiator, Ofer Dekel, that no negotia-*
> *tions have begun on the prisoner exchange. I don't understand what*

you are waiting for. Israel is prepared to negotiate and is waiting for you to submit your demands, including a list of the Palestinian prisoners you wish to have released. Don't you want the hundreds of Palestinian prisoners to be with their families for Eid al-Fitr?[2] What's the point of waiting? Enough suffering has occurred.

I understand that there are many issues involved and also power struggles between the organizations. Let's move forward. The decision is in your hands.

Ramadan kareem,[3]
Gershon Baskin

In addition, I wrote to Dr. Azzam Tamimi in London. By then, Tamimi was becoming an unofficial deliverer of messages to and from me whenever I contacted the Hamas leadership in Damascus, which refused to speak to me directly. Azzam responded, and I forwarded the letter to Noam; he called immediately and asked to share it with Dekel. I said yes, of course. Dekel, I learned, was preparing to go to Cairo to see Omar Suleiman.

Then I got a call from Nader El-A'aser. He wanted to meet and wouldn't answer any of my questions over the phone. He asked if I had tried to get a letter to Gilad. Yes, I said, and asked if he thought it arrived. He said no.

Years later, when I met Gilad for the first time in November 2011, almost a month after he was freed, I showed him the letter from his parents (along with about sixty pages of e-mails and other letters from a folder of more than seven hundred pages documenting my efforts to bring about his freedom). He had never received it. Throughout Gilad's years in captivity, the Schalit family made many attempts to deliver letters to him. The only letter that reached him was one that former us President Jimmy Carter personally took to Khaled Mashal in Damascus in June 2009. Imagine how Gilad felt – five years and four months in captivity and only one letter from his parents. I still wonder how he coped with the loneliness, and with having no control over his fate.

2. Eid al-Fitr is a holiday marking the end of Ramadan, the month in which Muslims fast from about 3 a.m. until sundown every day.
3. A blessing for the month of Ramadan.

I spoke to Ghazi that evening. He was surprised nothing was progressing. He had heard things were moving quite well. Ghazi, like me, is an optimist, often assessing situations more positively than they in fact are. Perhaps this shared quality helped to develop trust between us.

September 27. Another intense day with a flurry of phone calls, through which I learned that Omar Suleiman had sent a harsh letter to Mashal demanding Schalit's release.

In a phone call, Ghazi said he would really like to bypass the Egyptians; he too didn't have confidence in them and thought things could go much faster directly. He said he would also check on the letter for Gilad that I had given him.

But Noam was very nervous about bypassing the Egyptians. He said Dekel would refuse any lists from Ghazi. I said we could present the list and use it to verify information Dekel would receive from the Egyptians. I suggested to Noam that Dekel shouldn't be his only source of information. The issue was too complex, and there were too many conflicting interests between parties, and even within each one.

I believed Olmert didn't really want to negotiate the release of Palestinian prisoners with Hamas. For him this would strengthen Hamas at the expense of Fatah and Abu Mazen. Moreover, for any Israeli prime minister, negotiating with Hamas was the ultimate taboo. Negotiating with Hamas meant negotiating with terrorists, which goes against Israeli policy and principles.

For his part, President Mubarak wanted to control the process in order to make sure Hamas would not have a platform for success. At the same time, he wanted to assure Israel that Egypt was a superpower that could control Hamas. But Hamas suspected Egypt, had no trust in Israel, and held a very valuable asset – an Israeli soldier, whom it was in no hurry to give up.

I was convinced that the Israeli officials weren't being honest with the Schalit family. They wanted the Schalits and the Israeli public to believe Israel was doing everything humanly possible to bring Gilad home. Again the mantra was that if there was too much noise in the media about Gilad, Hamas would increase its demands. We were told that if Hamas sensed the Israeli public putting pressure on the government, Hamas would see its stock in Gilad rising even higher. It was better to be silent and let the officials, who knew what they were doing, do their job.

It made sense, but it was never true.

September 28. Israel's *Haaretz* daily reported that Abu Mazen had gone to Qatar to meet with Khaled Mashal. *Haaretz* also said Hamas had broken off talks with the Egyptians. I sent the article to Noam and told him that Azzam Tamimi had said more than a month ago that Hamas did not want the Egyptians to mediate, but wanted to bring in the Qataris.

Tamimi sent me an article from *Asharq Al-Awsat*, a Saudi-supported paper published in London, stating that Olmert had no intention of releasing Palestinian prisoners for Schalit. Tamimi wanted my opinion. I told him the article wasn't true: Dekel had full authorization from Olmert to negotiate a generous prisoner release. I was repeating to Tamimi the official Israeli position, but in my heart I didn't believe Olmert was prepared to negotiate.

Noam asked whether I could verify that Abu Mazen was in Qatar. Hanna Siniora spoke to Abu Hisham, Abu Mazen's political adviser, who confirmed that he was. Abu Hisham told Hanna that there had been progress in the negotiations. The reports that emerged continued to contradict one another.

I concluded that most media coverage of the case was false. Even the officials didn't know what was happening. All parties were spreading a huge amount of disinformation. Because the public was so anxious to hear about Gilad, there was an urgency to write news stories, but most of the time there was no real information. Most articles would repeat the same tidbit, which was frequently untrue. When journalists asked me what was going on, more often than not I would tell them I had no idea, even if I did.

Noam told me he was going to Paris to get the French government involved, since Gilad was a French citizen via his grandmother. The French, unlike any Israeli official, could go to Syria and influence the Syrian government to pressure Hamas. Noam was realizing that additional pressure had to be put on Hamas around the world.

I wrote to Khaled Mashal that we were encouraged by his meeting with Abu Mazen. I told him of Noam's upcoming trip to Paris. Perhaps Mashal and Noam could meet? I also suggested using Alastair Crooke (the now former British MI6 agent) to pass on messages. Alastair had been stationed in Israel during the Second Intifada, and had very good contacts within both the Israeli intelligence community and Hamas. In the past, he'd helped de-escalate some very difficult situations. When I spoke to Alastair, he said he would be happy to assist.

September 29. London's Arab media reported that negotiations were frozen. There was no contact between the Egyptians and Hamas. Hanna Siniora spoke to Abu Hisham and learned that Abu Mazen did not meet Mashal in Qatar after all. Abu Mazen had gone to Egypt. More disinformation? I didn't know whom to believe.

Ghazi remained convinced that, in a back channel with Dekel, he could speed up the process. I told him I would speak to Noam about the idea. He would also try to make sure Gilad received the letter.

I understood that using a back channel could cause problems with the Egyptians. Nonetheless, I was sure this was the only way we could make progress. Without a direct line of communication between Israel and Hamas, we were at the mercy of third parties with their own interests and a tremendous amount of disinformation. Any potential mediators from a third country – be it Egypt, Turkey, Qatar, or anywhere else willing to assist – were not coming to the table solely to bring Schalit home or release Palestinian prisoners. They were also interested in increasing their influence and power in the region and, in some cases, rebuilding Palestinian unity. To my mind, these additional issues only complicated the mission at hand.

Many people in Israel and around the world wanted to see Gilad released. Many in Palestine hoped to have their imprisoned loved ones released in return. And many political players in Cairo, Damascus, Amman, Paris, Washington, and London – to name a few – wanted to help, and perhaps to be heroes as well. Amid this complex, international web of concerned parties and conflicting interests, we had to find a way to bring Noam and Aviva's son home.

Chapter 6

Regional Players Sniff Out Starring Roles

By the beginning of October 2006, the possibility of an agreement to be mediated by the Egyptians seemed to be dissipating. Egypt was complying with Israel's demand to seal the Rafah border crossing between Gaza and Egypt, in accordance with Israel's blockade of Gaza, until Schalit was released. Even before the blockade, the tunnel trade – a robust flow of mostly illegal weapons and other contraband – was moving underneath the Egyptian-Gazan border along the Philadelphi Corridor.[1] With the blockade, the tunnel business had grown into a full-fledged underground economy, enabling Hamas to function financially. The governments of both Israel and the United States were pressuring Egypt to close the tunnels. This too, complicated relations between Hamas and Egypt.

Meanwhile, the Palestinians were busy grappling with their political disunity, focusing on talks between the Fatah movement of President

---

1. The Philadelphi Route, 8.6 miles long, is the border between Egypt and Gaza, where hundreds of tunnels have been constructed to supply the Palestinian-Gazan economy as well as to smuggle rockets and other weapons into Gaza from Sinai.

Mahmoud Abbas and Hamas, led by Khaled Mashal. The Qatari government had offered to mediate the dispute between the two organizations.

With all this going on, it was essential to find some way of opening a secret but direct back channel between Hamas and Israel. This is what I proposed to Ghazi Hamad, writing to him late at night on October 11 – for the second time that day.

October 11, 2006, 11 p.m.

Dear Ghazi,

I am more convinced than ever that we must find a way to conduct direct negotiations between you and Dekel. You have to convince your side that you will quickly produce results that will meet their demands. Israel too will resist, because it doesn't want direct talks with Hamas.

I am sure that if you came with another letter from Gilad and with the abductors' permission to negotiate on their behalf, we could convince Olmert to agree to the secret negotiations. This would have to be 100 percent secret. This way would be fast, and we could reach good results. Everything could be put on the table: the numbers, the names, the means of releasing Gilad and the Palestinian prisoners.

We have just a little time left until Eid al-Fitr. Let's not waste a single day. The best time for Israel to make a generous prisoner release is for the holiday.

Ghazi, I know you have jobs to do other than working on the Schalit case, but believe me, nothing is more important than this now. If it ends badly, it will be a disaster for all of us. If it ends well, the result will be all kinds of new political possibilities. Please give it your full attention. Get to the abductors and convince them to empower you on their behalf. Then it will be my turn to deliver.

We can succeed.

Best wishes,
Gershon

Ghazi responded by phone. While he concurred that the best way to move forward would be a secret direct back channel, he didn't think the leaders of Hamas would agree. I emphasized that he should tell them I was not an Israeli government official, but someone who directed a non-government organization working for Israeli-Palestinian peace. He said he would try to convince them, but I didn't sense much hope.

I was coming to realize that I had to gain credibility in the eyes of the decision makers on both sides – at times a seemingly impossible task. I had to persuade the Israeli officials that my contacts with Hamas led directly to those who were holding Gilad. And I had to prove to the Hamas leadership that I could reach – and influence – the highest-level decision makers in Israel.

On the Hamas side, I had to deal with the contradiction that Hamas wouldn't recognize Israel, yet wanted to negotiate with it. Hamas found its way around that little problem by demanding a third-party interlocutor, but also by allowing Ghazi Hamad to continue his contacts with Israelis such as me. I continued to insist that Hamas provide another sign of life from Gilad, as this would be the best proof that my channel led directly to the abductors. And if they could deliver it to me directly this time, Dekel couldn't claim I'd had nothing to do with it. Even though the September 9 letter from Gilad had already accomplished this, Dekel had discredited my efforts, I'd learned, by telling the prime minister and the Schalits that my role in securing that letter had been minimal.

It was important that my Hamas contacts came through multiple channels. If I could reach the most important figures, such as Khaled Mashal, and they would listen to me, perhaps it could lead to a breakthrough. The letter I passed from Noam Schalit to Khaled Mashal had done exactly that, leading to the release of Gilad's letter to his parents. So I wrote again to Mashal. Though I knew I wouldn't receive a direct response from him, I kept hoping my words would penetrate and influence the decision-making process of Hamas' top leadership.

October 13, 2006

Dear Mr. Mashal,

Nine people in Gaza were killed yesterday. It has been reported that since the kidnapping of Gilad Schalit, more than 250 Palestinians have been killed in Gaza. Is keeping Schalit in custody worth even one more Palestinian life? Israel will not stop its military pursuit of Schalit until he is either found or released. Until then, many more innocent Palestinians will die.

The Egyptian mediators tell me your side has not put any serious demands on the table. Despite statements by Azzam Tamimi that you are waiting for the Israeli side to make its offer, I know the Israeli side has already made a commitment to President Mubarak that there will be a significant release of Palestinian prisoners. The Egyptians are waiting for your side to submit a list of prisoners to be released.

It would be much easier and faster if you accepted my direct involvement in the negotiations. We want to close the deal by Eid al-Fitr. We had wanted to by the beginning of Ramadan, but that is behind us. Please, let's finish this already, for the sake of every innocent human life.

Gershon Baskin

In the following days, the violence between Hamas and Fatah increased. Gaza was beginning to look like a lawless land. Warring Palestinian factions seemed to have only one thing in common – an interest in attacking the enemy. More Qassam rockets were being shot at Israeli towns, prompting IDF retaliation against Hamas and other factions in Gaza. Meanwhile, Hamas boasted that it was prepared for any Israeli attack, and that the invading Israeli army would find Hamas fighters popping up from underground when least expected. Hamas also claimed that the entire Gaza Strip was booby-trapped with trip wires that would set off huge explosives, destroying Israeli tanks on the spot. The war of words was escalating between the two sides.

I couldn't sleep. I wrote to Ghazi before dawn, urging him to act.

October 16, 2006, 6:40 a.m.

Dear Ghazi,

The situation is getting worse, and it looks like Israel is planning a massive attack on Gaza. There must be something we can do to prevent further deterioration. Believe me, Israel's intentions are real. The reports of Hamas' defensive capacity against the Israeli army in Gaza are a lot of hot air. The only way to avoid disaster is to make real progress on the Schalit case. I think it's time to involve the prime minister, Mr. Haniyeh, directly, if he hasn't been involved until now. He has to use his authority to call on the abductors to make a deal with Israel now. Halas! [Enough!] It's time to reach the end. Israel's patience has come to an end. Please, do something.

Gershon

Completely frustrated, seeing disaster unfold before my eyes, I knew I had to reach Khaled Mashal directly. I asked Azzam Tamimi to speak to Mashal and see if it was possible to do something constructive. I then sent him an e-mail reinforcing what I had said on the phone, and hoping he would forward it to the Hamas leadership in Damascus.

October 19, 2006, 8:20 a.m.

Dear Azzam,

The negotiations seem to be frozen. We were hoping for a breakthrough by Eid al-Fitr. Do you have new information? Could you check with Khaled Mashal?

The Egyptians say they are not getting answers from the abductors on the proposals. The Israeli side, they say, is being responsive and ready to negotiate a prisoner release. I believe the best way to speed everything up is direct negotiation with someone from the Hamas government. I am almost positive that I can arrange a secret meeting between the Israeli negotiator and Ghazi Hamad, if Hamad is appointed to represent the abductors directly. This way we could conclude the negotiations quickly. I can also be directly involved to help the process. Please advise.

Best wishes,
Gershon

Azzam answered my e-mail two hours later:

October 19, 10:15 a.m.

Dear Gershon,

My information, as recent as yesterday, is that Omar Suleiman – who visited Damascus recently – has agreed with Khaled Mashal that the Egyptians will continue their mediation effort. What is missing in the process is Israeli agreement to the principle of a swap. So long as this is not promised by the Israelis to the Egyptian mediators, things will remain as they are. What you need to do is work on your own prime minister; he is the real obstacle. All he needs to do is agree to the swap, and then negotiations through the good offices of the Egyptians will immediately proceed.

Azzam

I conveyed Azzam's message to Noam Schalit. Noam believed the Israeli side had informed the Egyptians of its readiness to negotiate a swap of Palestinian prisoners for Gilad. This is what he'd been told by Ofer Dekel and by Prime Minister Olmert himself. It was unclear to Noam why Hamas was claiming there had been no Israeli decision. It was unclear to both of us why both sides were dragging their feet. Clearly, telling the truth, the whole truth, and nothing but the truth was not characteristic of the process of trying to conduct negotiations between Israel and Hamas.

October 19, 1:41 p.m.

Dear Azzam,

Noam Schalit is meeting with Olmert on Monday. He would like to have as much information as possible before the meeting. From what you know, has Israel refused a release of Palestinian prisoners simultaneously with the release of Gilad, or has Israel rejected the idea of releasing Palestinian prisoners entirely? Our understanding is that Israel has agreed to a prisoner exchange, but in two phases – releasing Gilad to the Egyptians, and then releasing Palestinian prisoners. We understand that previously Mashal rejected the idea of the two phases. Do [the captors] demand a simultaneous release, or can we talk about two phases, with Egyptian guarantees? Your answers to us are very helpful.

Gershon

Once again Azzam responded quite rapidly.

October 19, 2:05 p.m.

Gershon,

Simply, Hamas does not trust the Israeli government. Hamas wants the releases to be conducted in the same way as previous prisoner exchanges. So Olmert needs to tell the Egyptians he is willing to release prisoners in exchange for Schalit (who I'm told is in good health and being taken good care of). Hamas has not agreed – and I do not expect it will agree – to release Schalit into Egyptian custody first, in the hope that the Israelis might then agree to release some prisoners. The deal, I understand, would have to include agreement on the names of the prisoners to be released.

Azzam

"Hamas does not trust the Israeli government," I read aloud, amused, as if this were news. Of course Hamas didn't trust Israel, nor did Israel trust Hamas. (And Egypt had its own set of complex relations with both sides.) We had to break this vicious cycle. I was convinced that I could find a way, if only the Israeli officials would take me seriously.

The only good news was that Azzam had said Gilad was in good health and being treated well. At that moment, and many other times over the years, I doubted this was true. But his words provided some hope.

October 25, 2006

Dear Mr. Mashal,

Kul 'am w'intum bkheir.[2] My friends in Gaza and Egypt tell me there is a new initiative under way regarding something more comprehensive than a prisoner exchange. The Egyptians are behind the initiative and have received an Israeli promise to cooperate.

I understand that the initiative includes a plan for resolving the internal Hamas-Fatah conflict as well as a renewed tahdiyah [calm] in Gaza. As you know, there is growing pressure in Israel to launch a major ground operation in Gaza. The news media here are full of reports about the large amount of weapons smuggled through the Rafah tunnels. There is almost no reporting about the more than three hundred Palestinians who have been killed since the Schalit abduction. The rationale behind the offensive is to locate Schalit and confiscate as many weapons and explosives and as much ammunition as possible.

The alternative to all this death and destruction is to make a deal that would include a prisoner exchange, the prevention of a Palestinian civil war, and a temporary cease-fire that would allow everyone to breathe a little and prevent the deaths of so many innocent people.

Olmert, in my assessment, is prepared for both scenarios. I understand that you have been invited to Cairo for talks with the

2. A Muslim holiday blessing: "May every year find you in good health."

Egyptians. The time has come – it has been too long since the abduction of Schalit. Too many people have suffered. The future is in your hands.

Gershon Baskin

In November 2006, I heard from Israeli, Hamas, and Egyptian sources that Israel had transmitted an "agreement in principle" to the Egyptians for a very generous prisoner exchange for Gilad Schalit. The deal would have two phases. Hamas, I was told, had demanded – in addition to the release of all women and minor prisoners – that a total of one thousand prisoners be released in exchange for Schalit. Hamas had submitted a list of about 350 names for the first-phase release of 450 prisoners. Ghazi Hamad told me Israel had accepted only 200 of the names, and had demanded that most of these people be deported to Gaza. Their deportation was rejected by Hamas.

Meanwhile, Ofer Dekel told the Schalit family not to deal with me anymore. I was raising questions about the Egyptians' ability to deliver. I was raising doubts about Dekel's seriousness and Olmert's sincerity. Dekel and his team referred to me as a "disturbing element." That is exactly what I intended to be. I kept telling Noam and Aviva that they needed someone who could communicate with all sides. They needed to base their assessments on information coming not only from the Israeli prime minister, but also from Gaza, Syria, London, and other places where people had contacts and could pass on messages.

The Schalits were growing doubtful. They felt that Ghazi Hamad seemed well-intentioned, but Dekel had told them he had no influence. Yet they also had doubts about Olmert and Dekel, and felt that they were not being told the whole truth by Israeli officials. The Schalits continued talking to me, but I sensed that their confidence in me and my contacts in Hamas was waning. I continued speaking to Ghazi, at least every few days. I also spoke with Ahmed Yousef, Haniyeh's senior adviser. I wanted to keep my channels of communication open.

By now, Gilad Schalit had become part of my family. I was always conscious of him, wondering how he was doing, where he was being held. Did he have food? Did his captors talk to him? Was he learning Arabic? I kept in mind the promises of Ghazi and others that Gilad was being treated well. They told me Islam had strict laws governing the protection of prisoners, and Gilad was being held in accordance with them. I also knew that the Hamas leaders understood the value of the "asset" they were holding and would do their utmost to ensure his safety. At the same time, Gilad could be killed inadvertently by Israeli artillery fire on Gaza.

The rumors of an agreement that I heard throughout November didn't pan out, but in early December there was again talk of a deal in the works. On January 2, 2007, the Israeli newspaper *Haaretz* reported: "Hamas accepts Israeli offer of 450 Palestinian prisoners for Schalit."

According to *Haaretz*, Hamas would give Israel a video showing that Schalit was alive, and in exchange, Israel would release an as yet undecided number of women and minors held in its jails. Next, Schalit would be transferred to Egypt, then to Israel. At the same time, Israel would release the 450 Palestinian prisoners. Finally, about two months later, Israel would release another 550 prisoners. The list compiled by Hamas would include senior figures in the group's political and military wings, and leading Fatah members such as Marwan Barghouti.[3] *Haaretz* further reported that Omar Suleiman, the Egyptian intelligence chief, had just met in Saudi Arabia with two top Hamas officials – political leader Khaled Mashal and Palestinian Prime Minister Ismail Haniyeh, sourcing the information to Hamas spokesman Fawzi Barhoum.

Had the *Haaretz* article been written in October 2011, it would have been just as accurate in describing the basic framework for the deal. Why Gilad Schalit had to spend nearly five more years in captivity – not to mention the 1,027 Palestinian prisoners who got their freedom in exchange – is a troubling question that only Hamas and the Israeli leadership can answer in full. I will explore it in subsequent chapters.

The day after the news broke, Azzam wrote me from London:

> *My source says Barhoum has exaggerated the little progress that has been achieved in negotiating a deal. The source denied that a deal has been reached or is about to be.*

---

3. Convicted in 2004 of a terrorist attack in which five Israelis were murdered.

I passed Azzam's message on to Noam Schalit. The Schalits and I had learned not to get too excited by every piece of news. For them, the only measure of success was Gilad's return.

In the days to come, street fighting between Fatah and Hamas forces exploded. Gaza was engulfed in chaos. No one seemed to be in control. Aside from innocent Palestinians being killed by competing militias and gang lords, I believed Gilad Schalit was not safe. He could be used as a pawn between forces, just as Ron Arad was when imprisoned in Lebanon, until he disappeared.

January 7, 2007

Dear Ghazi,

Things are looking pretty bad in Palestine. You must do everything to develop some working relations with Abu Mazen. A Palestinian civil war is bad for us all, most of all for you Palestinians. There has to be a way to compromise. The decision to double the Hamas force is foolish and will only lead to more bloodshed.[4] I hope Haniyeh and Abu Mazen can find some accommodation between them for the benefit of the Palestinian people. The current situation cannot continue for long before it gets completely out of hand. I hope it is not too late.

On the Schalit case, it looks like once again everything has broken down. I know they've spoken again about the videotape in exchange for women and children. I told you I didn't think Israel would go for it. We need to move on the new letter from Gilad to his family – without anything in exchange. If you get this letter to me, not to the Egyptians, it will put me in a position to work independently with Noam Schalit to get enough public pressure from important people in Israel to finally conclude a deal. I can't make any promises, but I know that having the letter in my hands would significantly improve my ability to move things forward.

---

4. This round of inter-Palestinian fighting erupted when Hamas announced that it was doubling its security personnel against President Abbas' wishes.

> *Please, Ghazi, give it your best. Let's end this affair.*

Best wishes,
Gershon

Ghazi sent me a message that he was out of Gaza and would call in a few days.

In the meantime, Noam called to ask whether I could help him arrange a visit to Gaza. Given the turmoil there, no one in Israel would approve such a thing, and I doubted Noam would be willing to go through an illegal tunnel run by Hamas via Sinai. He agreed with me that he could go in only legally, through the Gaza-Israel crossing. Aside from the Israeli security hurdles, it was more than doubtful that anyone in Hamas would consent to see him in Gaza. But I liked his spirit, and in his place I would do exactly the same thing. I was also glad he'd asked for my help.

On January 13, I tried to get more information from the Hamas side regarding rumors in the Israeli press about progress in the talks. Again, I thought about how cynically everyone was using the media to spread misinformation. We were dealing with human lives! What an impossible situation for the Schalit family – every day new rumors, new hopes, and new disappointments.

I wrote to Azzam:

January 13, 2007

Dear Azzam,

Hope you're well. I need some information. The Israeli officials have told Noam Schalit that the Palestinian side has not yet provided the names of all the prisoners it wants released. I understood from other Palestinian sources that lists were submitted about three weeks ago. Could you check on this? It is most important.

Thanks,
Gershon

Azzam soon replied:

> *January 14, 2007, 11:16 a.m.*
>
> *Dear Gershon,*
>
> *My source says that Israel objects to the concept of Hamas submitting lists. According to the source, Israel insists that it alone will determine who should and should not be released from prison.*
>
> *Azzam*

I responded:

> *January 14, 11:20 a.m.*
>
> *Dear Azzam,*
>
> *Thanks. From my information, Israel insists on receiving the lists from the Egyptians, as Hamas would reject any list that [the Israelis] would prepare. I am more than willing to receive the lists from Hamas and deliver them to the Israeli side. They cannot refuse to receive the lists from Noam Schalit.*
>
> *Gershon*

I was incredulous. Gilad Schalit was in Hamas captivity. Nobody in Israel had any idea of his condition. Yet the main problem was who would submit the names of Palestinian prisoners to be released? Or whether the lists had been submitted at all? This was ludicrous!

There was a whole team of Israeli experts and intelligence officers working on the Schalit case. Even if some of them were probably busy devising a military operation that would allow Israeli forces to dash in and heroically pull Gilad out of some bunker, what was the rest of the team doing with its time?!

Chapter 7

The Road to Gaza Runs Through Damascus

In January 2007, the government of Spain convened a two-day conference to commemorate the fifteenth anniversary of the historic Madrid Conference on Middle East peace, which had led to the Oslo process, mutual recognition by the PLO and Israel, peace between Israel and Jordan, and a near deal between Israel and Syria. The Syrian Foreign Ministry sent two representatives to this gathering: Dr. Riad Daoudi, the ministry's legal adviser, and Bushra Kanafani, its director of communications and spokesperson. On the first day of the conference, I found myself in an elevator with these two officials and Israeli journalist Akiva Eldar. Akiva tried to speak to them and even offered his hand to Daoudi, but to no avail. The Syrians stared at the floor, refusing to even glance at us Israelis. Daoudi pushed the button of a floor below his in order to exit the elevator as soon as possible.

Despite this treatment, I knew that by the end of this conference, I had to speak to them about Gilad Schalit. The Syrians provided Hamas with a haven and a base; they could surely influence Hamas to be more forthcoming. I asked one of my Palestinian friends,

Walid Salem of East Jerusalem, to ask Dr. Daoudi to meet me in a secluded corner of the hotel, the Madrid Intercontinental, where we would not be seen.

Walid spoke to Daoudi and he agreed. We met in a dark side room of a banquet hall. There were chairs and tables, but we stood together instead. I shook his hand and thanked him for consenting to speak to me.

Daoudi listened intently, although somewhat impatiently – perhaps he worried about the impact of such a meeting if word of it got out. I came right to the point, asking him to consult President Assad about what Syria could do to resolve this situation. I stressed the pressure the people of Gaza were under, adding that the fastest way to relieve it was by completing the prisoner exchange, and to that end, it was necessary to press Hamas. Daoudi listened, said, "Okay," then departed. No promise, no handshake, but also no rejection. This would not be my last attempt to speak to Syrian officials – sometimes finding an interlocutor, and other times, encountering silence.

The ping-pong of mutual accusations continued for months, with no progress on the horizon. Passover was approaching, and in homes all over Israel an empty chair would be left for Gilad Schalit at the Seder table. Gilad was rapidly becoming an honorary member of every Israeli family, including my own.

I felt increasingly angry at everyone involved. I told Noam and Aviva Schalit to stop believing everything Olmert and Dekel told them. I told Ghazi that Hamas wasn't serious and didn't care about its own people and prisoners. And I wrote to Khaled Mashal asking if he didn't want to end this saga.

April 4, 2007

Dear Mr. Mashal and Colleagues,

Tomorrow evening Passover – our holiday of freedom – begins, and it would be nice to give the Schalit family some news of their son. It would be nice to give several hundred Palestinian families news of freedom for their children too. Why can't this deal finally be concluded? Don't you want it to end? I can help but you refuse. I don't understand. I will never publicize that you have communicated with me. Let's end this ugly chapter already, for the sake of the families.

Gershon Baskin

Throughout April, Noam and Aviva reported no progress. According to Azzam Tamimi, Hamas was receiving messages from the Egyptians that Olmert wouldn't release any Palestinian prisoners.

Late that month, I attended a conference in Ankara, the Turkish capital. For three days I sat next to Dr. Samir Taqi of Syria. Dr. Taqi was a cardiologist but also headed a strategic think tank in Damascus, and he and Daoudi had been appointed by President Assad to represent Syria in proximity peace talks with Israel. I befriended Dr. Taqi, and on the last day of the conference I spoke to him in confidence about Gilad Schalit. He promised to speak to Assad about the matter.

We never spoke again. But I believe Taqi kept his word – and the Syrian president refused to get involved. Assad had told former US President Jimmy Carter that the Schalit issue was Hamas' business – he would not intervene. Almost five years later, in April 2012, Taqi left Syria and joined the opposition fighting to overthrow Assad.

By the beginning of May 2007, the civil war in Gaza was in full force. Just walking the streets was dangerous. People were locking themselves in their homes. Everyone was trying to secure personal weapons. Nobody was working. Gaza was becoming a very unsafe place to live. In this atmosphere, the prospects for bringing Gilad home seemed bleaker than ever.

On May 20, I tried a new tactic. I published an open letter through e-mail to the people of Gaza. I asked my 150-plus friends in Gaza who received my letter to distribute it widely.

Dr. Mohammed Migdad of the Islamic University, a member of Hamas, inspired by this appeal, wrote me that he was contacting some of his friends from Fatah to see if they could do something together, such as a joint march or a joint call to both sides to end the fighting and negotiate an understanding. The fighting in Gaza was growing worse. Gaza was in total turmoil.

On June 7, after one day of major warfare on the streets of Gaza, Hamas fighters took control. Forces loyal to Mahmoud Abbas ran for the border. Some 120 Palestinians were killed, and more than five hundred wounded. The following week, fighting continued as Hamas consolidated its hold over the Gaza Strip. Using horrendous acts of violence – including throwing people off roofs – Hamas forces led by Ahmed Jaabri made it clear that he controlled Gaza. Jaabri was also holding Gilad Schalit.

On June 15, President Abbas pronounced the Hamas government in Gaza illegal, and official contacts between Ramallah and Gaza stopped. Israel declared Gaza a "hostile territory," although the Israeli legal system knows no such term. I was concerned that it might be more difficult for me now to maintain contact with Hamas leaders, even if for the sole purpose of trying to free Gilad Schalit.

The shake-up in Gaza introduced a new factor into the negotiations for Schalit. How would a prisoner exchange affect the power struggle between Fatah and Hamas? This consideration must have crossed the minds of all decision makers in Israel, the West Bank, Cairo, and Washington. There would probably now be additional pressure on Prime Minister Olmert not to deal with Hamas. Surely President Abbas would tell him not to do anything to strengthen Hamas, including – and perhaps especially – releasing Palestinian prisoners.

I also surmised that Egypt would no longer be in a position to mediate. The Egyptians had backed Abbas against the *coup d'état* of Hamas. Egyptian support for the Hamas regime would endanger that of President Mubarak, who was coping with increasing public backing of the Muslim Brotherhood, Hamas' parent movement. Soon after the coup, Egypt closed its official office in Gaza, and the Egyptian officers posted there returned to Cairo.

On June 20 I wrote to Ghazi:

Dear Ghazi,

I hope you and your family are well. You people have gotten yourselves into a big mess. I understand that Hamas did not intend this result, but when you play with fire you never know what will burn.

I think the people of Gaza are in for a very long, hard period. I also think Hamas will be increasingly isolated in the world, and the lives of Hamas politicians will become more and more difficult, both externally and internally.

I also fear for the future of Gilad Schalit. I wonder if the Egyptians are going to continue mediating for the prisoner exchange. I am willing to step in once again, and together perhaps we can achieve some results.

It would be very nice to hear something from Gilad. This week marks one year since his abduction, and his family has gone through more than enough (and so has Gilad). There are also thousands of prisoners waiting for this exchange to happen – so let's see once again if it is possible to move forward.

Gershon

Not wanting to "put all my eggs in one basket," I also contacted Dr. Ahmed Yousef again. Still senior adviser to Hamas Prime Minister Ismail Haniyeh, he had been appointed deputy foreign minister as well. Respected in some Western capitals, Yousef was often presented as the more reasonable face of Hamas. I had spent many hours in dialogue with him and respected him personally, even if I disagreed with him politically.

June 24, 2007

Dear Dr. Ahmed,

I want to repeat and emphasize what I told you yesterday (June 23) on the phone. I am convinced that if there is an offer of up-to-date information about Gilad Schalit – a video or a new letter handwritten by Gilad – then Olmert might be willing to release some minors and women prisoners. If you want me to be directly involved in this new effort, I am more than ready to do whatever possible.

I know you don't have direct contact with the abductors, but I assume that you have ways of getting to them. My information channels tell me that the Israeli security establishment knows where Gilad is being held, but for the time being its estimation of the costs and benefits of a military operation to release him is still in the negative balance. That could change, and therefore time is important.

Gershon

The next day, Hamas released an audio tape from Gilad. I don't know if my pleas for another sign of life had something to do with it. Hamas may simply have decided that since its takeover of Gaza, it needed to improve its image around the world.

I sat and listened in awe.

"I regret my government's lack of interest in me," we heard Gilad say on the tape. "You must meet the demands of the *mujaheddin*[1] to get me out of prison. Just as I have parents who miss me, so do the thousands of Palestinian prisoners, and they deserve to have them home. It has been a whole year, and my health continues to deteriorate, necessitating lengthy hospital treatment."

Gilad was clearly reading a script, but what a relief to hear his voice!

That same day, Prime Minister Olmert met with President Mubarak, President Abbas, and King Abdullah II of Jordan at a summit in Sharm el-Sheikh aimed at boosting Abbas' leadership of the Palestinian Authority and isolating Hamas. Following the meeting, Olmert announced that he would release 250 Palestinian political prisoners as a goodwill gesture to Abbas.

The following day was June 26, 2007. It marked a long, trying year since the abduction of Gilad Schalit. I felt we were no closer to bringing Gilad home than we had been on the day he was abducted. I sensed that Prime Minister Olmert had not come to terms with the need to make a deal with Hamas. Until he did, there would be no deal. Perhaps if Hamas were to demonstrate more flexibility, it would help convince Olmert to move forward.

The next day, I wrote again to Ahmed Yousef:

1. The "jihad fighters," a term coined by Islamic militiamen in reaction to the Soviet invasion of Afghanistan.

Dear Dr. Ahmed,

The presentation of the audio tape was a big success and has, I believe, contributed to the possibilities of moving forward. What's the next step? How can we move this process forward faster? Is Hamas willing to submit a new list of names?

The tape released today and the one-year anniversary of Gilad Schalit in captivity have created the environment for Olmert to make quick decisions. So what can be done to move forward? There is a need for direct contact and direct messages. Why don't you invite me to Gaza to work on this issue? I would present the invitation to Olmert in order to get clearance to come.

Gershon

Dr. Yousef answered that he thought it would be helpful if Israel submitted its own list of one thousand Palestinian prisoners it would be willing to release. But with no Egyptian office in Gaza anymore and the split between Hamas and Fatah being solidified, it seemed that all contacts and negotiations were off. My mind raced, trying to figure out how to break the stalemate.

July 7, 2007

Dear Mr. Mashal,

The negotiations are once again deadlocked. Last week Dr. Ahmed Yousef suggested to me a proposal for breaking the stalemate: Israel would submit a list of one thousand names of prisoners for Hamas to choose from according to the agreed number. I transmitted that message to Olmert. Ofer Dekel went to Omar Suleiman saying that Israel was ready to submit a list of names. Suleiman reported back to Dekel that Hamas refused to receive a list of names from Israel. Who is making decisions on your side?

Ghazi Hamad tells me that Hamas will indeed not accept a list from Israel. He insists that the problem now, after Israel has rejected 90 percent of the list Hamas submitted to it via the Egyptians, is that there must be an agreement on the criteria for prisoners. I explained to him that politically, Olmert can release only so many prisoners with blood on their hands.

I have always advocated direct back-channel negotiations rather than going through the Egyptians. Everything goes slower with the Egyptians, which makes concluding a deal much more difficult. Hamas also has an interest in ending the Schalit affair as soon as possible.

Ofer Dekel went to the Rimonim military prison, in the center of the country, to speak directly with some Hamas prisoners, so this shows that Israel is willing to speak directly with Hamas members.[2] I believe we could convince Olmert to approve a direct back channel. Ghazi Hamad and I could both help with this. He and I have been speaking about this idea for two weeks. He says he will check with people in Gaza if there is any chance of this happening. I have also begun checking on the Israeli side. This is the best chance we have of making a deal quickly. It is also the best way to know which channel is authorized to make progress – which is unclear today. It is time to end this chapter. It is also time for you to respond to me directly. I can help.

Gershon Baskin

As usual, I received no answer from Khaled Mashal. But about a month later, Ghazi called to say there was interest in "checking the possibility" of a direct, secret back channel. I contacted Noam, who said he was meeting with Dekel the next day and would raise the issue with him.

Noam told me Dekel would run the idea by Olmert. Several days passed. Then I learned that Dekel had not gotten a positive response from Olmert. But a few weeks later, I received a message through Noam

---

2. While Israel opposes direct contact with Hamas members, it has always spoken to Hamas leaders inside Israeli prisons. I suppose that in prison, Israel can make sure the Hamas prisoners know who is in charge. Nonetheless, Israel is fully aware that these inmates communicate regularly with the Hamas leadership in Gaza and Damascus.

that Israel was in fact prepared to investigate the possibility of a secret, direct back channel. I contacted Khaled Mashal once more, undeterred by his failure to answer my previous letters.

September 9, 2007

Dear Mr. Mashal,

It is almost Ramadan again, and virtually no progress has been made in negotiating a prisoner exchange. The situation for both our peoples is much worse than it was a year ago. The negotiations on the Schalit case have gone nowhere, with no hope in sight. Each day the situation seems even worse. The Egyptians don't want to be engaged anymore. Perhaps the Norwegians or the Turks or some other people and countries can take over?

Ofer Dekel has agreed to my pursuing the possibility of a direct, secret channel to complete the negotiations. I know that according to your side, you submitted a list of prisoners, and the Israelis only accepted forty of the names on the list and demanded that hundreds of others be deported. You are still waiting for the Israelis to accept your list, but that is not going to happen. The list contained too many names that no Israeli prime minister could accept and continue to survive politically.

Is that the end of the negotiations? Isn't it possible to work on other names? Israel could submit more names; your side could submit more names. Isn't it time to bring 400 or 450 Palestinian prisoners home to their families? Aren't they also longing to see their loved ones?

My wife's first cousin, Sasson Nuriel, was kidnapped and killed by Hamas. I have felt the family's pain. I don't want the same fate for Gilad Schalit. There is no reason he and his family should continue to suffer so much. They're no different from the hundreds and thousands of Palestinians who don't deserve to suffer.

We're not talking about peace. We're talking about the human side of this conflict. Islam guarantees the protection of prisoners, and for good reason. Islam is a humanistic religion; it puts people and humanity first.

*I propose that this direct channel work to reach an agreement.
I think that if you instruct Ahmed Jaabri or anyone else to work out
the details, we can make it work. You tell me where to come, and I'll
come. Tell me with whom to speak, and I'll do so. Let's negotiate a
final deal. I'm waiting for your response. I won't give up.*

Ramadan kareem,
Gershon Baskin

Khaled Mashal didn't answer directly, but Azzam Tamimi told me not
to give up. He said the basic problem was still the complete distrust
between the sides. Tamimi said that Mashal didn't like the idea of a
direct channel. He insisted on a third party. But few countries were in a
position to mediate. The European Union and the United States listed
Hamas as a terrorist organization, so their diplomats were forbidden to
contact Hamas officials. Four countries had decent relations with both
sides, however, and could play a mediating role: Russia, Turkey, Switzerland, and Norway. I decided to contact the Norwegians.

Ambassador Svein Sevje was a senior adviser to the Norwegian
prime minister. Sevje had contacts throughout the Arab world and knew
people in both Hezbollah and Hamas. Since coming to Israel after high
school to volunteer on a kibbutz, he had maintained many friendships
here. I had met him several times when he was advising the Norwegian
government on the Israeli-Palestinian peace process. He seemed able
to speak to many people in diverse quarters, so I decided to knock on
his door.

September 14, 2007

Dear Svein,

*I don't know if you know, but I have been deeply involved in the
behind-the-scenes negotiations with Hamas on the Schalit case. I
have been trying to open a direct, secret back channel. I am working
with a few people in Gaza, and we are trying to get the agreement
of Ahmed Jaabri as well as Khaled Mashal. I sent Mashal a fax and
an e-mail last week, and we verified that he received it. Ofer Dekel*

is willing to advance a direct, secret channel for negotiations. I am sure you and Norway could help. Certain people in Gaza want me to be directly involved. Mashal wants a third-party negotiator, and since the Egyptians seem to be out of the picture, Norway could step in and assist. What do you think?

Gershon Baskin

On September 17, Sevje answered me:

Gershon,

Our involvement in the Schalit case is, as you know, purely humanitarian. We have not been given a mandate by either Israel or Hamas to go between. Frankly, I see little that Norway can do which is not being taken care of by those already involved. The solution seems to rest on the "price," not on lack of contacts.

I hope to see you next time I'm in the region.

All the best,
Svein

I was disappointed in Svein's response, but glad when he asked to meet a couple of weeks later. He introduced me to Tor Wennesland, who would soon head the Norway office in the Palestinian Authority, a kind of embassy. Both Tor and Svein asked sharp questions about the negotiations and the positions of the various players. Svein said he would consult the prime minister and foreign minister in Oslo.

Two weeks later, he returned with a negative response – but an open door. Norway would mediate only if both sides requested that it alone take over the negotiations. This demand was not unreasonable, but I doubted both sides could agree on anything at this point.

In the next two months, October and November 2007, nothing moved even an inch forward. I couldn't understand why Olmert wasn't demanding that Dekel make a deal to bring Gilad home. The prime minister told the Israeli public that he had a picture of Gilad in his office and looked at it every day. In every speech, Olmert said the State of Israel was doing everything possible to bring Gilad home. With all due respect, I didn't believe any of it.

At the end of November, Olmert and Abbas became very busy with renewed peace talks. All attention turned away from Gilad Schalit to Annapolis, Maryland, where President George W. Bush was convening another Israeli-Palestinian parley aimed at re-launching the peace process. Neither Olmert nor Abbas wanted to reward Hamas with a large prisoner exchange in the midst of these efforts. Indeed, if these two leaders had anything in common, it was the desire to marginalize Hamas – not hand it another victory to boast about.

Meanwhile, I received a call from General Nader El-A'aser. He told me he was working directly with Egyptian Intelligence Minister Omar Suleiman. He said that Egypt was continuing to work on the negotiations and that I should send his regards to Noam Schalit. Clearly, even after the Egyptians had withdrawn from mediation, they were demanding that negotiations by any other third party be conducted under Egyptian auspices. With vital national and security interests in Gaza, Egypt recognized the importance of continued involvement and, if possible, control over these negotiations.

With apparently no progress taking place behind the scenes, I thought it might be helpful to launch a campaign that would attract attention in Gaza and around the world. I drafted a plan and sent it off to Gaza, Damascus, and politicians in Jerusalem, including Prime Minister Olmert and Foreign Minister Tzipi Livni:

January 8, 2008

Plan for Dealing with Gaza

There seems to be a lack of strategy in dealing with the situation in Gaza. It is necessary to ease tensions and avoid an ultimate, full-fledged Israeli invasion. Continued mortar and rocket fire from Gaza into Israel will provoke an Israeli invasion. Continued total closure of

Gaza and the economic siege will continue to provoke Palestinians to shoot mortars and rockets into Israel.

The continuation of the "underground" economy in Gaza endangers Israel, Egypt, and Palestinian society in Gaza. The closure of the Rafah crossing increases the role of the tunnels underneath the Philadelphi Corridor. An opening of the Rafah crossing should be consistent with a demand to close all tunnels.

An agreement on a bilateral cease-fire could be in the immediate interest of both sides. Israel is interested in ending the rocket fire from Gaza. Hamas is interested in ending Israeli incursions and air attacks against Gaza. Israel would require that the cease-fire include all organizations in Gaza and all rocket and mortar fire. If Hamas cannot impose the cease-fire on all organizations in Gaza, then the cease-fire on Israel's part will also be partial – rocket for rocket, so to speak.

It's possible to make a comprehensive package deal, with each part linked to the others:

1. *Bilateral cease-fire between Israel and Gaza – Hamas will impose the cease-fire on all organizations in Gaza.*
2. *Israel will allow the Rafah crossing and one crossing into Israel (for goods transport in both directions) to be opened under the following conditions:*
   a. *PA troops (loyal to Abu Mazen) will man the crossings and not Hamas troops.*
   b. *EU monitors will function on the Palestinian side of both crossings.*
   c. *Hamas will take responsibility for closing tunnels across Philadelphi – tunnel closures will be inspected by the EU monitors.*
3. *Schalit/Prisoner exchange – the implementation of the above will include the release of Schalit and an agreed-upon number of Palestinian prisoners by Israel.*

> *This deal could be negotiated through the back channel of Gershon Baskin and appropriate people selected by Hamas. The final deal would be concluded and agreed upon through the Egyptians.*

There seemed to be interest in these ideas in both Gaza and Israel, but a third party was needed to conduct direct negotiations. I once again contacted the Norwegians.

February 21, 2008

Dear Svein,

I would like to speak with you as soon as possible regarding the prospect of Norway mediating a cease-fire understanding between Israel and Hamas. I have launched a series of very serious conversations with all parties. It is clear that a third party must come in and tie the pieces together. Time is crucial, because we must prevent an all-out Israeli attack on Gaza. I just came back from Ramallah, where I met with Rafiq Husseini, chief of staff of the Palestinian President's Office. I have had several long conversations with Ahmed Yousef in Gaza. I am speaking to the Israeli side as well. I did propose that IPCRI mediate, but the parties here don't know how to relate to a non-state actor. There is clearly a need for Norway to step in as fast as possible.

Gershon

In the middle of this initiative, my parents were in a terrible car accident in Florida. My beloved mother didn't survive. Rita Baskin was by far the strongest influence in my life. She was an inspiration and role model for me, and losing her was devastating. She was always aware of my "hopeless" work for peace and, currently, for the release of Gilad Schalit. Although other people discouraged me or called me naïve, my mother was a constant source of encouragement, admiration, and support; her passing would make carrying on much more difficult. I received hundreds of condolences from friends in Israel and elsewhere, and many from Palestinians, including in Gaza and Hamas.

On April 1, Svein wrote to me:

> *Dear Gershon,*
>
> *I wanted personally to offer my condolences on the passing of your mother.*
> *I am now on a plane bound for Cairo. Will during the next day's visit Beirut, Damascus, and Amman before reaching Jerusalem on April 9. Will stay until April 16. Let us sit down and discuss the whole agenda.*
>
> *Svein*

I responded:

> *Dear Svein,*
>
> *I understand that the Egyptians are negotiating the cease-fire. I would have much preferred that Norway do so, but I guess the Egyptians wouldn't back down. The most important thing is that they reach an agreement. I am trying to work behind the scenes to move that possibility forward.*
>
> *Best wishes,*
> *Gershon*

On April 16, I contacted Noam Schalit by e-mail, predicting the Egyptians would fail. I told him about my proposal that Norway mediate. I believed Hamas would agree to a Norwegian role, but Olmert was less likely to do so. I suggested that we also had the possibility of a secret direct back channel between Ghazi Hamad and me, and that if Olmert were to agree, I believed Hamas would as well. Noam said we would talk when he came back from DC.

On April 23, I was filmed for the first time about the behind-the-scenes talks. I met the filmmaker, Irit Gal, through the Schalits. Aviva and Noam were interested in the film because it would expose the failures of Olmert and Dekel to Israeli television viewers. I was ready to tell the Israeli public that little was being done to bring Gilad home and that many opportunities had already been missed. I arranged for Ghazi to be interviewed too. I had hoped he and I would speak to each other in the film. However, Ghazi didn't want to be seen in direct contact with an Israeli, even a peacenik like me, so a Palestinian film crew in Gaza interviewed him. When the film aired on Israeli television, the government's response was that it damaged the cause, claiming that when Hamas saw Israeli public pressure on the government, they'd raise the price. This rationale turned out to be erroneous, but it successfully postponed any significant public debate.

I did arrange a conference call between Ghazi Hamad, Noam Schalit, and me, however. Noam was very angry and frustrated. Ghazi listened and suggested that Noam pressure Olmert to negotiate seriously. Ghazi said Gilad was in good condition and Hamas was taking good care of him. Noam said he wanted Gilad released. I understood that a secret direct back channel was not in the offing, but I wouldn't give up on the idea.

April 23, 2008

Dear Ghazi,

The filming went well today, even though we didn't get to speak on the phone. I wish we could do a lot more to bring about the release of Schalit. I still think the best way would be the direct back channel we've discussed so many times. The Egyptians claim to be making progress, but everything takes too long through them. I imagine that Khaled Mashal has to give the green light for the direct back channel, and he opposes any direct contact with Israelis. I'm sure that if you got an okay from your side, I could convince Olmert to allow us to try and move forward. I know the main problem is the list of names that are too difficult for Olmert to accept. Please think about how you and I can still do something to make a difference.

The next day Ghazi answered my e-mail:

Dear Gershon,

Thank you so much for your message. I am sorry I did not respond to your call yesterday, because I was so busy. I think we can make progress, but we need to be sure Olmert is serious about dealing with the names. I know it's very difficult to accept all the names but, for example, if they accept two hundred or three hundred of the 350, we can make a breakthrough. I hope you can talk to Noam and his friends about pressuring the government to show more flexibility, and I will do my best to push forward with people here.

All the best,
Ghazi

Passover was once against being celebrated, and Gilad was spending his second festival of freedom in captivity. The Israeli public was beginning to show more sympathy for the plight of the Schalit family, and it was essential to get the message to Prime Minister Olmert that it was long overdue for him to make the critical decision and bring Gilad home.

It was also time to try again to get the Hamas leadership to move forward, so I wrote to Khaled Mashal in Damascus:

April 29, 2008

Dear Mr. Mashal,

As you are well aware, the Egyptians are almost ready to present a package to the government of Israel regarding a cease-fire in Gaza. I have been deeply involved in these talks behind the scenes and have transferred messages back and forth from Gaza, Cairo, and Jerusalem.

There are great reservations on the Israeli side about the package, because Schalit is left out of the deal. Yet it seems to be in the interests of all parties now to advance a calming period. I know the Israelis have demanded that the Egyptians commit fully to stopping the smuggling of weapons into Gaza underneath the Rafah border. I know Hamas has demanded the opening of the Rafah crossing without any Israeli veto. I have heard Hamas has agreed to allow Abu Mazen's troops to be stationed in Rafah. The Egyptians have told me they will be making a very attractive package offer to Israel.

I know the Israeli side better than the Egyptians do. Even the most attractive package possible will be very difficult for Olmert and his cabinet to accept if Gilad Schalit is left in Gaza. I know the negotiations on Schalit are stalled. Olmert lacks the political strength to release many of those on the lists. This is the main problem, not the number of Palestinians to be released. Olmert can be more flexible on the number than on the specific names. Without more flexibility on your part, it will be next to impossible to arrive at an agreement. As part of the package deal including the cease-fire and the opening of the Rafah crossing, we must find a way to include Schalit.

Gershon Baskin

I met with several senior members of the Olmert government. I came away with a clear understanding that Israel would not accept a cease-fire agreement with Hamas. Even more particularly, everyone I spoke to said there could be no Israeli cease-fire with Schalit left in captivity. The official Israeli position was: If they stop shooting at us, we'll stop returning fire. Off the record, however, senior Israeli leaders were telling me that eventually Israel would have to go back into Gaza, remove Hamas from power, and find Gilad Schalit.

Following this Israeli rejection of the cease-fire proposal, I contacted my friend Nader El-A'aser in Egypt and outlined the complications to him. Olmert wouldn't accept an official cease-fire without any progress on Schalit, I explained. I also shared with him some other Israeli concepts that were coming into focus. Israel, I understood, preferred quantity over quality – meaning it wanted to release a generous number of prisoners but a very limited number with "blood on their hands." Israel was also floating the idea of a very gradual release – a few prisoners a week, to build support for President Abbas – over handing Hamas a "victory" in the form of a big, impressive one.

It was all so difficult and horribly maddening. I kept telling myself not to give up. My motivation to continue increased with the belief that I could do it. But how could I convince the Israeli officials to see what I saw? I needed to come up with creative ways of making the deal possible. I was consumed with thinking about how to reach a breakthrough. I vowed not to give up until Gilad was home.

Chapter 8

Tahdiyah: The Calm Before the Storm

In early May 2008, Israeli forces and Gaza militants were pounding each other in a deadly tit for tat. I wrote to Ghazi Hamad again to share some ideas about how we could move things forward.

May 11, 2008

Dear Ghazi,

I'm trying to think of new ways to move forward with the Schalit negotiations. I don't know what will happen in tomorrow's meetings with Omar Suleiman in Israel. He'll be presenting the Egyptian plan for the cease-fire and the opening of Rafah to the Israeli government. I already told you the deal will be difficult for Israel, because Schalit was taken out of the package. I hear that your side won't resume talks on Schalit until the Rafah border is open on a regular basis. I don't know 100 percent what's true and what's disinformation.

My concern is trying to move forward again in the negotiations. My working assumptions are the following:

1. Your side won't compromise on the list of names presented.
2. It is nearly impossible for Olmert to give in to this list.

I have already proposed one option – increasing the quantity of Palestinian prisoners to be released in exchange for reducing the "quality." I believe Olmert would release more prisoners if the list included people easier for him to release from a political point of view.

I don't believe your side will agree to this.

Another option is for Hamas to agree that all those released from the original lists will go to Gaza, not the West Bank.[1] This would make it easier for Olmert to carry the decision through and for it to be accepted by the Israeli security forces and by the public. Living in Gaza instead of the West Bank should be a lot more attractive to prisoners than serving a life sentence inside an Israeli prison. It should also be acceptable to Hamas, because it controls Gaza and can find many ways of rewarding those ex-prisoners there.

In regard to building public support in Israel for the release of Palestinian prisoners, it would be helpful if another action raised the emotional level of the Israeli public and got them in the mood to pressure the authorities to move ahead with the prisoner exchange. Phone communication between Noam Schalit and his son would be the absolute best. We need to find ways to get the talks moving again and bring them to a point of conclusion. I'm always ready to discuss additional ideas and do anything possible to move this along.

Gershon

---

1. In the agreement finally reached in October 2011, this was a key element. Hamas demanded that a majority of prisoners from the West Bank not be expelled to Gaza, so Israel agreed that 50 percent plus one of these prisoners would return home, while the rest would be deported to Gaza.

Olmert rejected Omar Suleiman's cease-fire proposals. I sensed that with each passing day Israel was getting closer to launching a full-scale war in Gaza. The Israeli public would fully support it, as would the Western world. No government can accept a barrage of missiles from a neighboring country or territory. Israel had to respond, and when it did, it would go in with force, with the intention of finding Gilad Schalit and bringing him home. I hoped we would bring him home alive, causing minimal death and destruction in Gaza.

But I wasn't optimistic. My information was that Israel knew where Schalit was being held. A reliable source informed me that a military operation had already been attempted, but it was halted in view of intelligence assessments that the place was booby-trapped with explosives, so there was no way the plan could succeed.

May 12, 2008

Dear Ghazi,

I told you Olmert wouldn't accept the deal unless the Schalit negotiations were included. I still suggest that you push on your side for a direct channel. I also think that the key to the negotiations might be if Hamas were to agree that all prisoners be released to Gaza – that would make it easier for Olmert, and I think being in Gaza beats serving a life sentence in Israeli prisons. That might be the only way forward.

Gershon

Two days later, a Grad rocket fired from Gaza hit Ashkelon. This was a serious escalation on the part of Hamas. It demonstrated that new, higher-quality rockets were being smuggled into Gaza via the tunnels from Sinai. It also showed Hamas' brazen willingness to provoke an Israeli counterattack.

May 14, 2008

Dear Ghazi,

After the Grad missile hit Ashkelon while Olmert was sitting with Bush, it seems that Olmert has received a "green light" from Bush to hit Gaza hard. The army is pushing for a large-scale ground operation. Politicians across the entire political spectrum are preparing the public for such an operation – just listen to Israeli radio. The drums of war are beating.

    I know the Hamas spokespeople are boasting, "We're ready for them – let them come!" but hundreds of innocent Palestinians will pay with their lives. When will this end? Yes, I know Hamas presented a cease-fire offer. You know what the problems are with the offer – I won't go into them again. I'm calling on you and your colleagues to show some responsibility toward your own people. It's time to end this senseless violence. It's time to send Schalit home and hundreds of Palestinian prisoners with him. Yalla[2] – get this done – for everyone's sake (and mostly for the sake of so many innocent Palestinian families in Gaza).

Gershon

Ghazi called me concerned about the possibility of an Israeli ground operation in which many Palestinians would be killed. He believed Hamas would accept a package deal including a full cease-fire, the end of the siege on Gaza, and a prisoner exchange. He said we had to deal with all three issues together. I told him I would contact Israeli leaders to see if Israel would consider such a package deal.

For the time being, there was no major Israeli offensive into Gaza, and the rocket fire calmed down. As far as I knew, no new negotiations on the prisoner exchange were taking place. Stalemate was the best way to describe the situation.

2. An Arabic expression used by Hebrew speakers as well, meaning "Come on, get moving!"

It seemed that a series of power struggles were developing within Hamas. It wasn't clear who was calling the shots and who had the authority to negotiate the prisoner exchange. I wanted to deliver a tough message to Hamas through Ghazi, but at the same time tell him I was beginning to hear more willingness from the Israeli side to demonstrate additional flexibility in order to break the deadlock.

June 6, 2008

Dear Ghazi,

From the latest information I have about the Schalit negotiations, there is a big question about who is in charge on your side. There have been no negotiations for months. No one in Israel knows who is making the decisions on the Palestinian side. There is a keen sense in Israel that on your side Ahmed Jaabri and probably Khaled Mashal don't want to reach an agreement. Schalit is a source of power for them and a kind of insurance policy against Israeli attacks.

Something has to be done to make sure the negotiators know who can make the decisions. The Israeli side, I hear, may be ready to demonstrate more flexibility than in the past. The best option would be the direct back channel – but your friends in Damascus seem to prevent that option. I told you I tried speaking with Abu Marzouk. I sent him a fax and an e-mail. I called twice. His office director told me to call back, and then I was told that he refuses to speak to me – this is not the first time. Ghazi, please do something to get an understanding on your side regarding who is in charge. We are almost two years since Gilad is in captivity.

Gershon

On June 7, 2008, one full year after Hamas ousted the Palestinian Authority, Prime Minister Olmert stated that Israel planned to reoccupy Gaza and replace the Hamas government with one representing the Palestinian Authority. It was also announced in the news that the Egyptian ambassador in Ramallah was pressuring the Palestinian factions to reconcile, accept a cease-fire, and avoid an Israeli attack on Gaza.

On June 18, an Egyptian-brokered "calm" (*tahdiyah*) between Israel and Hamas got under way. Israel refused to admit there was a bilateral agreement, stating only, "If they don't shoot at us, we won't shoot at them." In any case, the *tahdiyah* was intended to halt rocket attacks from Gaza in return for a halt of IDF operations in Hamas-controlled Gaza. Israel was to open border crossings, ending the blockade of supplies to Gaza. Hours before the cease-fire began, however, Amos Gilad, a senior official in the Israeli Defense Ministry, declared that the Rafah border crossing to Egypt would not be opened until Gilad Schalit was released. Hamas officials countered that Schalit would not be released until Israel freed hundreds of jailed Palestinians as per Hamas' demands. Amos Gilad stated that there was no alternative and that the truce was a step toward the release of Schalit. So Israel and Hamas agreed to stop shooting at each other and accept a period of calm.

I contacted General Nader El-A'aser at the Egyptian Embassy and, at his request, began sending him ideas on how to advance the negotiations for the prisoner exchange. We exchanged several e-mails and held phone conversations on various proposals. I wanted to share my ideas with the Hamas people in Gaza.

July 1, 2008

Dear Ghazi,

We have to get renewed negotiations completed as fast as possible. I have sent some ideas to the Egyptians. I want to know from your assessment, is there any chance Hamas will demonstrate some flexibility on the list of names already submitted? Will Hamas consider other names? Will it be willing to increase the number instead of some of the more difficult names on the list? What ideas do you have that could help the process? You know that the list contains some people who are directly responsible for the deaths of dozens of Israeli citizens – civilians, not soldiers – and it will be very difficult for the government of Israel to accept them. You know who some of them are – like Hassan Salameh and Abdallah Barghouti[3] *and others. At*

---

3. Throughout the process, Hamas demanded freedom for arch-terrorists, who were

this time, it will be easier to release the political prisoners, like the Hamas ministers and PLC members. Is there any way for Hamas to be more flexible in order to put an end to this story?

Gershon

Ghazi always responded to my calls for flexibility by saying that when Israel was serious about negotiating, Hamas would be flexible. I never understood what that meant. I often asked him if Hamas defined Israeli "seriousness about negotiating" as simply accepting all its demands. He always said Hamas was flexible but had its limits.

On July 16, a surprising announcement was made: Hezbollah and Israel had agreed to an immediate prisoner exchange. Conflicting reports had been circulating in Israel for months as to whether Ehud Goldwasser and Eldad Regev – the Israeli soldiers abducted shortly after Gilad Schalit – were still alive in Lebanon.

As the deal was implemented, we all sat by our radios and televisions, hoping for good news – a rare redemptive ending. Our faces fell as the coffins containing the two soldiers were carried across the Lebanon-Israel border. The remains of Goldwasser and Regev, we soon learned, were being exchanged for a Lebanese prisoner, Samir Al-Quntar. Al-Quntar was serving four life sentences for a grisly attack in Nahariya in 1979, staged by the Palestinian Liberation Front. He had murdered Eliyahu Shahar, an Israeli policeman, Danny Haran, thirty-one, and Haran's four-year-old daughter, Einat, whom he had bludgeoned to death with a rock. In addition, Al-Quntar had been convicted of indirectly causing the death of two-year-old Yael Haran by suffocation, as her mother, Smadar, tried to muffle her crying while hiding from him.

As part of the prisoner exchange, which Israelis had hoped would bring home at least one live soldier, Israel also released four Hezbollah

behind some of the most horrendous attacks in Israel's history, and were serving multiple life sentences. For Hamas, they symbolized the struggle against Israel, and it was determined to release them.

Dr. Gerhard Conrad

fighters captured in the 2006 Lebanon War and the bodies of 199 Palestinians, buried by Israel in the past three decades.

It was a lopsided exchange, and not the first one, in which Israel paid dearly for its ethos of leaving no soldier behind. Two years after the kidnapping in a Hezbollah raid near the Lebanese border, the Goldwasser and Regev families could have closure and lay their sons to rest – unlike the family of Ron Arad. But as we witnessed the transfer, I think the entire nation was asking itself if this would also be the fate of Gilad Schalit.

The main negotiator of the Hezbollah-Israeli deal was Dr. Gerhard Conrad, a German intelligence officer brought in by Ofer Dekel as an acceptable third party. Like Hamas, Hezbollah refused to have direct contact with Israel. I had tried to make unofficial contact with Hezbollah through friends in Lebanon, in particular through people connected to Hezbollah's allies in the Free Patriotic Movement (at-Tayyar), the Christian party headed by General Michel Aoun. I was turned down. At least Hamas was willing to have direct contact with me.

July 16, 2008

> *Ghazi,*
>
> *Now that the Hezbollah story is over, all attention is going to focus on Schalit. We have to get those negotiations going. Please raise once again the idea of direct negotiations. Can't you get Prime Minister Haniyeh to support it and push for it? It's time to finish this and get Schalit and the Palestinian prisoners home.*
>
> *Gershon*

On July 17, I wrote to Prime Minister Olmert and asked his daughter Dana to make sure he received the letter. The following is an excerpt:

Dear Mr. Prime Minister,

Today someone in Haniyeh's office asked me to find out if you would agree to a back channel that would bypass the Egyptians, perhaps with the assistance of the German mediator. I said I would check directly with you. I am convinced that Hamas will not substantially compromise on its demands and that Gilad is at risk. The high price that the State of Israel must pay for Schalit is known and will not change significantly. The room for flexibility is mainly in that Hamas may agree that many of the hard-core terrorists from the West Bank will be sent to Gaza. In my opinion there will not be much flexibility beyond that.

I understand that there is no real military option for bringing Schalit home. I don't know how much longer you will be prime minister, but Gilad was abducted on your watch, and it is your obligation to bring him home. You have two choices: either sacrifice him on the grounds that he was a soldier sent into battle, and soldiers may fall in the service of their country, or save his life and bring him home. Despite how difficult it is to consider giving in to Hamas' demands, the time to decide is now. You can save his life and bring him home. There might well be harsh criticism from some circles, but most Israelis will support you.

I once again express my willingness to work without rest in order to bring about a positive outcome. I am ready to travel to Gaza again. I am prepared to go anywhere in the world to try to speak to anyone from Hamas, in Damascus, if possible.

I call on you to display courage now, before it's too late. Leadership is not measured only by sending soldiers into battle; it is also measured by making fateful decisions for the country, controversial though they may be. Be a leader and bring Gilad home alive.

Gershon Baskin

Olmert never answered this letter, which Dana hand-delivered to him.
The following day I had an opportunity to meet the Turkish ambassador in Tel Aviv. I suggested privately that the Turks use their

influence with Hamas to help make a deal. He told me he was sure Ankara would agree if requested to act by both sides.

On July 19, I wrote to Dr. Ahmet Davutoglu, senior adviser to the Turkish prime minister and soon-to-become the very powerful Turkish foreign minister. We had met at several conferences in Turkey and had remained in contact.

> *Dear Dr. Ahmet,*
>
> *I am sitting with Noam and Aviva Schalit, parents of the kid-napped soldier Gilad. We are trying to think of ways to advance the negotiations for his release. The Egyptian mediators are mak-ing no progress. Turkey is perfectly positioned to move in and help end this story. You have relations with Syria and Khaled Mashal and Israel. We have to end this before Olmert leaves office. Please let me know your thoughts.*
>
> *Gershon Baskin*

Davutoglu's answer came shortly:

> *Dear Mr. Baskin,*
>
> *Thank you very much for your message. As you know, we tried to do our utmost for the Gilad Schalit case in the past, because we see it purely as a humanitarian case. We understand the feelings of the fam-ily. We still intend to contribute to a solution, and we have suggested this to the Israeli government. But we understand that the government wants to continue giving the Egyptian effort a chance. The existence of two channels in these types of cases might be counterproductive. If there is a request from the Israeli government, we will do everything possible to solve this problem.*
>
> *Sincerely yours,*
> *Ahmet Davutoglu*

It was increasingly clear that the relationship between Egyptian Intelligence Chief Omar Suleiman and the Hamas military wing – headed by Ahmed Jaabri, the person holding Gilad – was operating at only the most basic level. There had to be a way to bypass Egyptian control of the negotiations. The German mediator who had succeeded with the Hezbollah deal seemed like a natural replacement.

On July 20, I received an urgent phone call from Ghazi, who said he had convinced Prime Minister Haniyeh to examine the possibility of a secret Egyptian-bypass channel through the German mediator. I wrote Olmert another brief letter:

July 20, 2008

Dear Mr. Olmert,

Recently I have been receiving several phone calls a day from my contact in Haniyeh's office. He says he has convinced Haniyeh to positively examine the secret bypass channel with the German mediator. Khaled Mashal has also given a green light to such a channel. Mashal wants to know if you are willing to go ahead with the German channel. Mashal has also inquired if you would be ready to open a direct, secret back channel as an alternative.

I would like to speak with you or Ofer Dekel about this.

Gershon Baskin

Olmert never responded.

On July 30, Olmert announced his resignation, following his indictment on charges of taking bribes. The prime minister said he would step down after the Kadima party elected a new leader in September, and after a new government was formed.

On August 14, I had a long conversation with Ghazi. I pleaded with him to speak to Mashal about opening the back channel. We both acknowledged the truth: No negotiations were going on, and time was being wasted. He suggested that Hamas was annoyed at Egypt – and Ghazi himself was frustrated at the slow progress. He wanted to know whether I thought Olmert was really ready to pay the price. I wasn't sure, but I told him that Olmert did seem to want to end the story before leaving office.

On September 1, I drafted a proposal for an agreement between Israel and Hamas. I sent it to the Israeli leadership.

Schalit Deal – Secret

> *To:*
> *Prime Minister Ehud Olmert*
> *Foreign Minister Tzipi Livni*
> *Minister of Defense Ehud Barak*
>
> *The following is my proposal for advancing the negotiations for the release of Schalit:*
>
> *Hamas demands –*
> - *Release of 450 prisoners listed by Hamas (in the meantime there are only 350 names on the list).*
> - *Release of 550 prisoners after Schalit is freed, according to a list to be agreed upon by Israel and Egypt.*
> - *Release of all minor prisoners (about 150 – may partially overlap with Hamas list).*
> - *Release of all women prisoners (about 300 – may overlap with Hamas list).*
> - *Egyptian/International assurances of a continued cease-fire.*
> - *Egyptian/International assurances of no more targeted killings of Hamas leaders after the release of Schalit.*
>
> *Israeli possibilities –*
> *Israel should initiate this plan. The idea is to give Hamas "an offer it cannot refuse." The proposal should include two thousand names, as follows:*

- *About eighty names have been approved from the Hamas list.*
- *There are about seven hundred Gazan prisoners in Israeli jails, who can be released to Gaza regardless of their crimes, because Gaza is completely sealed, so the risks to Israel are low.*
- *Some seven hundred to eight hundred administrative detainees have not been brought to trial for various reasons and require only the defense minister's decision to release them.*
- *The Hamas list can be increased if Hamas agrees that West Bank prisoners will be sent to Gaza.*
- *It is possible to reach the number two thousand by including the most veteran prisoners as well as the sick and elderly. Hamas will emphasize "high-quality" prisoners and therefore not agree to those with short sentences or those nearing the end of their terms.*
- *The list must include the Hamas politicians – members of Parliament and ministers.*

We should use the month of Ramadan to complete the deal, so the prisoners can be home for Eid al-Fitr at the end of the month.

Hamas is interested in an Egyptian bypass channel because of the problems it's having with Egypt. The Turkish prime minister is prepared to appoint his senior adviser – who's been running the proximity talks with Turkey – if both sides agree.

Sincerely,
Gershon Baskin

I spoke with Dr. Tal Becker, Foreign Minister Livni's senior adviser and head of negotiations with the Palestinians. He told me he would discuss my letter with her but thought Olmert wasn't interested in any cease-fire arrangement with Hamas; he didn't trust them. Becker also said Livni supported a military operation in Gaza that would bring the Hamas government down.

"What about Gilad Schalit?" I asked.

He had no response.

On September 17, Kadima held its primaries. Livni won. On September 21, Olmert resigned as prime minister. He was to remain in office until Livni formed a government – something she never succeeded in doing.

In November, fighting flared up again between Hamas and Israel after Israeli forces bombed a tunnel used for smuggling weapons. Israeli ground forces and artillery entered Gaza for the first time since mid-June. Hamas responded with a barrage of Qassam rockets and mortars into Israel. Over the next two months, clashes continued along the border and eleven Palestinians were killed. From November 4 until mid-December, Hamas fired more than two hundred rockets into Israel.

Ghazi contacted me in mid-December, requesting that I inform Olmert that Hamas was once again proposing a package deal that would include a full bilateral cease-fire, passage for people and goods, and advancing the prisoner-exchange negotiations for Schalit. I relayed the message to Olmert, Livni, and Barak, but as usual got no response. On December 18, Hamas officially announced that the cease-fire had ended, launching more than two hundred rockets and mortars into Israel in one day. Ghazi contacted me once again saying Hamas was serious about returning to the cease-fire, but with the other elements as well.

At an Israeli cabinet meeting on December 21, both Defense Minister Barak and ISA chief Yuval Diskin confirmed that Hamas was trying to improve its position by linking the cease-fire to other issues. On December 23, Hamas declared a unilateral, twenty-four-hour cease-fire to test Israeli willingness to reach an understanding.

The next day, Israel launched an airstrike on what it claimed to be a group of militants preparing to attack. Hamas retaliated by shooting another eighty rockets into Israel. On December 25, Barak warned Hamas to hold its fire – or suffer the consequences.

On December 27, Israel launched Operation Cast Lead – a full-fledged aerial bombing campaign followed a week later by a full-scale ground operation. Although no formal announcement was made that the IDF was preparing to locate Gilad Schalit and bring him home, those intentions were clear from the military plans. Several members of the Israeli government also told me that Olmert and Barak intended to rescue Schalit.

I hoped that they would, and that Gilad would survive the Israeli bombing and any Hamas retaliation. But I was not at all convinced that Gilad Schalit would be alive at the end of Cast Lead.

Chapter 9

Dead Ends and New Openings

On February 10, 2009, Israel held elections. The right-wing bloc triumphed, enabling Likud leader Benjamin Netanyahu to form a new government.

Prime Minister Benjamin Netanyahu

In the final days of his term, Prime Minister Ehud Olmert decided not to agree to a prisoner exchange, because Hamas insisted on conditions he couldn't accept. Olmert wouldn't take the risks involved in the deal, and the security heads seemed to support him. The Schalits were crushed. They had generated a lot of public pressure on Olmert's cabinet to bring Gilad home while it still had the chance.

I was convinced that Olmert's "red lines" for a deal with Hamas would be liberal compared to Netanyahu's. The new prime minister had always been outspokenly against prisoner exchanges. He was known around the world for his position that responsible governments should never negotiate with terrorists. With this in mind, I decided to try one last time to impress upon the Hamas leaders the urgency of moderating their demands before it was too late. In retrospect, my assumptions about Netanyahu were wrong. However, when Netanyahu took over, nobody – including himself – thought he would compromise on this issue. Based on this assessment, I wrote to the Hamas leaders:

March 22, 2009

Gentlemen,

This is it – the last stretch of reaching an agreement on a prisoner exchange. It can be done, but you cannot get 100 percent. You have forced a very hard deal on Israel, and you can get a lot more than anyone would have thought possible.

I know you're not afraid of threats from Israel, nor am I the messenger of threats. But you must be aware that the Netanyahu government will not make the same kind of deal as Olmert. Deals also have a timing of their own, and what is possible today may not be tomorrow. Sometimes it's wiser to get what you can today.

Everyone says Hamas has a different way of looking at time. I am quite sure that's true. The families of the prisoners don't have such a different view of time, though. They want their loved ones home now. They want them out of prison, even if some of them will be sent away from home temporarily.

Regarding Israel's insistence on deporting 144 prisoners from the list you submitted, I suggest that you consider an arrangement that would be time-limited – a number of years – and not permanent. This might make it easier for Israel to accept.

In case you think you'll get a better deal from Netanyahu, read what he has to say about prisoner releases in his book A Place under the Sun. *In short, Netanyahu was 100 percent opposed to the 1985 "Ahmed Jibril" exchange.*[1] *People around Netanyahu say he wants the*

---

1. The deal negotiated with Ahmed Jibril's Popular Front for the Liberation of Palestine, in which Israel released 1,150 prisoners in exchange for three Israelis.

deal to be completed before he takes office, because afterward it will be a lot more difficult to conclude it. You know this as well.

Netanyahu will seek to prove that he isn't like Olmert. He'll use the military to make his point. You're probably saying there's no difference – you had the war in Gaza under Olmert. True, but don't underestimate Netanyahu and his political allies. Netanyahu won't hesitate to resume assassinating Hamas leaders. He'll have strong backing in his cabinet to do that, and if Schalit is killed as a result, he'll be considered a shaheed [martyr], and it'll be easy for Netanyahu to tell the people of Israel that he didn't give in to terrorism.

So if you want your prisoners released, it is time to be more reasonable and come to a final deal. There is no time left. If you would like to pass messages through me, I am more than willing to relay them. You can also pass on messages to me through Azzam Tamimi in London or through Ahmed Yousef in Gaza.

Gershon Baskin

On March 31, Netanyahu took office. I was very doubtful that any progress would be made, and more convinced than ever that Gilad would not be coming home. I expressed this sentiment to both Israeli and Palestinian friends and leaders.

In the first week of April, Ofer Dekel asked Netanyahu to relieve him of his duties. Dekel had been handpicked by Olmert – a personal friend – but he'd failed to bring Schalit home. The Schalit family had few kind words for Dekel. In an interview I conducted with Noam Schalit after Gilad was released, he complained that Dekel had been very sparing of information. He'd reprimanded the Schalits for their public campaign, claiming it had hardened Hamas' position. Dekel had also attacked me and my role, complaining to the Schalits that all kinds of "self-appointed mediators" were causing damage. Noam Schalit thought Dekel's ego had gotten in the way.

Throughout Olmert's tenure, I felt that the key to Gilad's release was in the prime minister's hands. Had he had the political courage to make the deal, Hamas would have made significant compromises. Ghazi Hamad and Azzam Tamimi had repeatedly told me that when the Israeli side was ready to be serious, Hamas would demonstrate significant flexibility. But it just didn't happen.

I was furious that no deal had been completed in the final days of the Olmert administration. I considered it a complete failure of leadership on the prime minister's part. (I know the Schalit family too was livid that Olmert left office while Gilad remained in Gaza.) Mostly I was afraid Gilad would be forgotten, because Netanyahu would not negotiate with Hamas. I was also angry that Hamas didn't understand that with some compromise on its part, a deal could have been made with Olmert. I wanted to share my anger, frustration, and even despair with my Hamas contacts. I even hoped it would prompt a reality check on their side, and perhaps they would become more reasonable in their demands.

With Netanyahu now at the helm, I was very pessimistic. In the end, of course, Netanyahu surprised us all and demonstrated real leadership. He went against his own principles in support of social solidarity, and in keeping with Israel's unwritten covenant to leave no soldier behind. But it took more than two years for that to happen.

During April 2009, I began speaking with people in Netanyahu's government to assess how the new cabinet would handle the Schalit issue. It was quite clear that Netanyahu would use the image of his right-wing government to try to scare Hamas into being "more realistic." It was important for me to get the message to Hamas leaders that they were in for tough times. My message was harsh, because I wanted to apply pressure on them from the outset about the new Israeli government.

Hagai Hadas

National Photo Collection

On May 31, Netanyahu put Hagai Hadas in charge of the negotiations. The Israel Foreign Ministry webpage reported: "Hagai Hadas, 56, has held a variety of positions in the Mossad and is considered an outstanding intelligence and special-operations man. He retired from the Mossad in January 2006, after holding a very senior position."

Shortly after his appointment, Hadas contacted Noam Schalit. Hadas said that Gilad Schalit and his family were at the center of affairs and that freeing him was a moral mission of the highest order. He pledged to do his utmost to unite all relevant bodies, noting, "We have a great obligation to our fighters, and it is in the spirit of this commitment that I intend to act."

I had never heard of Hadas, but I had to reach him. How do you find a Mossad agent in the twenty-first century? Facebook! Hadas' Facebook page didn't have much information, but it did provide the name of his town. So I dialed Information and asked for the number of Hagai Hadas in Maccabim (a city in the center of the country). Simple.

I called Hadas, introduced myself, told him what I had been doing, and asked to meet him. Hadas informed me that a German mediator was handling all contacts with Hamas and that my involvement was not necessary or desired.

From that day on, I kept trying to convince Hadas to listen to me. He served as the prime minister's special envoy for releasing Gilad Schalit from June 2009 until he resigned in failure in April 2011. He consistently refused to listen to or meet with me. Like Ofer Dekel before him, he did not recognize that I was handing him a direct line to the people holding Gilad Schalit. I couldn't understand Hadas' insistence on not meeting or even talking to me.

The Schalits found Hadas to be a refreshing change from Dekel, however. He provided them with information. He initiated contact with them. They felt that under Hadas the end might be in sight.

Hadas worked through Dr. Gerhard Conrad, who had succeeded in negotiations with Hezbollah. Hadas' first "achievement" was to invent the formula by which Dr. Conrad was the negotiator, but negotiations would take place under Egyptian auspices. Egypt remained the most important country in the Arab world, and although Hamas and the Egyptians had conflicting interests, the continued Egyptian role was essential, however problematic.

I wasn't sure Egypt was interested in an agreement that would increase Hamas' popularity around the Arab world. I shared these thoughts more than once with Noam and Aviva.

Noam said that Hadas seemed very serious and more committed than Ofer Dekel. Hadas gave the Schalits more confidence in the negotiations, and they were encouraged by the high level of German support for Conrad. German Chancellor Angela Merkel personally provided Conrad with the full backing of the German government, including all expenses paid. Conrad flew frequently to Israel, Gaza, and Cairo in a private German jet. He showed great intensity and commitment. After Olmert and Dekel, Netanyahu and Hadas brought new hope.

I checked in from time to time with Noam Schalit, Ghazi Hamad, Azzam Tamimi, and others, but there seemed very little I could do. Noam was turned against me and my intervention by Olmert and Dekel, and now by Hadas as well. Whenever I spoke to him and Aviva, I was made to feel that I was intruding, that my information wasn't serious. They always told me my Hamas contacts weren't the decision makers regarding Gilad; only Jaabri was, and I had no contact with him. When I reminded them about the first letter from Gilad, which had to have come with Jaabri's agreement, Noam once again told me that Dekel had denied my having anything to do with the letter. He told them the letter was produced through the efforts of the Egyptians. That was completely false; the Egyptians themselves were surprised when the letter showed up at their office in Gaza that Saturday morning, September 9, 2006. The Schalits also asked if I had contacts with Hamas Foreign Minister Dr. Mahmoud al-Zahar. I did not.

Dr. Conrad was in direct contact with al-Zahar, a member of the Hamas Shura Council, the supreme decision-making body of Hamas. He had apparently been appointed by the Hamas leadership, including Jaabri, to head the negotiations for the prisoner exchange.

Dr. Mahmoud al-Zahar

I remained quite convinced that Netanyahu would not negotiate with Hamas. And then a surprise came. On October 2, 2009, Hamas transferred a videotape of Gilad to Israel. The Schalits were brought to the Ministry of Defense in Tel Aviv to watch it, and then a decision was made to allow the whole country to view the tape. The Sukkot holiday was drawing near as Israeli television aired the special broadcast, but despite the late hour people all over the country gathered to see and hear Gilad Schalit. Dressed in an army uniform, he spoke for two minutes, expressing hope that the Netanyahu government would make the deal. It was a moment of great optimism.

I was convinced that Hamas had released the tape because a deal had been made and in a few weeks we would see Gilad back in Israel. Netanyahu even agreed to release nineteen women prisoners in exchange for the video – something Olmert had refused to do. Perhaps I had misjudged Netanyahu?

But then nothing happened. There was no deal, and Gilad remained somewhere in Gaza. Ghazi Hamad told me Conrad was visiting Gaza frequently. Hadas told me, always by text message, that everything was in the German mediator's hands. The media reported that progress was being made. My own sources in the Israeli intelligence community relayed that the German government was investing considerable resources in ensuring Conrad's success. I heard from various Palestinian sources that Conrad and al-Zahar had developed a genuine friendship. I viewed that as a good sign. In my experience, there was entirely too little trust between the parties in these negotiations. If al-Zahar trusted the German negotiator, that could only help. Eventually, however, the friendship between al-Zahar and Conrad worked against the deal, because Jaabri grew suspicious of whom Conrad was really working for, making Jaabri wary of al-Zahar as well.

Through late October, I was getting reports that the German channel was deadlocked. Conrad had not been seen for weeks at a time. I had no idea what was happening. Hagai Hadas refused to speak to me. Each time I approached him, he responded with "There is an official track through the Germans – don't interfere."

Ghazi believed no negotiations were taking place and the German track had failed. I told him I would see if there might be another suitable mediator acceptable to both sides. Ghazi agreed that it would be useful to investigate other possibilities of moving forward. He added that if the Russians would step in, they could be quite effective.

It turned out that something was indeed moving. In November, Conrad gave the parties a draft agreement. Jaabri rejected it, and so did Israel. Conrad returned a month later with a new draft. This time Jaabri broke ranks with al-Zahar. The Hamas leadership in Damascus supported the agreement, as did al-Zahar. Hamas and the foreign media reported that Jaabri had fired al-Zahar from the negotiations and instructed him not to interfere. Then Jaabri told Conrad not to come back. The Israeli reaction was that there was an agreement on the table, and now we would wait for Hamas to respond to it.

Two months later, I met with a senior intelligence officer in the Russian Embassy in Tel Aviv. I did so after speaking with Noam, who confirmed that the German track seemed dormant. Israel's official position was that we were waiting for Hamas to respond to the German proposal. This would remain the official position from December 2009 until May 2011 – almost a year and a half.

January 31, 2010

Dear Ghazi,

I spoke twice yesterday with the intelligence chief at the Russian Embassy in Tel Aviv. He has already spoken with his superiors in Moscow. If the Russians express an interest and a willingness to step in as mediator, I will try to get the green light from Netanyahu.

If Netanyahu agrees, my proposal will be for the Israeli and Palestinian delegations to make a commitment to go to Moscow, remaining there as long as it takes to reach an agreement. The two parties could be put up in nearby safe houses, with the Russian mediator shuttling between them. There should be a commitment from both sides to bring this issue to a conclusion and not drag it out for more time. I would like to propose that you and I be included in the delegations as people who can bridge gaps and work to reach agreements.

Gershon

The Russian intelligence officer visited Moscow and presented the idea of a Russian track. He came back with the same answer I had received from the Norwegians and the Turks: They would be happy to assist if both parties formally request their involvement, and if they are the only negotiators working on the case.

I contacted Hadas, who responded like a broken record: "There is an official track of negotiations through the German mediator." I knew Conrad had essentially finished his role and that Israel was waiting for Hamas to respond to the German proposal. I wrote to Netanyahu and to Defense Minister Ehud Barak, informing them that the Russians would be willing to step in and assist. They replied that my letter had been referred to the person responsible for dealing with this issue – meaning Hadas. Dead end.

Five long months later, my good friend Mohammed Najib, Middle East correspondent for *Jane's Defence Weekly*, went to Damascus to interview Khaled Mashal. He said he would gladly deliver any message I had for Mashal.

Najib returned to Jerusalem on June 26 and told me that when he'd tried to hand my letter to Mashal, the latter had raised his hands and said he wouldn't touch it. He was probably thinking it contained some deadly chemical material. (More than a decade before, the Mossad had almost killed Mashal on a busy Amman street using a toxic chemical. The Mossad agents were apprehended by the Jordanian police, and Israel was forced to provide the antidote that saved Mashal's life.) Mashal agreed to have Najib read the letter out loud, however.

June 6, 2010

Dear Mr. Mashal,

I am writing to you once again about Gilad Schalit and the prisoner exchange. Ever since Hamas abducted Schalit, as you know, I have been trying to secure his release. Too much time has passed without any progress. It is time to make the deal. Too many people are suffering – not only the Schalit family, but the hundreds of Palestinian families waiting to reunite with their loved ones, and the 1.6 million Palestinians in the Gaza Strip, who are suffering from economic isolation. It is clear that you place the problem on the shoulders of the Israeli government. It is equally clear that Israel places it back on you. The German mediator seems to have completed his work without an agreement. Each side is waiting for the other.

The Shura Council must make a decision, and everyone

must agree on an acceptable offer to allow Schalit and hundreds of Palestinian prisoners to reunite with their families. Your word and your decision are crucial. If there is to be a true negotiation, that automatically assumes you won't get 100 percent of what you demand. There must be compromise. You say time is on your side, you can wait until Israel gives in. But look how many people are suffering.

True, the economic siege of Gaza is not only the result of holding Gilad Schalit, but that is the pretext. Israel's position on the Gaza siege is not being challenged by the international community because Schalit is in Gaza. Why do you offer Israel this pretext? Isn't it time to push for the siege on Gaza to end? I know Palestinian suffering won't end with the release of Schalit, and your political struggle will continue long afterward, but why allow this case to drag on?

The siege on Gaza will lessen after Schalit is released. This won't solve the Palestinian problem, but it will ease the situation for the people of Gaza, who are under your direct control.

Your demands are far beyond what the government of Israel can accept. Surely it's possible to offer something that will be a huge victory for Hamas but one that Israel can also accept. Waiting without real negotiations will solve nothing. We have a long, hot summer ahead of us. The time for reaching an agreement is now.

Israel may attempt a military rescue, even if the price tag is the killing of Schalit. People around Netanyahu strongly advise him to do that, because they would rather have Schalit labeled a dead "hero" than give in to Hamas demands. Don't believe Israel doesn't know where Schalit is. If it doesn't know, it will soon. A military rescue will cost you your most valuable bargaining chip. Free the hundreds of Palestinian prisoners now, while you have that card in your hands. Don't be too greedy or too confident.

You can lead Hamas to make the right decision now. If you give the green light, this can be done. I would suggest that you empower Ghazi Hamad to negotiate the deal with me – with your approval in hand; I will get the green light from the Israeli government. Then we can put a speedy end to this nightmare. I urge you: Do what's necessary to end this story now.

Gershon Baskin, PhD

Chapter 10

A Possible Breakthrough

Inside Hamas there were reports of growing tension between the chief negotiator, Mahmoud al-Zahar, and Ahmed Jaabri, who held Gilad Schalit. The rumors suggested that al-Zahar supported the German proposal but the rest of the Hamas leadership opposed it. The disputes within the Hamas leadership led to indecision, so while Israel had given Dr. Gerhard Conrad a green light to continue negotiations, Hamas offered no response.

On July 4, 2010, Ghazi sent me a new proposal. He said it had the support of Schalit's captors, meaning Jaabri. Since Hagai Hadas had rejected every attempt to propose a new mediator, Ghazi suggested working through Conrad, putting him back on track and indicating areas that needed additional work and areas of flexibility. Ghazi believed that if Israel showed additional flexibility, it would close the gaps inside Hamas. He had been appointed the political liaison for dealing with border crossings, including the Rafah crossing to Egypt and the tunnels. In this capacity, he was in regular contact with Jaabri. Ghazi began talking to Jaabri about Schalit and how to conclude a deal with the Israelis. This is what Ghazi sent me:

Hamas' position:

1. *Commitment to renew and intensify negotiations through an agreed-upon mechanism;*
2. *Negotiations only through the German mediator;*
3. *Commitment to provide new ideas to move the negotiations forward, submitting these ideas to the German mediator;*
4. *Make the necessary efforts to show flexibility;*
5. *Negotiations to begin based upon the points agreed upon in November 2009 (the German proposal);*
6. *Identification of points of contention with a view to reconsider and find solutions;*
7. *No security restrictions on the prisoners released;*
8. *Commitment to provide every assistance to the German mediator, and to reconsider its positions on many points relating to the terms of the deal;*
9. *Negotiations on the following basis;*
   a. *Reducing the number of prisoners to be deported to Gaza or abroad;*
   b. *Reducing the number of prisoners Israel refuses to release;*
   c. *The release of girls and women;*
   d. *The release of all prisoners incarcerated for more than fifteen years.*

I immediately wrote to Barak, Conrad, Hadas, and Nader. To start, I had a suggestion for Barak. Given that each side claimed to be waiting for an answer from the other, we needed to find a breakthrough formula. My proposal was that both parties submit a new paper to Conrad at the same time, presenting new positions within the limitations that everyone was aware of. To jump-start this, Ghazi Hamad had already sent me a paper written together with Jaabri. I also raised the idea that both parties return to negotiations in the same place, perhaps Egypt, so the deal could be concluded faster.

Barak's answer was more than disappointing. His office director wrote me a terse reply: "Your letter has been passed on to the official dealing with this issue" – in other words, right to Hadas.

July 4, 2010

Dear Nader,

I am sending you a text I received from Ghazi Hamad this morning. It has been approved by Ahmed Jaabri. The purpose is to find a mechanism by which to invite Dr. Conrad to return to the region in order to restart negotiations, with the knowledge that both sides are prepared to present new ideas and positions. Hamas wants the invitation to go to Conrad from both sides simultaneously.

Can Egypt transmit the messages between Israel and Hamas to get Conrad to come back?

Gershon

Nader replied that he would check with his superiors to see how Egypt could assist in getting the negotiations back on track. But there was no further Egyptian response. I decided to once again write to Barak:

July 5, 2010

Dear Mr. Barak,

I was more than disappointed by the answer to my last letter. I thought you would be a responsible adult and find a way to advance the deadlocked process. There is a real possibility of returning the negotiations to positive tracks and bringing Gilad home.

Hamas has requested a signal that Israel is willing to be more flexible than in the previous proposal. Hamas will then also declare its willingness to be more flexible. Due to honor games and foolish "Middle East bazaar" rules, both Israel and Hamas are preventing the return of the German negotiator. Meanwhile, Gilad continues rotting in the dungeons of Hamas in Gaza.

We need to break these rules. If Israel passes a message to Jaabri – through me or anyone else – that it is prepared to submit *an improved proposal to the German negotiator, then Hamas will do the same. We need to stop the game of who goes first. Why don't you utilize me to help?*

Gershon Baskin

Once again, a senior assistant to Barak replied, stating that the minister had forwarded my message to his representative dealing with the Schalit negotiations.

What was happening was hard to believe.

Negotiations through the German mediator had broken down. There had been a German proposal on the table since December 2009, which Hamas had rejected without formally saying so. And, as reported, Jaabri was apparently so dissatisfied with the plan that he'd fired Mahmoud al-Zahar and instructed him to stay out of the issue. Jaabri was without a doubt the strongman in Gaza. He had the real power, commanding tens of thousands of armed Hamas combatants, including the people holding Gilad Schalit. This move was thus interpreted in Israel as another clear demonstration that Jaabri simply didn't want to reach an agreement.

I texted Hadas and tried speaking with him. Hadas texted back but refused to speak to me. I spent almost two hours texting back and forth with him, pleading that he meet with me. He maintained his position: There is an official track. There is a German mediator. I kept saying the German track was dead. Something had to be done to get it started again. I didn't suggest that I replace Conrad. I simply wanted Hadas to understand that we now had direct contact with Jaabri and it should be used. He refused.

On July 6, with no negotiations in the works, the Schalits took to the streets. They marched from their home in Mitzpe Hila, way up north, all the way to Jerusalem. Tens of thousands of Israelis joined them. Public support for the Schalit family had reached a new high. "Free Gilad Schalit" posters appeared all over the country. People tied yellow ribbons to their cars. The Schalits appeared on television all over the world. They set up a tent next to the prime minister's residence and vowed not to leave until Gilad came home.

The Schalit campaign activists swelled all around the country, but mainly in Jerusalem. A large sign marking the number of days Gilad had been missing had been posted in front of the prime minister's residence since the first year of his captivity. Now, in addition, people were demonstrating every Friday at noon, closing the street in front of the house, shouting, "Gilad is still alive!"

The campaign was making an impact. Polls showed that most of the public favored a deal with Hamas.

Feeling the pressure, Netanyahu spoke to the public about the issue for the first time, laying out his "red lines" for a prisoner exchange. "I see, as does every Israeli prime minister, the security of all of the state's citizens. Israel is willing to pay a heavy price for the release of Schalit, but not any price," he stated at a press conference. Nonetheless, Netanyahu said he had agreed to the latest offer from Hamas.

This was the first official statement acknowledging that Conrad had placed a full offer on the table. "The German mediator's offer, which we agreed to accept, called for the release of one thousand terrorists. This is the price I am prepared to pay to bring Gilad home. I said yes to the deal, and it is ready for immediate implementation," Netanyahu explained, outlining what he was and wasn't willing to compromise on:

"There are prices I am not prepared to pay, and they are not included in this difficult deal .... I stand firm on two basic principles: The first principle is that dangerous terrorists will not return to Judea and Samaria [the West Bank], where they can continue to harm Israel's citizens." The second sticking point he mentioned was that "arch-terrorists" would not be freed as part of the deal.

With the document I had received from Ghazi on July 4, I knew I was holding something of great value, and I believed Ghazi when he told me it had come with Ahmed Jaabri's full agreement. To my mind this was a breakthrough – perhaps the final path on the long road to bringing Gilad home. I was ready to re-enlist with all my time and energy. I decided to contact everyone once again.

July 19, 2010 [SMS]

To: Dr. Gerhard Conrad, Hagai Hadas, Ghazi Hamad (for Ahmed Jaabri), Nader El-A'aser, Noam Schalit

Dr. Conrad has received a message from Hamas with six different points, indicating a willingness to continue the negotiations and reach an agreement. The message came through me, not directly from Ahmed Jaabri. Dr. Conrad says he must hear directly from Jaabri and not from me in order to take action. Jaabri's reservations regarding direct contact stem from his concern that the request to renew negotiations must come from both sides and not just from him, which he perceives would weaken his position. My suggestion is that Mr. Omar Suleiman initiate direct contact with Jaabri following assurances from Israel that both sides are prepared to resume negotiations and make compromises to reach an agreement so the exchange will take place at the beginning of Ramadan. From that point, both sides will invite Dr. Conrad to return in order to resume and complete the negotiations. Gershon Baskin. PS I am not attempting to negotiate, only to advance the negotiations.

Conrad responded that he must receive an official request from both parties. "Jaabri has my phone number; he knows how to reach me," Conrad told me. Ironically, Jaabri told Ghazi the same thing: "Conrad has my phone number; he knows how to reach me." Obsessed with appearances and how they could weaken or strengthen one's positioning, each kept waiting for the other's call.

I replied to Conrad:

July 20, 2010

Dear Dr. Conrad,

I receive daily messages that both sides are prepared to return to serious negotiations and to improve their previous positions in order to reach an agreement by the beginning of Ramadan. Mr. Jaabri has not been convinced to take the first step of requesting that you return to resume the negotiations. I have been assured that if you ask both him and Mr. Hadas at the same time whether they agree that you should return to resume negotiations, the answers will be affirmative.

Dr. Gershon Baskin

On August 3, I met with Ahmed Sadat, grandson of former Egyptian President Anwar Sadat and a political adviser in the Egyptian Embassy in Tel Aviv. Meeting in a well-known Tel Aviv restaurant, I handed him the paper from Jaabri. He was surprised, but he also believed that even if Jaabri put it on official stationery, or sent it directly to Conrad, it would not produce a breakthrough. Nonetheless, he took the paper and said he would speak to Cairo about it.

On August 8, Ghazi sent a note directly to Conrad, in Arabic (sending me a copy to pass on to the Israelis):

1. *Hamas says the soldier is alive and in good condition, confirming that he is being treated well and will not be harmed.*
2. *Hamas is committed to negotiations with the German mediator, and is as committed to the efforts of the Egyptians and any other efforts.*
3. *Hamas hopes a prisoner swap will be accomplished soon.*
4. *Hamas seeks direct contact with the German mediator as soon as possible, unless there is a new Israeli stand, based on what was agreed upon in Cairo and Gaza (during the German mediator's latest visit).*
5. *If a deal is reached, Hamas will have several points to be amended through negotiations.*
6. *Hamas wants to discuss and review several practical means in this regard.*
7. *Several points that are to be built upon:*

First by Israel –
a.*Reducing to a reasonable minimum the number of detainees Israel refuses to release;*
b.*Reconsidering the number of detainees to be expelled to Gaza or abroad;*

c. *Release of all women detainees;*

d. *Israel should not object to the release of detainees who have served more than fifteen years in jail.*

Second by Hamas –

a. *All detainees to be released should sign a pledge not to return to any activities against Israel's security;*

b. *All detainees to be released and returned to their homes in the West Bank are obligated to be present at police stations for a certain period;*

c. *Hamas agrees to the expulsion of a number of dangerous people, whom Israel completely refuses to release unconditionally;*

d. *Hamas will be ready to negotiate and discuss excluding detainees from within the Green Line in the deal; however, they are to be released after three months using a certain mechanism with guarantees from the International Committee of the Red Cross or [other international guarantees].*

Ghazi received a response from Dr. Conrad and e-mailed me a summary, asking me to forward it to the officials in Israel:

1. *The ideas he [Conrad] received were important but unofficial, and he appreciates efforts to move the issue.*

2. *He will think seriously about what has been proposed in order to decide what to do next.*

3. *He has also received ideas from the other [Israeli] side.*

4. *He believes it is better to contact him directly, especially the parties he has already dealt with [al-Zahar and Jaabri].*

5. *He expects the proposed ideas will return to where negotiations stood in November 2009, but believes the Israeli side is building its positions on the latest proposals of December 2009.*

I tried to get Ghazi to spell out what Hamas perceived to be the gaps between their position and the Israeli one based on Israel's willingness to accept the German proposal from December 2009.[1]

---

1. It is important to note that Hamas was now relating to the German proposal as a

On August 15, Ghazi replied:

1. *Israel refuses to release seventy prisoners on the list of what Conrad calls the VIPs.[2] This number is very large, and unacceptable to Hamas. In the past, Israel refused to release 120, but now the number rejected is seventy.*
2. *Israel insists on deporting 240 West Bank prisoners to the Gaza Strip. This is too many for Hamas to accept.*
3. *Israel insists on deporting about 120 prisoners outside the Palestinian territories.*
4. *We can discuss how to find alternatives. The most important issue to Mr. J.[3] is reducing the seventy removed from the list.*

We seemed to have actually begun a kind of unofficial negotiation. Ghazi was laying down the terms on how to reach an agreement. There were no official talks taking place, and this channel of mine with Ghazi could actually produce results. At the same time, I had no way of getting Hagai Hadas to change his position.

About two months after Gilad came home, I showed the above document to David Meidan, who succeeded Hadas in April 2011. He was astounded and said that this document was not so different than the one we produced a full year later, described by Netanyahu as "the breakthrough document."

The next day I once again approached the key people by text:

German-*Israeli* one, believing the German mediator was coordinating his proposals with the Israelis and even acting on Israel's behalf. A complete confidence gap had developed between Conrad and Jaabri.
2. I learned from David Meidan, see below, that the German mediator, Dr. Conrad, had referred to the Palestinian prisoners with the most Jewish blood on their hands as "VIPs." I was completely disgusted by the thought that the more Jews they killed, the more important they were. I complained to David, but he said it was already the accepted terminology. These arch-terrorists were the most difficult for Israel to release, both for security reasons and because of the political fallout that would be experienced by any Israeli prime minister for releasing people who had killed so many Israelis.
3. Mr. J. is what Ghazi often called Ahmed Jaabri in our phone conversations.

August 16, 2010 [SMS]

To: *Noam Schalit, Dr. Gerhard Conrad, Mr. Hagai Hadas,*
Mr. Ghazi Hamad
Ghazi Hamad and I have been encouraged to continue unofficial dis-
cussions on ways to move the prisoner-exchange negotiations forward
and to communicate new ideas to the people copied on this message.
Hamad is in direct contact with Ahmed Jaabri. Hamad spent more
than two hours with him two days ago and speaks with him daily.
Jaabri has encouraged the exchange of ideas and is willing to receive
any ideas we come up with.

We (Ghazi and I) strongly believe both sides are willing to
move forward in order to conclude the agreement. We believe it is
possible to reach an agreement by Eid al-Fitr.

Neither side wants to appear to be taking the first step. We
call on Dr. Conrad to take the initiative and come back, meet with
each side separately, define new areas of compromise, and work out
an agreement.

I have received signals from Hamas that if Israel removes forty
names from the VIP list (instead of seventy), it would be acceptable.
Hamas is also willing for the VIPs to be deported to Gaza or abroad.
Jaabri wants those who have already served the longest time and those
with the longest sentences to be included, even if deported.

These are the first ideas. More will come. Gershon Baskin

Chapter 11

Two Narratives of Mutual Blame

O n a hot August day in 2010, I decided to summarize where we were. Here's what I wrote:

The prisoner-exchange negotiations have been frozen since December 2009. As can be expected, there are at least two narratives explaining why there is no progress. Each side blames the other. Each side has said to me, "The ball is in the other's court."

These are the two narratives I have heard:

The Israeli narrative:
Negotiations reached a breakthrough with the release of the videotape of Gilad on October 2, 2009. Work done by the German mediator Dr. Conrad brought about significant progress toward an agreement. In November 2009, the deal worked out by Dr. Conrad was brought to the inner cabinet (the septet), where intensive deliberations brought a three-to-three split, with Netanyahu casting the deciding vote against

the deal. The septet demanded new negotiations, the deletion of some ten names from the list of arch-terrorists, the removal of all Israeli Arabs from the list, and to deport – either to Gaza or out of the region – 224 Palestinian prisoners.

On the basis of the Israeli objections, Dr. Conrad submitted a new version in December 2009. Israel indicated a positive response, while Hamas has not given any answer. Since then, Israel has had regular contact with Dr. Conrad and has informed him that it is willing to adjust the December 2009 proposal.

The Israeli side has indicated its confidence in Conrad as the mediator.

The Hamas narrative:
Following the Israeli agreement to release nineteen women prisoners, a videotape of Gilad was released by Hamas on October 2, 2009. Negotiations progressed and in November and December (in Cairo and Gaza), a deal was worked out and believed to have the agreement of both sides. Mahmoud al-Zahar met with Khaled Mashal in Damascus and convinced him to accept the deal. (This was before Ahmed Jaabri threw al-Zahar out of the negotiations.)

The deal included all 450 names that Hamas wanted, with 97 of the West Bankers to be sent to Gaza, and another 550 names to be released in phase two.

When the Israeli cabinet rejected the offer, the German mediator submitted a new proposal. From Hamas' perspective, the ball is in Israel's court, because the Israeli side rejected the deal that had been worked out. Chief Hamas negotiator Ahmed Jaabri says he gave Dr. Conrad a direct phone number to use when he hears the Israelis are serious about making a deal. Jaabri is still waiting for the phone call from Conrad.

Dr. Conrad:
Dr. Conrad has indicated that he is willing to continue the negotiations when he receives clear indications that both sides are willing to go beyond their previous proposals to reach an agreement. Dr. Conrad has indicated that he must receive these signals either from officials or from persons authorized by officials in Hamas. He has indicated

that Ahmed Jaabri has his phone number and knows how to reach him. Conrad seems unwilling to take the initiative to restart the talks, but is waiting for both sides to approach him.

I sent this summary to Ghazi, who replied with the following correction:

The Hamas narrative:
When the Israeli cabinet rejected the offer, the German mediator sub-mitted a new proposal. Hamas responded that the original agreement had to be the basis of a deal, and that it would not agree to a proposal made after an agreement had been reached.

This was not true, because people *outside* the Hamas leadership in Damascus – Mashal et al. – rejected the proposal. Ghazi's correction suggested there was no conflict within the Hamas political leadership. This was not what I'd understood.

He added: *Hamas has indicated its confidence in Conrad as the mediator.*

This sentence was suspicious, because by now Jaabri was convinced that Conrad was more in line with Israel than with Hamas. The German channel ended because Jaabri no longer trusted Conrad. The real reason for the lack of trust only became evident to me in May 2011, as we shall see.

What seemed to be lacking in this saga was the "responsible adult" who would cut through all the nonsense and tactical positioning and get to the heart of the matter. That person, I hoped, would be Ehud Barak, the former prime minister and current defense minister. So once again, I appealed to his intelligence and good sense.

August 21, 2010

Dear Mr. Barak,

Over the past month that I have been trying to renew the negotiations for the release of Gilad, I have been passing messages from a repre-sentative of Ahmed Jaabri to Hagai Hadas and to Gerhard Conrad. All my attempts have failed.

On July 4, 2010, I turned to you, also without success. The answer I received from your office was at best laconic. As you know, since January there have not been any real negotiations. Your direct involvement is needed now. If there were negotiations taking place through the German negotiator, at least there would be some hope for a positive outcome. Without any negotiations, Gilad continues to rot in Gaza. The declaration that the State of Israel is doing everything possible to bring him home is a lie to the entire public.

Mr. Barak, the time has come to stop depending on the officials responsible for this file, who until now have completely failed. The messages I receive from Hamas indicate its willingness to renew negotiations and complete a deal for a prisoner exchange. Jaabri has refused to turn directly to Conrad because he says the conditions Prime Minister Netanyahu has made do not allow for negotiations. At this point, Jaabri will not issue any unilateral compromises. But he has asked Ghazi Hamad to approach people in Israel to search for a mechanism for renewing the negotiations.

Hamad has approached me, and for more than a month we have been searching for ways to move forward. He is prepared to speak with an official appointed by you, in secret, direct talks. Due to the trust that has developed between Hamad and me over the past four years, I can also assist.

Hagai Hadas refuses to speak to me or to examine the Hamas proposals I send him, because – as he says – they are not coming via the German mediator. This refusal seems illogical, given that it prevents potential advancements in the negotiations.

I am turning to you because I believe the prime minister is not currently interested in advancing an agreement with Hamas. You have also declared, "Not at any price," but this deal is not "any price." The price has been set and agreed to. It is essential that you directly involve yourself and help push for a positive decision.

As the most senior member of the government after the prime minister, and as a former prime minister, you must not refrain from direct action toward a deal. The messages Ghazi Hamad is sharing come directly from Ahmed Jaabri. He will hear from your representative, and messages will be passed on directly to Jaabri. This of course

*demands the highest degree of secrecy, as neither side is interested in
exposing any direct contacts between them. The passing of these messages is solely for completing the Schalit deal.*

*I request that you meet me as soon as possible, or that we
speak by phone, so we can advance my proposal.*

Gershon Baskin

I received no substantive answer from Barak, only that the letter had
been received and that he would read it. His office sent me another
terse response, thanking me for the letter but again indicating that Hagai
Hadas was the special emissary responsible for the return of Schalit.
Hadas didn't even bother responding to the letter.

I had to get Hadas to listen to me. I knew people who had worked
in the Mossad and who respected me. I asked them to speak to Hadas
on my behalf.

August 29, 2010 [SMS]

To: Ghazi
*I spoke this morning with someone who worked with Hagai Hadas in
the Mossad and knows him well. He agreed that if I got a new picture
of Gilad or a letter from him, it would make all the difference, and I
would be brought "inside" with a much better chance of influencing
the process. Gershon*

By this time, Jaabri had lost all confidence in negotiating. He refused to provide any additional sign of life. According to Ghazi, Jaabri believed that the
last sign – the video from October 2009 – had caused Israel to drag its feet
rather than speeding up the negotiations. Seeing that Gilad was alive and
well, according to Jaabri, reduced the pressure on Israel to conclude the deal.

Another Ramadan came and went. Eid al-Fitr passed and Hamas
didn't bring its prisoners home. Gilad was still in captivity. That year, Rosh
HaShana and Eid al-Fitr happened to fall on the same day. Four years in
captivity. I knew a breakthrough was possible. Hamas was finally ready to
really negotiate. A deal could be made. I was convinced of it.

Despite my many failed attempts to speak with Hagai Hadas and convince him to give a direct back channel a chance, I decided to try again. The prime minister's military attaché delivered the following letter:

September 28, 2010

Dear Hagai,

Last week Dr. Conrad made a private trip to Gaza to visit Mahmoud al-Zahar in the hospital. He did not meet Ahmed Jaabri. I understand that Jaabri doesn't want to see Conrad anymore and has no confidence in him as a fair mediator.

There are no negotiations. Ghazi Hamad is acting with authority from Jaabri. According to him, Hamas is willing to advance the negotiations and demonstrate flexibility. Hamad has been asked to check if Israel is also willing to demonstrate more flexibility. You have seen the document Hamad sent Dr. Conrad, indicating the points Hamas has requested to advance. Clearly, they indicate an opening. Hamad emphasizes that the basis for reaching an agreement is narrowing the number of names Israel has removed from the list and Hamas' agreement for them to be deported to Gaza or abroad.

Hamad repeatedly says Jaabri is prepared to speed up the process. Hamad says he has received permission from Jaabri to meet with you and me directly; he is prepared to do so at the Erez crossing or in another location that would provide the security for him to return safely to Gaza. It's possible to request that Dr. Conrad return to close the final elements of the deal.

If, because of the Israeli government's policy of no contact with Hamas, you cannot or will not meet Hamad directly, he has requested that the dialogue be conducted with a non-official. I am ready to take on that mission anytime.

There is an opportunity here to end this horrible story – perhaps the first real chance in a long time. I don't know how you can refuse. What do you have to lose?

Gershon Baskin

But Hadas did refuse. He responded by text message that there was an official channel through the German mediator. Hagai Hadas was the key to opening a secret direct channel. Never had Ghazi been more explicit in Hamas' willingness to open such a conduit for negotiations. Ghazi even expressed his willingness to meet Hadas with the full authorization of Jaabri. Hadas' refusal made no sense to me. Yet it seemed that nobody in the Israeli government would demand an explanation from Netanyahu as to why the process was dead, and why no one was doing anything about it.

Israel's government ministers and security officials continued telling the public and the Schalit family that they were leaving no stone unturned to bring Gilad home. As I heard their statements, all I could think was: lies, lies, lies. I couldn't understand why Israeli officials weren't jumping at the opportunity Ghazi Hamad had laid at their feet.

The Schalit family campaign was running on ritual: demonstrations in front of the prime minister's house every Friday at noon; volunteers there every day, giving out flyers and yellow ribbons. The number of days in captivity was repeated on many radio and television programs. Many people made a statement in their Facebook profiles by swapping their own image for one of Gilad.

I began attending the Friday demonstrations. I saw Noam and Aviva there all the time. They seemed more helpless and desperate than ever. I had a hard time looking them in the eye. Aviva looked completely lost. Noam was constantly on the phone, being interviewed and trying to draw attention and sympathy to their personal crusade. He seemed so overwhelmed. How could any parent survive so long under these circumstances?

I felt genuine anger – first toward Hamas, then toward Hagai Hadas, Ofer Dekel, Ehud Olmert, Ehud Barak, and Benjamin Netanyahu. I also felt frustrated that even the Schalits didn't take me seriously. They kept telling me Ghazi Hamad was the Yossi Beilin of Hamas – a reference to the leader of Israel's leftist Meretz and the initiator of the Oslo process, who enjoyed respect but had no influence.

A year had gone by since the video of Gilad had produced so much hope. Ghazi said he would try to produce a new sign of life, but Jaabri was disappointed by the results of the previous sign. I reminded Ghazi that Netanyahu did release nineteen women prisoners in exchange for the videotape. Yet I knew Ghazi would not succeed.

October 25, 2010 [SMS]

To: Conrad
Dr. Conrad, my understanding is that you made no progress on your
last visit. I understand that Hamas indicated some willingness to com-
promise on key issues, but you got nothing new from the Israeli side.
My Egyptian contacts tell me you are threatening to resign in order
to apply pressure on the parties. We can also apply pressure. Would
this be helpful? Gershon Baskin

Now Conrad was also ignoring my messages and phone calls. I
understood that Hadas had told him not to respond to me. I went to
Berlin for a conference and proposed to Conrad that we meet. He
didn't respond.

In early November, I learned from Nader El-A'aser that the
Egyptians were ready to take over if asked. He complained that the
German negotiator had simply disappeared after the parties rejected
his efforts.

I passed this information on to Hagai Hadas via text message:

Dear Hagai, Following the desertion of the arena by the German
mediator, I understand that the Egyptians are prepared to take full
responsibility for the negotiations – if requested to do so. They also
believe they are the only ones capable of applying real pressure on
Hamas to conclude the deal. Gershon Baskin

Hadas didn't respond.

By the beginning of 2011, there was no negotiation, no mediator, no
process, and no contact between Israel and Hamas. For more than six
months, things stagnated. I had come to the heartbreaking conclusion
that Netanyahu had given up on bringing Gilad home alive. I expressed
this sentiment in my *Jerusalem Post* column, "Encountering Peace":

Encountering Peace: The Forgotten Soldier

*Gilad Schalit isn't home yet because
no one wants to give Hamas a victory.*

Who really wants Gilad Schalit released, except his family? Apparently no one. "The State of Israel is doing everything possible to bring Gilad home." Come on, who are they kidding? After four and a half years, a few kilometers from the border, in an area under our complete external control, sits an IDF soldier, one of us, one of our children, sent to defend us, in captivity by our enemy with no real sign that he'll be coming home in the near future.

Before I start on the Prime Minister's Office, let me put the blame where it really belongs – on Hamas. But criticism of Hamas isn't going to pressure it to change its demands for Schalit's release

He could have been home long ago; the price tag has been known for more than four years, and it hasn't changed. I personally received the first list of Hamas' demands, which I passed on to the Prime Minister's Office, and the price remains today as it was then – in fact, as I will show, Hamas has made some compromises, but still Schalit remains in captivity

Hamas even indicated a willingness to conduct direct, secret talks to conclude a deal – I know because I delivered the request. The response: We have an agreed-upon mediator – a German former intelligence officer – and everything must go through him.

Let's be brutally honest – Schalit isn't home yet because no one wants to give Hamas a victory. Egypt, which has provided the umbrella for the negotiations, has the Muslim Brotherhood to worry about. The recent elections there clearly demonstrated the political manipulations the regime is willing to undertake in order to prevent any kind of political victory for Hamas' elder brother. Jordan, like Egypt, doesn't want to see celebrations of Hamas' success in bringing about the release of Palestinian prisoners.

Mahmoud Abbas and the Palestinian Authority work overtime to crush Hamas influence in the West Bank. The release of hundreds of prisoners to Hamas is perceived as a direct threat to the Abbas regime.

The Americans don't want a Hamas victory, and why should they care about a single IDF soldier anyway?

Ehud Barak, leader of the dying Labor Party, certainly doesn't want to be perceived as the man who gave in to Hamas. Ehud Olmert didn't want that either, though his negotiator almost closed a deal.

Who in the government wants the reputation of being soft on terror? Our prime minister has certainly calculated the political costs of a deal and has concluded that "business as usual" is much better than paying the price to bring Schalit home.

What does "business as usual" mean? That we will continue to lie over and over again that we are "doing everything possible to bring Schalit home." We will continue making speeches about the high moral code of the IDF, and how we don't leave any soldier behind. We will continue to whisper, "We shouldn't discuss this issue in public, because the negotiations are secret, and the price will rise."

We will continue to employ a former senior Mossad official and pay him more than NIS 300,000 a year, plus a team to work with him, so we can justify our claim of leaving no stone unturned.

No negotiations are taking place. The German mediator, Dr. Gerhard Conrad, has basically stopped trying, knowing the process is stuck almost where it was more than a year ago. Egyptian security officials claim they could conclude a deal, but no one will appoint them to take full charge, and without that they will play only a passive role. (If they can deliver as they claim, why won't they? Because they also don't really want to.)

In July 2010, a letter from a senior Hamas official was delivered to Conrad after its contents had been authorized by Hamas strongman – and the person believed to be holding Schalit – Ahmed Jaabri, in which Hamas agreed to moderate some of its demands. I received a copy and delivered it to the prime minister and the minister of defense. Jaabri was willing to accept that a certain number of prisoners on the Hamas list would be removed, and that Hamas would agree that about thirty of the West Bank prisoners could be released to Gaza or sent abroad. Israel's position was that more than ten names on the Hamas list be removed entirely, and that more than 120 West Bank prisoners be expelled to Gaza or abroad.

On the basis of the letter and other indications, Conrad tried to renew the process, but came to a dead end on the Israeli side. I recently spoke with that senior Hamas official, who continues to state that Jaabri is now willing to accept even more deportees to Gaza and abroad, but Israel continues refusing to enter serious negotiations.

Without declarations, without ceremonies, without a funeral and a flag over a casket, Gilad Schalit is nonetheless being treated as a soldier who fell in defense of his country; it's much easier to quell the national conscience than to make the tough decisions no one wants to make.

The problem is that Schalit is still alive, he's still a soldier, he's still one of our sons, and our conscience should not allow us to conduct business as usual for even one more day.

Abbas and the PA will survive the momentary Hamas victory. Egypt and Jordan will not collapse if hundreds of prisoners are released to Hamas. Our security forces can deal with any released prisoner who really presents a threat. The IDF will be free to take care of Hamas' military wing after Schalit's release without fearing that its actions will lead to his death. What will not survive is the moral code of the IDF, the covenant between the state, the people and the army – and our good conscience.

On April 13, 2011, Hagai Hadas informed Netanyahu that he would like to step down as special envoy. Hadas had failed to bring Gilad Schalit home. His failure reflected not only his unwillingness to think outside the box and grab any and every opportunity before him, but also Netanyahu's failure to give him the mandate to complete a deal with Hamas. The key to a deal between Israel and Hamas was in Netanyahu's hands, and he never gave that key to Hadas. My anger at Hadas, though, was primarily because he never even gave me a chance. Instead, he formed a team of "negotiations experts," using valuable government resources and money. But rather than make a deal, they spent their time trying to understand how a deal could be made. Many of these so-called experts teach negotiations and conflict resolution at various universities but have never actually negotiated anything themselves.

On April 18, Netanyahu's office announced that David Meidan, a senior Mossad official, had replaced Hadas. Once again, my hopes rose. I decided that by the end of the day, I would be in contact with Meidan.

April 18 was the eve of Passover, the Jewish festival of freedom. It would be another Passover in which Gilad was underground in Gaza, while his family and about a hundred activists in the campaign for his release held their Seder – their reenactment of the exodus from Egypt – on the street in front of Netanyahu's official residence.

Chapter 12

Tuning In to the Back Channel

David Meidan was the first person in charge of Gilad's file who was not a former official, but an active one. He headed "Tevel," the Mossad division responsible for liaison relationships with allied governments on counterterrorism. Dekel and Hadas had each been appointed after being denied a promotion. But Meidan was still in active service and was the equivalent of a general in the Mossad. In intelligence circles, he was highly respected, not a powerless go-between.

This time Facebook didn't help me find his phone number. But I knew someone with the same last name who had served in the Mossad – Pini Meidan. After leaving the Mossad, Pini had been a foreign policy adviser to Ehud Barak. In 2000–2001, I was a member of a team of experts on Jerusalem that helped develop Israel's positions on the capital for the negotiations with the Palestinians

David Meidan

in Taba, Egypt, in January 2001. Pini Meidan met with our team, and that's how I met him. Later, he joined forces with Barak's former chief of staff, attorney Gilead Sher, as part of a team of experts participating in various Israeli-Palestinian meetings. I had recruited both of them for a project on permanent-status negotiations.

On April 18, the day of David Meidan's appointment, I called Pini and asked whether he was related to David. He said no and asked why I wanted to know. I said it had to do with Schalit. He asked whether I wanted him to make contact with David. Pini spoke to him, then sent me his phone number, with a message that he was waiting for my call.

I called immediately, introducing myself as a veteran peace activist who co-directed an Israeli-Palestinian think tank. I told him of my communication with Hamas since the first week of Gilad's abduction. I said I was still in contact with senior Hamas officials and could help bring Gilad home.

David replied that, having just been appointed, he did not yet have a desk, a phone, or a secretary. I should contact him again in two weeks. It was Passover, a time of year when Israel barely functions for up to three weeks – most schools and government offices are closed, and everything gets put off until after the holiday. Still, I could think of nothing but Gilad Schalit and David Meidan. I couldn't wait for those two weeks to pass.

When they finally did, I called David again. He said he needed another week to get organized. I had learned the meaning of patience by then, and settled in to wait.

In the meantime, I called Ghazi Hamad and told him a new man had been appointed to the job, and perhaps we had a new chance at success. He told me immediately that Jaabri was prepared to renew negotiations. I asked him what the gaps were and what Jaabri was willing to do. He said nothing had changed since December 2009. Still, I was encouraged by Ghazi's belief that we could move forward. I also understood that he had direct contact with Jaabri and that our connection was strong and based on trust. We could make the difference.

I called General Nader El-A'aser in Cairo, now head of the Israel and Palestine desk in Egyptian General Intelligence, and told him I had renewed my attempt to free Schalit. Nader told me Egypt was prepared to resume its mediation role. I was quite aware that Egypt in April 2011 was very different from the Egypt that had existed immediately after Schalit's abduction. With Mubarak no longer in power – he had been ousted in February – and the Muslim Brotherhood on the rise, the Egyptian role could be quite useful. I would always prefer a secret direct channel with Hamas as the surest, fastest way to move forward, but in the end we would need the Egyptians to conclude the deal, because Hamas and Israel would not sign anything between themselves. The Egyptians would also be necessary to oversee the implementation of the deal. But first, I wanted Ghazi and myself to make a breakthrough. I knew we could do it.

I sent a text message to David. Texting between us became a regular activity. I would start each morning with a text message to him, and he would respond immediately. We would text throughout the day. Several weeks later, David commented, "We are making history – I don't think negotiations were ever carried out by text messages."

That day, I wrote to him:

To: David
From the information I have, the Egyptians are prepared to replace the German mediator in intensive negotiations until an agreement is reached. The Egyptians pressured the Hamas leadership to sign the reconciliation agreement with Fatah, and are prepared to pressure Hamas with regard to Schalit.

I assumed that as Meidan took responsibility for negotiations with Hamas, he would be studying the file. There must have been thousands of pages of notes and dozens of people to speak with. As the outgoing director of Tevel, he must also have been contacting other intelligence services – those involved in the case in the past, and those that could assist now. These contacts likely included Russia, Turkey, Norway, Britain, and of course the Egyptians. I further assumed that he'd received offers of assistance from many others like me – self-appointed mediators. I hoped Hagai Hadas wouldn't poison Meidan's opinion of me and I would have a chance to prove that my contacts did lead to Jaabri, and that the relationship I had developed with Ghazi Hamad over a five-year period would be helpful in bringing Schalit home. I continued texting Meidan that my channel was real and should be used.

On May 2, exactly two weeks after David Meidan's appointment – and our conversation – I was at a conference of the United Nations Alliance of Civilizations (UNAOC) in Doha, Qatar. I remember the day quite well, because other than being my birthday, it was also the day I heard that the United States had killed Osama bin Laden. I was one of two Israelis at this conference. Apparently there had been an argument between the UNAOC and the Qatari government about our participation. Although the government had approved our visas, when we arrived at the Doha airport we weren't listed among the conference participants, and it took almost an hour before getting permission to enter the country. When we arrived at the hotel, our names were again not listed. It took until after midnight before the issue was straightened out and we got our rooms. Despite all these complications – and the news about Bin Laden – all I could think of was speaking to David Meidan. I finally borrowed someone's phone to call him. He told me he needed another week, but if I had more contact from Ghazi or Jaabri I should text him. That was encouraging.

I was speaking with Ghazi several times a day, then reporting to David about our conversations. Mostly Ghazi was telling me about being in close contact with Jaabri, with whom he was now spending more time, especially in the evenings. David responded with encouraging text messages, sent within minutes of my messages to him. He said Israel was serious about moving the negotiations forward and bringing Gilad home.

I kept sending messages, waiting impatiently for the week to pass. It seemed like an eternity. I wondered what it felt like for Gilad.

Finally, on May 8 (one day early), I called David. He suggested that we begin by trying to get a sign of life from Gilad. He thought it was the right place to start. I began once again asking Ghazi for a new sign of life from the abducted soldier. Ghazi said he would try, but he wasn't optimistic. He reiterated that since there was no trust, he didn't think Jaabri would agree. I explained to David about the problems caused by the lack of trust. He nonetheless encouraged me to pressure Ghazi. David told me he was serious about negotiations, and I should tell Hamad that he, Meidan, had a clear mandate from Netanyahu to bring Gilad Schalit home. This was an important message.

It soon became clear that Jaabri would not offer another sign of life. I told Ghazi we needed another starting point. After speaking with Jaabri, Ghazi came back with the message that Hamas would be more flexible on the categories of prisoners delineated in the German proposal. The reference to that proposal was significant, because Israel had been waiting two years for Jaabri to respond to it. Jaabri had done so "unofficially" one year earlier, but no one on the Israeli side had been willing to listen. Now David Meidan was listening.

The following day, a short piece in *Haaretz* indicated that Hamas wanted the Egyptians to re-enter negotiations on the prisoner exchange. I told Ghazi we should make a real effort to convince both Jaabri and Meidan to use us. Ghazi spoke to Jaabri, and he agreed that Ghazi and I should try to advance the discussions on the principles of the prisoner exchange.

May 9, 2011, 5:45 a.m. [SMS]

To: David
David, in addition to what was published in Haaretz *this morning, Jaabri has expressed his agreement that Ghazi Hamad and I be part of the negotiations with the Egyptian mediation. That way we can have direct contact behind the scenes and find ways to cut corners. We can speed things up and overcome misunderstandings that could easily become obstacles during the negotiations. This proposal stems from the trust built between us during the years since Gilad's abduction. Think about it. Gershon Baskin*

David responded that I should continue talking to Ghazi and impress upon him the importance of starting with a sign of life as a humanitarian gesture. David told me to tell Ghazi that Israel would reciprocate with its own humanitarian gestures.

From Ghazi's conversations with Jaabri, it became clear that although Jaabri had rejected the German proposal in December 2009, he was prepared to use it as the basis for future negotiations. It was also clear that the document Ghazi had sent a year before, indicating Jaabri's willingness to restart the negotiations with demonstrated flexibility, was still valid. Ten months had been lost.

Ghazi spoke about improving the German proposal, as he had in July 2010. He said Jaabri wanted Israel to be more flexible on several issues. I knew he referring to what Israel called the "arch-terrorists." He added that Israel should agree to reduce the number of prisoners who would be deported abroad and of West Bankers to be deported to Gaza. Ghazi also mentioned the issue of prisoners who were Palestinian citizens of Israel and residents of East Jerusalem, whom Israel refused to release.

Israel had traditionally refused to include citizens or permanent residents of Israel in any prisoner exchange. I never understood this position, though Israel presumably wanted to prevent Hamas from winning hearts and minds in Jerusalem and in Israel proper. Israel expects its Palestinian citizens (about 21 percent of the population) to demonstrate more loyalty to their state than to their people, the Palestinians, and when they violate that code of behavior, to be severely punished. Perhaps this treatment is also meant to deter them from joining the enemies of the state. This issue would resurface throughout the negotiations.

Hamas aimed to demonstrate its concern for all Palestinians – Israeli citizens, Jerusalemites, and West Bank and Gaza residents – as well as demanding that prisoners from all Palestinian political movements be included in the deal, including Fatah, with which it had recently begun a reconciliation.

The most important thing for me was the indication that Ghazi was becoming very close to Jaabri. He told me he was speaking with him every day and spending a lot of time with him talking about the prisoner exchange and trying to understand Jaabri's position and on what issues he was ready to demonstrate flexibility. Ghazi was also beginning to understand Jaabri's "red lines," on which he would not compromise. If Ghazi now had direct contact with the person holding Schalit, this was extremely encouraging.

Meidan told me that if Hamas was willing to base the negotiations on the German proposal, and to show flexibility, then progress could be made. He said it was essential that I transmit that message to

Hamas. For years Hamas people had been telling me that when Israel was serious about negotiating, they would be willing to demonstrate flexibility. Now was the time to test their sincerity.

I decided to speak to Nader El-A'aser in Egypt. "Ghazi and I speak every day," I told him. Nader replied, "Gershon, you are speaking to Ghazi at least five times a day. We are all listening!"

That surprised me. I assumed Israel was listening; I figured the Americans were, too. The fact that the Egyptians were listening indicated that I was finally being taken seriously and we might actually succeed.

As my relationship with David Meidan developed, I grew certain that Ghazi and I could close the gaps and reach a breakthrough. I wanted to meet Ghazi face-to-face. I needed time to sit with him and discuss how we could work together as a team that would have direct contact with both sides. I asked David for permission to go to Gaza. I thought that by meeting in person, Ghazi and I could come up with some new proposals. David replied:

May 26, 2011, 7:47 a.m. [sms]

From: David
Gershon, I am not the address for approving your travel. Also, I didn't ask for new proposals. There is a proposal on the table, which they should relate to through the official channels. David Meidan

I texted back:

May 26, 2011, 7:51 a.m. [sms]

To: David
David, this has been the approach for almost five years, and the results speak for themselves. There is a possibility of thinking outside the box and a readiness for the first time by those who are holding Gilad to bring about a happy ending to this long, sad saga. We can end this. We need to demonstrate courage, flexibility, and new thinking. I don't

work against Israeli interests and won't do anything that isn't fully coordinated with you. I only request that you consider my offer.
Gershon

David then told me that only the head of the ISA, Yoram Cohen, could authorize my going to Gaza. I thought that if David had wanted me to go to Gaza, it would not be a problem of who has to give permission. Perhaps this was a kind of test? I don't think he knew I had the phone number for the head of the ISA and would actually write a letter.

May 26, 2011 [fax]

Yoram Cohen, Head of the ISA
Re: Request to enter Gaza or El Arish [in Sinai] to conduct talks on the Schalit issue

Shalom,

I just finished one of many conversations with David Meidan and Ghazi Hamad. Since the abduction of Schalit, I have been involved on the margins of negotiations, due to the relationship that has developed between Ghazi Hamad and me. This relationship led directly to the first letter from Gilad, which came out of Gaza September 9, 2006, following my visiting Gaza, meetings I held with Ghazi Hamad and other Hamas people, and the connections that have continued since then.

In recent weeks, our discussions have focused on new ways to restart the negotiations. Our goal is to bring this unfortunate chapter to a rapid and positive conclusion. Hamad has direct contact with Ahmed Jaabri, who has encouraged him to continue working with me to advance the deal and conclude it.

Hamad and Jaabri are developing a proposal that amends the last German proposal. I am passing messages to them, based on my conversations with David Meidan, that the prime minister will not accept a new proposal and that they must base their offers on the German one.

David Meidan has accepted the continuation of my contact with Hamad. I asked him to allow me to go to Gaza to meet Hamad face-to-face. Hamad and I agree that this is the best way to advance a deal. During our meeting, he would be able to pick up the phone and call Jaabri, and I could speak with Meidan at the same time. There is an alternative proposal for us to meet in El Arish or in Cairo, but I prefer not to involve the Egyptians. I prefer to keep our channel without a third party for the time being. We both believe in and want to help renew the negotiations.

I understand that the ISA has the authority to allow my travel to Gaza. I am prepared to go there at any time. I can meet Ghazi at the Erez crossing or at his house. There is a real chance, perhaps the first in five years, that Hamas will demonstrate a more serious and flexible approach. We should exploit this opportunity and the trust between Hamad and me. Please grant me permission to travel to Gaza.

Sincerely,
Dr. Gershon Baskin

As expected, I received no answer from Cohen. The ISA is not authorized to have direct contact with civilians. Normally, I would communicate with the ISA through the office of the prime minister's military attaché. This time I didn't want more people to know about my channel of communication with David Meidan. I didn't know who on the Israeli side was aware of our contact, and I didn't want to open the door to people who might cut it off. Had I wanted to push the issue I could have, but I focused on listening very carefully to Meidan, understanding him as much as possible, and acting in good faith in order to build trust between us. Though Meidan had begun to trust me and to understand that my channel with Ghazi Hamad could be useful, I was well aware that the Israeli military/security/political establishment still viewed me as an outsider, a civilian, and a peacenik to boot. These officials probably thought it more than strange that I spoke about trust in Ghazi Hamad. I knew this would be extremely difficult for them to digest.

In our daily text messages and phone conversations, David Meidan continued asking me to try getting a sign of life from Gilad – anything that would prove he was alive and well, and would verify that Ghazi was in contact with Jaabri.

But Ghazi was having trouble convincing Jaabri to comply with the Israeli request. David tried to make it easy by having me tell Ghazi we could work out something reciprocal. David specified what he had in mind. Since Gilad's abduction, the Hamas prisoners in Israel had been denied family visits. David was aiming high, suggesting that Hamas allow a Red Cross visit to Gilad. If Hamas complied with that, David was willing to allow family members to visit Hamas prisoners. And if Hamas allowed a video conference with Gilad, David would allow the Hamas prisoners' families to hold a video conference.

Jaabri refused to allow Schalit any visitors. Hamas had maintained total control of any information on Schalit's location, and Israel had not discovered his whereabouts. Jaabri would do nothing to compromise this secrecy. Ghazi did tell me the Egyptians had received assurances from Hamas that Gilad was alive and well and that it had no intention of hurting him. He was too valuable a bargaining chip to be damaged.

Ghazi wanted to move the conversation away from the sign-of-life issue and focus on the principles of the negotiations. He repeatedly said that if we could get Israel to be flexible on some of its refusals, he could get Jaabri to be flexible, too. He suggested that I speak with David about the specific issues that caused problems in the German proposal.

I communicated these messages to David, but I also got something in writing from Ghazi. He sent a document in Arabic, which set in motion a very tough, six-week negotiation over the principles for reaching a deal to bring Gilad Schalit home.

This was Ghazi's initial letter outlining these principles:

June 3, 2011

The final deal must include the following changes in the last [German] proposal:

1. *Prisoners who have served more than fifteen years should all be released;*

2. *Include Israeli Arabs and prisoners from East Jerusalem in the deal;*
3. *Reduce the number of people on the Hamas list whom Israel refuses to release;*
4. *Include all women and minor prisoners;*
5. *Reduce the number of West Bank prisoners that Israel insists on deporting to Gaza;*
6. *Reduce the number of prisoners that Israel insists be deported abroad.*

I sent this message to David, then transmitted his response back to Ghazi:

June 6, 2011

1. *Israel will go to Egypt for indirect proximity talks – conducted by the Egyptians, for however long it takes to close the deal – only after 95 percent of the points are agreed to (in negotiations between Baskin and Hamad), not before.*
2. *We must resolve the points of disagreement without beginning a new negotiation. The gaps must be closed based on the existing German proposal.*
3. *It has been agreed to in previous negotiations that Gaza and the West Bank are one territorial unit comprising Palestine. A West Banker who is sent to Gaza is going home to Palestine; he is not considered "deported."*
4. *Regarding prisoners who have served fifteen years or more, 90 percent of these are already on the list.*
5. *Israel is extremely serious about economic development and otherwise easing the lives of people in Gaza after this story is behind us. This is the key to the future. Israel will allow real economic development and reconstruction to take place in Gaza after Schalit is back home.*
6. *The Israeli side finds it extremely difficult to be flexible when there has been no sign of life from Schalit for 1.5 years. If Hamas is really interested in Israel being more flexible, it will send a sign of life and well-being from Schalit now. This will improve the chances of more flexibility.*

I added my own impressions:

> *I think that now your side should be specific in the changes desired. For example – if you want to decrease the number of deportees, what number would be acceptable? It may be wise to attach a time limit on the deportation.*
>
> *Regarding the names Israel removed from the list, I suggest that you now send the specific names you want put back on it, with a note that you agree that they will be deported for an agreed period of time. Suggest the period of time that you propose.*
>
> *It's time to get specific. The last message was good but too general.*
>
> *Gershon*

Ghazi was encouraged by what he heard from me. Meidan told me to emphasize that if we reached agreement on principles, it would take three days of intensive negotiations to close a deal. Meidan once again said that the prime minister was very serious about bringing Schalit home. He told me to pressure Hamad, imploring him to be practical, to understand Netanyahu's readiness to make a deal but also his limitations. Netanyahu could not give Hamas everything it demanded. Hamas had to make compromises, too.

Ghazi replied by e-mail on June 13, 2011:

> 1. *My friend [Ahmed Jaabri] is very willing to start serious negotiations and discuss details in depth.*
> 2. *He will show flexibility in many of the points in order to reach a deal.*
> 3. *He supports the channel between you and me and believes it can contribute much to removing many of the obstacles.*
> 4. *On the subject of a sign of life, he is not opposed in terms of a preliminary step, but says he has already submitted a letter from the soldier Schalit, an audio tape, and a video, without receiving positive steps from Israel in return.*
> 5. *He believes that addressing the whole deal will be better than wasting time on the details of a sign of life, but is ready to deal positively*

with this if there is a good response from Israel. For example, Israel is believed to be extremist on the subject of the 1948 detainees (Palestinian citizens of Israel), although some of them have been in prison more than thirty years, and some are over eighty. Why does Israel insist on keeping them in prison? If Israel is serious about releasing these detainees, he is ready to take concrete steps toward giving a sign of life as a strong impetus to negotiate.

I followed up Ghazi's e-mail with a phone conversation. I reviewed every point, so I could judge where there was room for compromise and finding solutions. Some of the points he made were sound. For instance, it didn't make sense to me to exclude Israeli citizens from the list. Ghazi spoke about the Younis family – prisoners from the Israeli village of Arara who had killed Avraham Bromberg, an Israeli soldier, in 1981. Three members of the Younis family were convicted of Bromberg's murder, and they had been in prison twenty-eight years. According to Ghazi, one was quite ill with cancer, and another had lost his sight. They posed no security problem to Israel. If these three prisoners could take the place of younger, potentially more dangerous ones, why should Israel object to releasing them only because they held Israeli citizenship?

I wrote to David with my assessment:

June 13, 2011

Dear David,

The following is my summary of a meeting last night between Ghazi and Jaabri, as reported to me by Ghazi. He says Jaabri's biggest problem is the complete lack of trust in the Israeli side. Jaabri says the Israeli side is constantly requesting a sign of life, which he is willing to give, but only after Israel demonstrates that it's serious about reaching agreement on the prisoners.

He does not believe Israel wants to close a deal. He wants to know what will happen concretely after he gives a sign of life. Jaabri repeated several times the fact that "we have no trust in the Israeli side." He says that the large number of West Bank prisoners whom Israel insists on sending to Gaza is also a problem. He understands the Israeli sensitivity on the issue, but 208 prisoners are too many for him to accept. He is asking for flexibility from Israel on this number.

Ghazi says Jaabri is willing to accept that 50 or 60 percent of them be sent to Gaza, but not as many as Israel now demands. In short, Jaabri is willing to enter negotiations to close the deal with the understanding that both sides will be flexible.

Ghazi is convinced that Jaabri is serious.

Gershon

My mind was working overtime. My daily regimen included swimming early in the morning. I'm usually bored while swimming, but these days all I could think about was coming up with creative ideas to get the negotiations moving. I had to keep proving the reliability of this channel of communications. We had to reach a breakthrough. We were making progress, but not significant enough and not fast enough. Ramadan was approaching. I once again set my sights on the target date of completing the deal by then. Perhaps Hamas would also agree that it would be great to bring its prisoners home for Ramadan.

On June 19, I came home from the pool and put on paper my own proposal for moving forward. It was a summary of all the issues discussed and the specific offers made by David, which I was authorized to submit to Hamas, along with specific requests I'd received from Hamas, which were central to its demands. I sent the proposal to David and Ghazi:

June 19, 2011

GB Proposal for Moving Forward

Principles:
1. The basis for renewing negotiations is the last German proposal.
2. Hamas will provide a sign of life from the soldier, for which Israel will:

    a. *In exchange for a video, release one extra prisoner (beyond 450) selected from the list of 450, or a humanitarian case such as the Younis' father.*

    b. *In exchange for a visit by the International Committee of the Red Cross, allow a visit of all Gaza families (two people per family) with close relatives in Israeli prisons.*

3. *Direct, secret meetings will begin between David Meidan and Ghazi Hamad (with the presence of Gershon Baskin), at an agreed location, to advance and conclude the negotiations. It is agreed that at those meetings the following issues can be dealt with:*

    a. *The number of West Bank prisoners being sent to Gaza;*

    b. *The number of West Bank prisoners being sent abroad;*

    c. *The length of time that released prisoners from the West Bank must stay in Gaza or abroad;*

    d. *A Palestinian proposal that specific people who have been removed from the list will be released and deported abroad.*

4. *The Palestinians also propose that specific prisoners who are Israeli citizens be released at a later, agreed-upon time. This would not be directly connected to the prisoner exchange and would occur under the application of Israeli law, e.g., presidential pardon. If agreed to by Israel, this release would include specific, agreed-upon individuals who have served more than fifteen years.*

5. *As agreed to by Hamas, all released prisoners will sign a personal statement that once released they will cease all aggressive activities against Israel and Israelis. Furthermore, all prisoners released in the West Bank will be required to report to the local Palestinian police station an agreed-upon number of times per week for an agreed number of years.*

If the undertakings in this document are agreed to by both parties, provision of the sign of life from Schalit will be completed within one week of signing this paper.

Date: _____

_____	_____
Hamas	*Israel*

The intensity of these exchanges was building. I was supposed to attend a conference in Barcelona on the Arab Spring, but as we seemed to be heading toward negotiations, I canceled my trip. David wanted me to find out if Ghazi would come to Israel. I knew that would be difficult for him, because of his fear of entering Israel and also because Jaabri would not authorize him to do so.

David didn't want to go to a third country. While no longer head of the Mossad's Tevel division, a post he'd relinquished prior to becoming the prime minister's special envoy on the Schalit case, he was still a high-ranking Mossad officer. As such, he couldn't conduct talks in a third country without informing the local intelligence organization.

David was serious about using our direct, secret back channel to conclude the negotiations quickly. For the first time, the Israeli side was accepting my proposal. After five years, the approach I was convinced would work was finally becoming an official channel. For Ghazi and me, this channel had existed all along – our leaders just had to tune in to it.

Chapter 13

Proximity Talks and Café Chats

I played it straight with Ghazi. Sensing that things were finally moving, I was canceling my participation in important conferences, putting everything else in life on hold. I wouldn't leave town for even five minutes.

June 19, 2011 [SMS]

To: Ghazi
Ghazi, I am willing to hop on a plane to Egypt to meet with your people – if you think it would advance something. I have canceled my trip to Barcelona, so I'm around.

Gershon

I followed up with an e-mail:

June 20, 2011

Ghazi,

Please give me an answer in the morning if you're willing to come meet David and me. David has made an offer that no other Israeli mediator has made – to hold face-to-face talks with you to end this sad chapter of our histories. He has made it 100 percent clear that he wants the people in Gaza to have a much better life – but first we have to end the Schalit affair.

Five years we have known each other because of the Schalit affair. We can do it. We have to do it. It's time to put a little trust in this process we have created. It's time for your leaders to trust you more than they do. It's time for you to trust me more than you do. It's time to be reasonable.

Your people are going to get 450 Palestinian prisoners, most of whom are serving life sentences. Then another 550 prisoners. It's time to stop being greedy. The best thing is to agree to the document I sent you, and I'll work on convincing David to accept it as well. In two weeks we can have an agreement. That's all we need.

I want you to come to Erez for a secret meeting in the next few days. Let's get this done.

Gershon

Three days later I received the third of seven documents from Ghazi, with Jaabri's agreement on the principles for reaching the final round of negotiations. I asked Ghazi to send me the documents in Arabic, because it was essential that every word be precise. The Hamas people were clearly taking our channel seriously. In fact, they had essentially begun negotiating, through Ghazi and me, the real deal that would bring Gilad home.

June 23, 2011

Official points:

1. *We are seriously prepared to start marathon negotiations aimed at releasing the soldier Schalit in exchange for releasing Palestinian prisoners.*
2. *The negotiations should not start from scratch, but be based on what has been agreed upon by both parties. However, the points of disagreement should be defined and minimized.*
3. *The negotiations should deal with all the points of disagreement.*
4. *We prefer to negotiate through the good offices of the Egyptian mediator, in the manner we've agreed upon, namely: both parties should be present in Egypt, and the mediator will go between them presenting the ideas and proposals suggested by one party to the other.*
5. *We support the communication channel between Ghazi and Gershon in order to exchange ideas and decrease the points of disagreement.*
6. *The proposals which reflect our official stance, are as follows:*
   a. Israel takes upon itself –
   – To decrease the number of prisoners it refuses to release;
   – To decrease the number of those who will be deported to the West Bank or abroad;
   – To accept the principle of releasing prisoners from the 1948 territories (pending an agreement between us).
   b. The Hamas movement will consider your demand for a sign of life, but that will have to be negotiated.
7. *If both parties agree upon the above points, the marathon negotiations can start immediately.*
8. *We are prepared to submit a revised list of prisoners to be released within two weeks (since a number of prisoners from the original list have been released or have died during the past year).*

The following day, David responded to Ghazi's letter in a long phone conversation with me. In addition to responding to all the relevant issues, David stressed that all communications must be fully accurate and that absolutely nothing must be leaked to the media. These conversations must be top secret. Any leaks would put an immediate end to this channel.

Things moved forward in the course of my conversation with David. I summarized his points and put them in an e-mail to Ghazi. Here are some excerpts from that e-mail, dated June 24:

> *Dear Ghazi,*
>
> *In response to the Palestinian letter of June 23, David accepts that we are talking about a package of understandings that will enable the final round of negotiations to begin. Israel is prepared to give assurances in any form that Hamas wants that this is a package; in other words, the commitment is to deal with all the issues based on the understanding that what has been agreed to in the past will not be re-opened. Israel does acknowledge and relate to the specific issues in the last Hamas paper, copied below. It is important for Hamas to understand that there are certainly issues on which Israel can and will be flexible, but also issues on which flexibility is quite limited.*
>
> *With respect to the points raised by Hamas:*
> 1. *New names – Since the last list was received in February 2011, a few prisoners have been released as part of the regular process of completing their terms. Any who have been released can be replaced by other prisoners in the same general category. This is not a problem for Israel.*
> 2. *Women prisoners – This will not be a problem, and the women can all be included in the final deal.*
> 3. *Israeli Arabs and East Jerusalem prisoners will be dealt with as agreed in annex 13 of the German paper;[1] in other words, they*

---

1. This point seemed quite significant to me. I was curious about its details, but more so, I was curious about the many annexes in the German draft. What exactly did they include, and why were they drafted this way? This would be very important in understanding why Hamas rejected the German proposal and how that caused problems within the Hamas leadership. More on this later.

are not part of the deal, but Israel will look at the specific cases brought up, on a humanitarian basis: those who have served long prison terms, those who have served most of their term, etc. Israel is prepared to offer guarantees to a third party, such as the German government, that it will fulfill this commitment after the deal for Schalit is completed.

4. Israel insists that a sign of life come at the beginning of the process, or immediately after the talks are renewed (as a commitment that Hamas must fulfill). Israel insists on this for several reasons:

   a. There has been no sign of life since September 2009. Hamas cannot expect Israel to negotiate in good faith without confirming the soldier's well-being.

   b. It is a humanitarian need to provide the soldier's family with knowledge of his well-being.

   c. It will create a better atmosphere for the rest of the negotiations.

   d. It is the first step toward building the trust necessary to complete the negotiations.

   e. It is essential to establish the source of authority[2] in these negotiations – in other words, this will prove that this negotiating track leads to those who make the decisions regarding Schalit. Without a sign of life, it is difficult to accept that this or any channel is the one that should be used in negotiations.

5. Israel believes it is possible for Hamas to arrange a visit to Schalit by the International Committee of the Red Cross or any other reliable third party. It is possible for Hamas to arrange this without risking that the meeting place will be discovered by Israel. David says to take your time – take a few days and make all the arrangements you need to make. From a technical and safety point of view, it can be done. Israel would view this very positively, and it would certainly influence Israel's ability and willingness to demonstrate

---

2. David Meidan referred to Ahmed Jaabri as the source of authority. According to the Israeli understanding, Jaabri had been the sole objector to the German proposal, and he had blocked all agreements until now, so Israel had to be sure he clearly supported the current process.

> *flexibility on other points. Israel stands behind the offers it has made in exchange for the sign of life.*

6. *Reducing the numbers of deportees – This is one of the more difficult points. David says we must be creative and think of ways that will not endanger Israel's security or undermine Hamas' honor. It is almost impossible for David to relate to this point as a "principle." It would be much easier to deal with specifics. I propose, for example, that certain people (and name them) would be deported to Gaza for five years, others for eight years, others for ten. Additionally, present specific names of those you would like to be allowed to remain in the West Bank as well as a mechanism to ensure that they not endanger Israel's security. He said several times that we must be creative on this point.*

7. *Restoring names that were removed[3] – This is the most difficult point, and David suggests lowering expectations. There is almost no flexibility on this point, mainly for internal Israeli reasons. It is extremely difficult to reinstate names that were removed. He says Hamas should be aware that this is almost impossible and drop the demand. Some creativity is possible here as well, without high expectations and without greed. I would add that if you present a few names of those who were removed and propose that they be deported to a specific country forever, perhaps some flexibility can be shown.*

8. *Hamas should remember that the list of names accepted by Israel includes 94 percent of the prisoners in Israel who are serving fifteen years or more, meaning that almost all of them killed Israelis. (The other 6 percent are made up mostly of Israeli Arabs and East Jerusalemites.) So Hamas is getting almost all the really hard-core prisoners who are most difficult for Israel to release.*

9. *The negotiating channel – The Egyptian track is slow and complex, and the Egyptians are not always consistent in the way they try to move things forward. If this is Hamas' choice, Israel will agree, but it would much prefer to move as quickly and directly as possible. If the Hamad-Baskin channel is acceptable, this will be demonstrated by*

---

3. These names were known to the Israeli public as the terrorists responsible for most of the Israelis killed in the past thirty years.

the sign of life and by the Hamas decision makers' sending a direct message – written and signed or authorized by whoever has direct power to make decisions for Hamas – to be passed to Hamad and on to Baskin for David Meidan.

David suggests that negotiations be carried out by phone, Skype, or video conferencing. Baskin and Hamad can meet in Erez and be in direct contact – each with his own side in real time – in order to complete the negotiations in a matter of days. It is possible to reach a deal. If Hamas wants the deal to be implemented through a third party, such as Egypt, that is fine and could be helpful. It could also be implemented through another third party – this is not a problem. But the more direct the negotiations, the faster and easier it will be to conclude them.

Two days later, after Ghazi presented this document to Jaabri, we received this (in Arabic):

June 26, 2011

We want to hear from the Israeli side three positive statements on issues of principle for us. After we hear these three positive statements, we are willing to open up intensive negotiations to complete the deal. The following are the three statements:

1. *Israel is willing to release 1948 prisoners; the exact mechanism can be agreed upon in the negotiations.*
2. *Israel is willing to reduce the number of prisoners removed from the list; the exact number and names can be discussed in the negotiations.*
3. *Israel is willing to reduce the number of prisoners deported to Gaza; the exact number and names can be discussed in the negotiations.*

After receiving these three positive points of principle, we can open the negotiations. Once the negotiations have begun, Hamas will deliver a sign of life from the soldier.

> *We encourage Ghazi Hamad and Gershon Baskin to continue working together to reduce the gaps between the parties. We would like the negotiations to be intensive, and we would like to conclude the agreement as soon as possible.*

David requested that this document be sent from Hamas officials, indicating that it was the official Hamas position. Ghazi sent me the following document, after telling me Jaabri backs every word of it.

June 26, 2011

1. There are positive signs indicating the will to begin serious and quick negotiations, as evidenced by the continuation of the Ghazi-Gershon channel.
2. There is some progress on some points but not enough clear definition.
3. The answers are general. There are no decisions regarding accepting or rejecting them, which does not allow us to know exactly what the final position on all points will be.
4. We emphasize the importance of concluding the process of setting out the principles for beginning the negotiations. We remind you that without agreement on the principles we sent you, it will be difficult to begin negotiations.
5. We repeat and emphasize the importance of agreeing to these principles and leaving the details to the negotiations:
   a. Reducing the number of those to be sent to Gaza and abroad;
   b. Reducing the number of those Israel refuses to release;
   c. Releasing detainees from Jerusalem and from the 1948 areas in an agreed-upon framework;
   d. Continuing the issue of providing a sign of life at the outset of the negotiations.

When you agree to these principles, we will be prepared to begin the negotiations in a serious and continuous fashion, until closing the deal.

Our opinion is that negotiating through an Egyptian mediator is best, and we can agree on the principles for speeding up the negotiations and reaching conclusions quickly.

After I received this document, Ghazi assured me once again by phone that Jaabri stood behind every word, but would not sign anything being sent to the Israelis. He said he knew the Israelis could verify the document's accuracy.

David and his team were not quite sure how to view these messages. There were positive elements in them, but the Israelis were concerned that Jaabri would do what he had done in the past: keep changing the points of reference. David told me the Israeli side was not convinced that Jaabri really wanted a deal.

The Israelis were concerned that Jaabri's refusal to provide a sign of life indicated he wasn't serious. David was also concerned that Jaabri's insistence on going to Egypt meant Hamas wasn't ready to deal. With the revolution in Egypt and the unclear political situation there, Israel wasn't happy about being dependent on an Egyptian mediator. I shared this opinion, especially because the direct channel Ghazi and I had established was working so well.

June 27, 2011

Dear Ghazi,

The test of leadership is always when it comes to making difficult decisions. In this regard, your leaders have failed the test, which may have very grave consequences for them personally and for the people of Gaza.

Greed is one of man's worst characteristics, and in my humble opinion, the leaders of Ezzedin al Qassam are demonstrating the worst form of greed. There is a deal on the table that isn't 100 percent of what you wanted. It can be slightly improved. In my assessment, it won't be there much longer. Your people can bring about the immediate freedom of one thousand Palestinian prisoners. Their families and the Palestinian people will grant Hamas a huge victory for this achievement. But for five years your friends have chosen to postpone this decision.

This deal can be completed in a week, but your people must be more practical and understand that they have pulled the rope as far as it will go without breaking.

Gershon

I was beginning to sense a loss of patience on David's part. Voices in Israel were calling for the destruction of the Hamas government and the renewal of targeted killings. I felt a great urgency to move forward quickly. I needed to offer a new initiative. The next day I wrote a proposal to both sides:

June 27, 2011

1. *Both sides agree to renew negotiations immediately.*
2. *What has been agreed to by both sides will not be re-opened.*
3. *Hamas will submit its demands for changes based on specific details and not principles, including the names of prisoners to be included in the deal and the names of those who they agree will be deported abroad or to Gaza, and the others who should be allowed to go to their homes in the West Bank.*
4. *Once negotiations begin, Hamas will present a quality sign of life of the soldier – Israel will respond with a humanitarian step as was proposed in the last days through the Hamad-Baskin channel.*
5. *The negotiations can begin with the Hamas submission of its written demands. Those demands can be submitted from Hamad to Baskin who will bring official first response from Israel.*
6. *The negotiations can proceed by telephone/Skype – at set times for hours with ability to receive immediate responses from Meidan and Jaabri.*
7. *Once the gaps are narrowed and near reaching agreement, both sides will go to Egypt to conclude the agreement with the Egyptian mediation.*

David told me to move from demanding a sign of life to a more practical discussion on the modalities of the negotiations. He said I should try to get Ghazi and Jaabri to agree to a mechanism for direct talks.

June 28, 2011

Good morning Ghazi,

I want to write to you what David told me on the phone last evening, so it will be 100 percent clear. This is his suggestion regarding the order of what we should do:

1. *First we should agree on the mechanism for the negotiations – how we will negotiate.*
2. *Second we should agree on the agenda for the talks – their guiding principles.*
3. *The timetable David would like to achieve is:*
   a. *By the end of this week, to agree on the mechanism;*
   b. *By the end of next week, to agree on the principles;*
   c. *To sign, seal, and implement the deal by the first day of Ramadan – which I think is August 1.*

This is an ambitious undertaking, but we can do it.

Regarding the mechanism, he prefers that we move forward and negotiate directly, without a mediator. He suggests that we do so by video conferencing and that the documents be exchanged by fax or e-mail. He suggests that you and I sit in front of the video, so the negotiations are not directly between Hamas and Israel – which I think is the preference of your leadership. David has no problem dealing directly with you or with anyone else in Hamas who has the ability and authority to make decisions, even Mr. J. But assuming that this is difficult for your side, he has proposed that you and I be in the front and that he and whoever on your side – Mr. J. or anyone else – be in the background, out of view of the video camera, so we can maintain the indirect nature of the talks.

If we decide on proximity talks, he prefers not to hold them in Egypt. He says that would be a big waste of time. He suggests that he sit in Erez and the Palestinian side in Beit Hanoun or somewhere else near Erez, inside of Gaza, and that the mediator go back and forth between Erez and Gaza. He has no objection to Egyptian mediation, but he really thinks that holding talks in Cairo will be inefficient and cause big delays. He also emphasizes that when necessary to consult the decision makers, it will be much quicker if the talks are held here.

I suggest that we begin this way and see how it progresses. If we feel a need to meet face-to-face, I'm sure David and J. will see that as well and authorize our travel.

> *Let me know what J. thinks as soon as possible – the goal is to settle on the mechanism by the end of this week, and it is now Tuesday.*

> Gershon

Ghazi told me Mr. J. preferred to go to Egypt. He didn't want direct contact with Israel. He encouraged the channel with Ghazi because I wasn't an Israeli official, but closing the negotiations had to be done in proximity talks through the Egyptian mediator.

It was becoming clear that the new political realities were having their impact. The Muslim Brotherhood was rising in Egypt following the fall of Mubarak. Hamas leaders were spending more time in Egypt; it was apparent that they wanted to empower their political allies there to play a greater regional role. Hamas officials were now free to travel to Cairo via the Sinai, and from Cairo to anywhere in the world that would allow them entry. The isolation of Hamas was coming to an end, and the new Egypt was playing a central role in facilitating its "normalization" in the region.

With a sense that we were making real progress, I tried to translate David's offers and Hamas' willingness to negotiate into a formal agreement.

June 29, 2011

Dear Ghazi,

Please see the attached draft agreement. Let's try to get Jaabri and Meidan to agree and to sign this today. I am sending it to David now as well. Gershon

Draft Agreement: Renewing Negotiations

1. *Both sides agree to renew negotiations immediately.*
2. *Negotiations will begin through direct communication between Dr. Hamad and Dr. Baskin.*

3. *Communication will take place electronically – by phone, video conference, fax, and e-mail. Hamad will be in direct contact with and receive instructions and authorization from the Palestinians directly responsible for the prisoner exchange. Baskin will be in direct contact with and receive instructions and authorization from David Meidan.*

4. *Hamad and Baskin will set an agreed-upon schedule for intensive talks aimed at reducing the gaps between the current positions.*

5. *When sides are nearer to closure, the parties will request that the Egyptian mediator step in and close the deal through proximity talks. For the sake of efficiency and effectiveness, the parties will request that these talks be carried out locally, with the Egyptian mediator shuttling between Gaza and Israel to advance the agreement more quickly.*

6. *As soon as agreement on the mechanism is reached, Hamad and Baskin will seek to agree on the principles and agenda for the rest of the negotiations. The aim is to complete that task in one week.*

7. *Both sides will work toward completion and implementation before the beginning of Ramadan.*

Signed and approved by both parties on June 29, 2011

I pretty much knew Jaabri wouldn't sign. I was less sure about David, but I thought that if Jaabri signed, Netanyahu would authorize David to sign too. It was David who was pushing to get agreement from Jaabri on the mode of negotiations. I was trying to speed things up by putting them down on paper.

Now that the Hamad-Baskin channel was being taken seriously, it was vital that Ghazi and I view ourselves as a team. We had to share information openly with each other. We had to understand that we were not really negotiating with each other – we were a pair of mediators whose job was to solve problems. We had to understand the positions and limitations of both sides, and to propose solutions. We had to be honest with each other and understand that only through the trust developed between us could we foster understanding between the two sides.

I demonstrated how we could be a binational stakeholder mediation team by sharing with him how I understood the positions of both sides, especially the Israeli one.

July 3, 2011

Dear Ghazi,

I just had a long conversation with David. I canceled my travel plans to Vienna (for a conference on the Arab Spring and arms control), because I don't want to be away if the opportunity arises to begin the negotiations. We have some problems to overcome, though.

David told me the Israelis doubt Jaabri's ability to say yes. This is a big dilemma for Israel. The people on David's team and in the intelligence community do not believe Jaabri will compromise on anything.

Everyone is convinced of your good intentions; of your desire to help bring this chapter to a happy end. But people here are not convinced that you have the influence to bring Jaabri to an agreement, and some question whether our track is just a cover to get more Israeli concessions.

I told David what you tell me all the time: that Jaabri is behind our channel and that he wants to reach an agreement. Still, I have nothing concrete to back up what I'm saying.

This would all change if you could deliver a concrete sign – such as a sign of life from Gilad. The Israeli side wants to know whether, when you and I talk, you can bring along someone from the "core" – someone like Mahmoud al-Zahar – who is not known as a moderate like yourself. This would prove that the more hard-line people won't sabotage any progress we make. The Israelis say this based on experiences.

The main thing is to prove we can produce results....

Ghazi, we can succeed – I know it. David really appreciates what we're trying to do, but he too needs to have some proof that we can bring about an agreement from Jaabri.

> *What do you suggest? This is extremely frustrating, because*
> *I know we can do it!*

Gershon

Ghazi responded immediately that he knew Jaabri was very serious. He said Jaabri didn't want to involve other people from the leadership at this point; it would make our talks more difficult. He stressed that we had to make more progress on the principles. He didn't rule out providing a sign of life once the proximity talks got under way.

Ghazi kept referring to the principles and to points he had already repeated so many times. It was tough, slow, and frustrating, but I was becoming more confident that we could succeed. Ghazi was fully committed, and I felt the same commitment and confidence from David Meidan.

Later that day, David called to say it was time to meet me face-to-face. There had to be a sense within his team that my channel was serious enough to be formalized.

We met July 6 in a coffee shop on a main street in West Jerusalem. It seemed like a strange place to meet. We were dealing with top secret issues, and Jerusalem is a very small town. I'm quite well known there, and sitting with a top Mossad man whose picture had been in the newspapers quite a bit since being appointed to the position of dealing with Schalit meant that we were sure to be recognized.

In any case, there we sat. We spent the next few hours getting to know each other. We were solidifying our relationship, adding faces to the phone calls and endless texts and e-mails. He wanted to know all about me. I gave him my full personal and professional history.

David told me that when I first offered to help, most of his team thought it was a crazy idea. The establishment views any peace activist as an anti-Zionist (or post-Zionist) anarchist who always sides with the Arabs against Israel. It was difficult for the officials to see beyond this stereotype. David also explained to me that after I first approached him, he kept telling me to call back, because he'd wanted to study the Schalit file. It had taken Hagai Hadas about a month to turn the file over to David and finally step down. David hadn't want to initiate anything until Hadas was out of the picture.

When David told me he had a clear mandate from Netanyahu to free Schalit, I knew we would succeed. "Failure is not an option," I said, trying to keep my voice down. "We are bringing Gilad Schalit home!"

I always believed that the missing element over all of these years was a leader's decision to pay the price that had essentially been known officially since January 2007, and unofficially just a few months after the abduction. The price of releasing Gilad was clear and calculated, but no leader had made the decision to pay it. Now it was time to make it happen.

David asked how I was surviving financially. I told him I drew a modest salary as the co-director of IPCRI. He asked if I needed help covering my expenses. I told him I wouldn't take money for that. But I had one request: When Gilad crossed the border into Israel, I wanted to be there. David said that if he had a say in the matter, I would be.

We parted with a sense that we were about to make history, that something good would come out of our relationship, a relationship built through mutual respect and a determination to bring Gilad home.

Chapter 14

Waiting for Mr. J.

I woke up feeling more enthusiastic than I had in a long time. It was as if a cloud had lifted. It was July 7, 2011, and David Meidan and I had just set a target date for the deal to take place: August 28 – Gilad's birthday.

July 7, 2011

Dear Ghazi,

I was very encouraged by my meeting with David yesterday. August 28, 2011 – Gilad's birthday – is our target date!

> *Now it seems that the ball is in Jaabri's court to come up with a proposal that can be the basis for closing the deal. David's words were this: He should present a practical and realistic understanding of Israel's limits and not go too far.*

The following points won't be a problem:
1. *Women prisoners – they'll all be released;*
2. *The 1948 borders and East Jerusalem are not part of the deal, but Israel will deal with them afterward through the framework of Israeli law – meaning shortening sentences and presidential pardons.*

On the other two big issues, I would recommend a "practical and realistic" position from your side.

I believe Israel will compromise on the number of people deported to Gaza. The VIPs are the biggest problem, and it is more political than security, because they will all be deported. Try to deal with those who have served the longest sentences. Don't bring in those who killed dozens of Israelis during the Second Intifada.

Gershon

Later that day, Ghazi sent me the following document:

July 7, 2011

Hamas Proposal

First – General principles:
1. This proposal can be built on what was agreed upon between Hamas and Israel during the term of Prime Minister Ehud Olmert.
2. Israel agrees to reduce the number of detainees to be deported to the Gaza Strip and abroad.
3. Israel agrees to the release of detainees from within the 1948 areas, according to a mechanism both sides agree on.[1]
4. Israel agrees to add more people to the VIP list.
5. Israel agrees to release all women detainees.
6. Israel agrees to release all detainees arrested before the signing of the Oslo Accords.
7. Israel agrees to release all detainees who have served more than fifteen years in jail, taking into consideration that some of them should be addressed as part of the final deal.

---

1. Annex 13 of the German proposal stated that 1948 prisoners and East Jerusalemites would be released not as part of the deal, at a later date, and in accordance with Israeli law. Meidan was willing to add international guarantees to this mechanism.

Second – Details:
1. *Reducing the number of those to be deported from 208 to 70;*
2. *The issue of the detainees from within the 1948 areas is to be resolved based on the following vision:*
   a. *Principle of agreement on their release according to a mechanism to be agreed upon. We can discuss several options for balancing Israel's demands and ours.*
   b. *Hamas should ensure the actual release of those detainees.*

Practical proposal:
We can start resolving the main issue, that of the VIPs. Israel should present a list of those it agrees to release, and we are ready to discuss it. We are also ready to agree on deporting detainees who Israel believes pose a great danger. Our agreement in this regard is final, without specifying deportation duration. They can be deported to the country Israel finds suitable.

The number of detainees Israel sees as dangerous should not exceed the "number of fingers on a hand" (such as Hassan Salameh, Abdallah Barghouti, Abbas Sayyed, and Ibrahim Hamed, on whose deportation we can agree).

I called David and read him the document. He told me to fax it to his office. I knew this document was quite serious. It had some good points, but the last sentence – dealing with those defined in Israel as arch-terrorists – was very problematic. Israel would never release those prisoners. They had masterminded many deadly attacks on Israelis, and were sure to return to terrorism once they got out of jail.

David then told me to tell Ghazi that he and the State of Israel refused to receive the document. He told me to say that if the Hamas people thought they'd get the prisoners mentioned in the document released, they had better stop the negotiations immediately. David asked me to be firm and direct. If they wished to reconsider, they should send a new document without those names. If not, better to end now, and Israel would have to reconsider its position.

Ghazi and I proceeded to have our most difficult conversation in the five years we'd been in contact. I repeated David's words.

"Israel refuses to even receive the document," I explained. "I read it to David over the phone. There isn't a single Israeli prime minister who could release those people. They are responsible for the deaths of hundreds of Israelis. Even if Israel's most left-wing politician, Yossi Beilin, were prime minister, he couldn't release them."

Ghazi was listening.

"Ghazi, a deal is more possible now than at any time in the past five years. Netanyahu is ready to release prisoners that Olmert would not. David Meidan is the most serious person appointed so far. He has a mandate from the prime minister to conclude the deal."

Still silence on the line.

"Tell Jaabri to be more practical," I continued. "He has to compromise, too. Israel will not accept all his demands. He has to understand that."

Ghazi understood the message. And I soon understood that this attempt to reinstate people who had been rejected from the list in the past was a test of how far Israel would go. Ghazi told me he would speak to Jaabri.

Later that night, Ghazi called me back. Jaabri would drop those names. Now Ghazi started to talk business. He laid out the gaps between the Hamas side and the Israeli position and began to signal where Hamas could be flexible. Ghazi said he and I should propose ideas on how to close the gaps. We should reach for the middle ground.

Our conversation continued the next morning by phone. Ghazi wanted to concentrate on the VIP list. He suggested that Israel release twenty-five of those on the list. That was the middle ground – twenty-five out of fifty – but I knew this number was still too high for Israel to accept. David had been telling me that Netanyahu and the security people objected to releasing the VIPs; they were simply too dangerous.

I relayed Ghazi's proposal to David and, to my surprise, he didn't reject it. He told me to tell Ghazi that it would be difficult for Israel to accept, and that we should try to get Hamas to agree to less.

Throughout the day I spoke with Ghazi several more times, primarily about the VIP issue. By late in the evening of July 8, he still wanted twenty-five VIPs released, but said Israel could select them from the original list of fifty in the German proposal – and almost all could be deported from the area forever. This was a new element. Hamas would agree that those Israel considered most dangerous would be banished from Palestine permanently.

The next morning, I sent Ghazi the following message:

Dear Ghazi,

David is meeting with the decision makers tomorrow morning. He thinks the number twenty-five may be too high, but he will give that number. He would like to receive an offer (in Arabic) saying more or less the following:

Closing the Deal

We agree that –

1. *Israel will release 50 percent of the VIP list (twenty-five people).*
2. *Israel can select them.*
3. *Hamas understands that most will be deported outside the country.*
4. *Israel will begin the process of reducing sentences and pardoning seven 1948 prisoners.*
5. *Once these points are concluded, Hamas will provide a current video of Gilad in which he will speak, get up from his seat, and walk around. The video will be kept from the media, and there will be no leaks from the Israeli side.*

As emphasized, the number twenty-five may be too high for Netanyahu to accept, but David is trying to get acceptance for this.

The next and last issue on the agenda will be the number of deportees to Gaza. David is studying the subject; I also suggest that we think of some creative ideas.

We need to begin thinking about closure (and I'm cc'ing David on this). Here are some points to consider:

1. *Will a final agreement document be signed? By whom? David and Jaabri? Gershon and Ghazi?*
2. *How long will it take for Israel to organize the full prisoner release?*

3. Which third party will receive the prisoners – Red Cross, UN, Egypt?
4. We need the text that all released prisoners will sign undertaking not to return to violence against Israel or Israelis. Is there a draft of the text? Can we see it now? What about prisoners who refuse to sign? Are they to be removed from the list?
5. Informing the PA in the West Bank about the deal and about the arrangements for prisoners released in the West Bank to check in with a local PA police station (how many times per week?).
6. Where will Gilad be transferred back to Israel? Who will receive him?
7. What next? Can we leverage the end of this chapter to bring about economic development/infrastructure projects for Gaza?

I am sure there are many more issues to consider. I just wanted to raise these now, so we begin thinking about them.

Gershon
cc: David Meidan

After meeting with the decision makers, David told me to keep working on reducing Hamas' expectations. Hamas had to understand Israel's limitations on releasing so many prisoners. David told me that over 90 percent of the 450 prisoners listed had Jewish blood on their hands. This would be very difficult to present to the Israeli public. Israel would also have to ensure that the released prisoners not endanger the public.

Ghazi was convinced that these people had already served so much time that they just wanted to go home, resume their lives, and leave their past behind. He said they would all be obligated to sign an oath not to return to violence. I told him, with all due respect, that no one in Israel took those oaths seriously. If we're living in an environment of peacemaking and accepting each other, then the violence won't return. But if we continue to live in this environment of war and conflict, some of those released will return to violence and try to kill more Israelis. This was the reality, which was why the most important thing to Israel in this prisoner exchange was to minimize the risk.

Throughout the years of the Second Intifada (2000–2005), only one suicide bomber came out of Gaza hidden inside a double wall of a shipping container in the Ashdod port. It probably wasn't for lack of volunteers. Israel had tightened its closure policy, and fewer Gazans had access to Israel. With no actual border between the West Bank and Israel, on the other hand, Israel had a porous buffer at best to West Bankers looking to enter Israeli cities and blow themselves up in crowded areas. That no Gazans had been suicide bombers was the best testimony to the need to send as many released prisoners to Gaza as possible. But when discussing the matter with Ghazi, I added that Gaza and the West Bank were both Palestine – the 1993 Oslo Accords said so. The prisoners were therefore not being deported, one could argue, but just being relocated to another part of Palestine. Once the security situation changed, I said, they would presumably be allowed to live anywhere in the future Palestinian state.

I could smell a breakthrough. We were approaching the document of principles on which a final deal could be negotiated.

David said to continue trying to get a written document from Ghazi indicating what would close the deal for Hamas.

July 11, 2011 [SMS]

To: Ghazi
We're making good progress. It is now really important that David get everything in writing, and that it reflect what Jaabri says. David requested again your list of the fifty, so both sides can deal with the same list. I can ask David for Israel's list of fifty too. Once he receives the last request in writing, he will be able to respond officially after consultations with the Prime Minister. Thanks. Gershon

Later that day, I received another written document from Ghazi.

July 11, 2011

To promote the humanitarian aspect (of the deal) in both parties, build a bridge of confidence between them, and consolidate the negotiations for the release of the soldier Schalit and Palestinian prisoners, we propose the following:

1. *Sending a paper stating Israel's readiness to release twenty-five prisoners on the VIP list;*
2. *Releasing five of the 1948 prisoners, among them members of the Younis family, who have spent more than twenty-eight years in prison, and particularly those who are ill;*
3. *Releasing another five sick prisoners, or prisoners who have lost their eyesight, among whom are:*
   a. *Blind prisoners Abada Blal, Ala' el-Bazian (in prison for about twenty-seven years), and Abd el-Aziz Amru;*
   b. *Ahmed El-Najar.*

On our part, we undertake to send you a video clip that shows Schalit moving about and in good health.

I viewed this new exchange in writing as a very advanced stage of formal negotiations. Jaabri was responding positively to the Israeli wish to put things in writing and be specific. I knew the Israeli officials saw this as real engagement on his part. They were still not convinced that Jaabri was prepared to make an agreement, but they were beginning to see signs of change.

July 13, 2011, 6:15 a.m.

Good morning Ghazi,

Some thoughts and suggestions that may help to make the final proposal more acceptable on the Israeli side:

David spent much of yesterday going through the lists of names, and now that he is much more familiar with them all, he believes it will be quite challenging to overcome the security difficulties of getting them approved. Nonetheless, he is sincerely encouraged by our working on a complete package deal that will finally bring this issue to closure.

He strongly suggests, as I've told you, that the paper you send me say something like:

This proposal represents the complete package for resolving the prisoner exchange. Once all the issues in this deal have been concluded and agreed upon, we are prepared to immediately implement the agreement, which will end the captivity of the soldier.

All words indicating the end of the chapter, the conclusion of the negotiations, etc., will increase the power of those inside the Israeli system who want the deal to be concluded.

Keep in mind that Prime Minister Netanyahu is in principle against this deal. He will be pressured into accepting it if this process is seen and understood by him to be the real end and not simply another round of negotiations in which Hamas is trying to extract more concessions from Israel (this is how some opponents of the deal view it, telling Netanyahu that Hamas will not agree to end the chapter).

In the next few days, David proposes that you and I spend several hours in a video or Skype conference. David will be in the next room and able to relate specific details and names, and you should have direct, immediate access to Jaabri.

Lastly, I suggest that when you deal with names and numbers, try to justify why you're selecting certain people – for example: they are sick, old, have served long terms, and were arrested before Oslo.

David says there are many East Jerusalemites on the VIP list and many names from the Second Intifada. If there are specific people you want on the list, write their names – as you did with the sick and blind people.

Please do not put back the four names that Israel absolutely refuses to release. We are now in a position to make real progress and conclude the deal. We have to be sensitive to each other's political and security constraints.

We can do this!

Thanks,
Gershon

The next day, the breakthrough document arrived.

July 14, 2011

Final Proposal for Closing the Deal

General principles:
1. *Reduce the number of those sent to Gaza and abroad;*
2. *Release 1948 detainees in a way agreeable to both sides;*
3. *Remove the refusal to release some of the VIPs, deporting them with the agreement of Hamas;*
4. *Release those who have served more than fifteen years;*
5. *Release those arrested prior to the Oslo agreement;*
6. *Release residents of the Gaza Strip;*
7. *Release the women and minors;*
8. *After reaching agreement on these points, Hamas will be prepared to release a sign of life from the soldier and information on his condition.*

Details:
1. *The 1948 detainees*
   a. *Releasing prisoners from the 1948 areas;*
   b. *Releasing 50 percent of the 1948 detainees before conclusion of the deal, in a way that is in accordance with Israeli law;*
   c. *Releasing the remaining 1948 detainees after the signing of the deal, accompanied by the necessary guarantees acceptable to Hamas.*
2. *The VIPs*
   a. *Releasing twenty-five to twenty-eight prisoners on the VIP list of fifty;*
   b. *Israel has the right to select the names of those to be released;*
   c. *We will agree to the deportation of some of them.*
3. *The deportees*
   a. *Israel will reduce by 50 percent the list of those to be deported from the West Bank to Gaza (from 208);*
   b. *The names of those to be deported will be agreed upon.*

This document was based primarily on continuous phone calls over the past few days. The first thing I noticed about it was that Ghazi had referred to twenty-five to twenty-eight VIPs, after we had agreed on twenty-five over the phone. This was Hamas' last attempt to add a few more names.

There were several significant things about this document. Most noteworthy was the title, written as David had demanded: "Final Proposal for Closing the Deal." This proposal put on paper Hamas' final demands. Never in five years had the Hamas people been willing to say what would close a deal for them. This was a breakthrough.

The other quite significant element was Hamas' agreement to allow Israel to select the names from the VIP list, and the fact that this list was the one from the German proposal, containing fifty names. Could Israel live with the proposal in this document?

David called me after receiving the proposal. It was clear from his tone and his words that a breakthrough had been made. He wanted Ghazi to have the document put on official Hamas letterhead and have Jaabri sign it. He wanted to bring it to Netanyahu, and it would be much better to have it as an official Hamas document.

I called Ghazi and told him what David had said. Ghazi assured me that the words in the document were Jaabri's and that he stood by every one of them. Nonetheless, Ghazi said he would try to get this document on official stationery. But he wanted reciprocity. David understood Ghazi's request – he also needed to get Israel's position on letterhead.

Personal/Sensitive

Tel Aviv, July 14, 2011

To: Mr. Gershon Baskin (Jerusalem)
Re: Steps to close the deal

I hereby certify receipt of the document "Final Proposal for Closing the Deal" in Arabic from July 14, 2011. On the basis of authorization that the paper in fact does represent a proposal for closing the deal

= אישי / רגיש =

תל אביב, 14/7/2011

לכבוד :

מר. גרשון בסקין (ירושלים)

הנדון : <u>צעדים לסגירת העסקה</u>

הריני לאשר קבלת נייר "הצעה להשלמת העסקה באופן סופי" בערבית, מתאריך
.14/7/11

בהינתן אישור רשמי כתוב שהנייר אכן מהווה הצעה לסגירה אשר מאושרת ביד
מקור הסמכות העליון לנושא (א"ג), נוכל להתחיל במשא ומתן מיידי בסוגיות
הרלבנטיות.

בשלב ראשון, ינוהלו השיחות בערוץ אשר בינך ובין עיאזי חמד, באמצעי התקשורת
הנוכחיים ו/או ועידת וידאו (כגון סקייפ).

כמובן, יש להמשיך ולהקפיד על דווחים כתובים לשם הדיוק, ובעיקר על מידור
וחשאיות מירביים.

בברכה,

דוד מידן,
הממונה מטעם ראה"מ לנושא

Letter from David Meidan; "Steps to close the deal"

and is certified by the source of authority (Ahmed Jaabri), we can begin negotiations immediately on the relevant issues.

In the first stage, the talks will be run in the channel between you and Ghazi Hamad, in the current manner of communication and/or video conferencing such as Skype.

Of course, you should continue insisting on written reports for accuracy's sake, and – most important – on total secrecy.

Sincerely,
David Meidan
Prime minister's envoy for the case [of Gilad Schalit]

Now Ghazi had to comply with his side of the deal, but there were problems. Jaabri refused to sign. No one in Hamas would give an official paper. Ghazi again promised me that Jaabri agreed to every word in the document, but he wouldn't sign anything.

Ghazi began evading my phone calls and wouldn't respond to my text messages. I could hear David's voice in my head: "We have serious doubts about whether Jaabri is capable of making a deal."

The next few days were painful and frustrating. I couldn't sleep, and thought only about whether or not the whole thing was possible.

July 17, 2011, 5:45 a.m.

Ghazi – I want you to understand the pressure. The intelligence assessment in Israel appears to be that you have not received clearance for our channel and have not been given authority.

I don't know if it's being blocked by Mashal or someone else in Damascus, or by Jaabri or al-Zahar in Gaza, but someone has blocked this channel.

If we don't prove our channel is real and authorized, the Israeli officials will search for another way – and maybe not one based on negotiations.

Please confirm receipt of this message.

Gershon Baskin

The next day, I tried to make it easier for Ghazi by sending him the letter from David above as an example and enclosing the kind of text I needed to receive from him:

July 18, 2011

> *The following is more or less the translation of the letter I received from David. We need a parallel letter to you from J. that looks like this:*

> *To: Dr. Ghazi Hamad*

> *I hereby confirm receipt of the letter from David Meidan to Gershon Baskin, indicating that Baskin is authorized to conduct direct negotiations on the prisoner exchange with Hamad.*

> *I confirm that the document sent by Hamad to Baskin on July 14, 2011, "Final Proposal for Closing the Deal," is an official document that I have authorized to be sent to the Israeli side.*

> *I also confirm that Dr. Ghazi Hamad is fully authorized to advance the negotiations toward the completion of the prisoner-exchange deal through his contacts with Dr. Baskin. This is the track that Hamas is supporting to reach the conclusion of the deal in the shortest time possible.*

> *Signed by A. J.*

> *Ghazi – If you can get this kind of letter to me soon, you will see the most serious response from the Israeli side in five years. We will be able to move forward and complete the deal quickly.*

Ghazi made contact – to tell me he had to travel and would be away for at least a week. His trip was a combination of personal travel, a conference in Turkey, and Hamas negotiations with Fatah. As deputy foreign minister of Hamas, Ghazi had his own portfolio to deal with. He was not officially in charge of the Schalit file. But I still needed answers from him, and he was the only person in Hamas I could speak to directly about these issues.

July 19, 2011, 5:30 a.m. [SMS]

To: Ghazi
I sure hope that you respond today to my text messages – I need to make plans, and so does the Israeli team. The Israelis really question whether Jaabri is with us – no one questions your positive position.

Ghazi texted back:

July 19, 2011, 5:45 a.m. [SMS]

From: Ghazi
Dear Gershon, I don't see a big difference between us on how to start negotiations. When I come back to Gaza, I am sure we will move forward. Let me check all details with Mr. J. Regards, Ghazi

The next day, I met with the Israeli team in a garden restaurant in Hod HaSharon. The team was composed of David and two others: A., a colonel in military intelligence, and Y., a senior officer in the ISA. We spent several hours together, speaking mainly about the state of the negotiations and the "Jaabri challenge." Was the man capable of making an agreement?

I wanted to understand the context and history. It was essential that they explain why the process broke down after the submission of the German proposal in December 2009. What had angered Jaabri so much and put him in confrontation with the entire Hamas leadership, leading to the sacking of al-Zahar? Jaabri had even forced his will on Khaled Mashal, who had favored accepting the German proposal with some modifications. Mashal backed down, Jaabri asserted total authority, and from that moment on, he was in complete control of the Schalit file. Consequently, no negotiations had taken place until Ghazi and I opened the new channel after David Meidan was appointed in April 2011 – a year and four months later.

David told me the German proposal was 150 pages. I couldn't believe what I was hearing.

"Did Dr. Conrad think he was arranging a merger between Daimler-Benz and Siemens?!"

My interlocutors smirked.

"No, really," I continued. "This is a prisoner exchange. The document can't be more than five or six pages. Hamas has no legal department to analyze 150 pages of a German proposal. Did Conrad think Jaabri was a lawyer?"

Now I understood why Jaabri had rejected the proposal, and why he'd thrown out the negotiator who had become friends with Conrad. Jaabri obviously assumed that the German proposal was actually an Israeli one, and that al-Zahar was working with the Israelis. There was no way Jaabri could have dealt with a legalistic document written in German style. The Germans had been complexifying things that needed to be made simple.

The team members agreed that the breakdown had been caused largely by Hamas' inability to deal with the proposal, but they also insisted that Jaabri was incapable of reaching a final decision. Although they couldn't crack the code behind his behavior, they believed a deal was probably impossible. Y. from the ISA was the most pessimistic. He didn't think Israel could release the people Hamas was demanding. The risks were too high. A. from military intelligence believed the risks could be contained, but he just didn't believe Jaabri was willing to conclude an agreement.

David Meidan was more optimistic. He also believed Jaabri was behind Ghazi's breakthrough document, even if he refused to sign it. David wanted to relate to the document as the official position, supported by Jaabri. But the team still told me to pressure Ghazi to get something official.

After this long meeting, I explained to Ghazi how the Israelis saw things. While they trusted him, they doubted Jaabri was genuinely interested in an agreement. One even posited that Jaabri saw Schalit as a kind of life insurance policy – as long as he held Gilad, he believed Israel wouldn't go after him. Most important, the Israelis wanted Hamas to have an identifiable negotiating team – ideally with Jaabri on it. Would he be willing to participate by video conference or Skype? Finally, I told Ghazi that according to the team, it was almost impossible for Netanyahu to agree to release more people from the VIP list – people responsible for the murder of numerous Israelis.

On July 20, I passed a message on to Ghazi that David was ready to invite the Egyptians to mediate in order to break the stalemate and begin the marathon talks.

Internet chat early morning, July 31:

Gershon: Hi, Ghazi. You're very busy lately.

Ghazi: Hi.

Gershon: Why so busy?

Ghazi: I am involved in the problems between Gaza and Ramallah, Egypt, etc.

Gershon: I see, big problems. How were the talks in Istanbul? I never asked you.

Ghazi: They were political discussions about reconciliation.

Gershon: Yes, I know. Were they productive? Who came from Fatah?

Ghazi: Many leaders from the West Bank, Lebanon, Syria.

Gershon: Did you make progress? On reconciliation?

Ghazi: Noooooooooo.

Gershon: Thought so.

Ghazi: We are still moving in a circle.

Gershon: David is hopeful that we can begin intensive marathon negotiations on Wednesday. For this to happen there has to be a positive answer from your side to the Egyptians – is anything happening in this regard?

Ghazi: I talked to Nader. He told me he is in contact with our side to check its acceptance of a new mechanism and will discuss other details and how to find the way forward.

Gershon: Has your side given the Egyptians an answer?

Ghazi: Not yet, but I think J. wants to understand the new mechanism before he will discuss it with Nader.

Gershon: What doesn't he understand?

Ghazi: Nader didn't give clear details.

Gershon: I think if we knew what was unclear, we could find the answers for J. That's really what our job in this is all about – clearing up misunderstandings, making things clearer, and helping to find solutions.

Ghazi: So he will see how we could discuss the names, lists, and how to move the ideas from Gaza to Israel.

Gershon: I think David wants Nader to come and to start going back and forth from Wednesday. He can start on either side. The Israeli side is basing the talks on the paper you gave me. They can go issue by issue, maybe starting with 1948 and East Jerusalem, or whatever your side proposes. We know the issues.

Ghazi: I hope this time we can make a breakthrough.

Gershon: I think we can. We have to get J. to say to Nader: Come – we want to start.

Ghazi: I will be with him all the time to give my advice. He will do that.

Gershon: Great. And I'll be with David, and we have the green light from both to communicate directly. Will Ramadan slow things down?

Ghazi: No…

Ghazi: He told me he would like to work twenty-four hrs.

Gershon: Great.

Just then Gaza's electricity went out – not an uncommon occurrence – so we completed the discussion by phone.

In the weeks to come, I was still pushing Ghazi to make sure Jaabri stood behind the paper. David had taken the July 14 document to Netanyahu and received his full agreement to close the deal with Hamas on that basis.

David was prepared to move to the next stage. I had to close the deal on the modalities so we could meet and conclude the work. But with Ramadan in full swing, and Ghazi apparently leery of Jaabri for reasons I did not understand at the time, Ghazi wasn't responding to my calls or text messages.

Ramadan began August 1, 2011. During this month, especially when it falls in the summer, life slows to a standstill. Muslims fast from dawn until sundown. Smoking is also prohibited, which for many people is harder than not eating or drinking. The first week is the hardest. People wake up for morning prayers at sunrise and then go back to sleep. Many stay inside most of the day. Those who have to work do so for a few hours and usually don't accomplish anything. Ever since Israel bombed the Gaza electric plant following Schalit's abduction, Gaza has had great electricity shortages, usually for about eight hours a day. There are few working air conditioners. A summertime Ramadan makes the fast that much harder.

I wondered how Gilad was surviving the heat. I wondered if they made him fast during Ramadan along with his captors. I assumed he was getting at least one very good meal every day: Every sundown is a feast. Palestinians save their money for the month of Ramadan so they can cook the very best specialties. I know many people who plan to lose weight during Ramadan but usually don't, because the food is so good and so plentiful that they cannot resist.

In the evening, especially in Gaza, people go to the mosque for prayers, discussions, and social gatherings. Then they get together with friends and family and eat fruit and snacks until going to sleep, much later than usual. This is especially true for political figures like Ghazi. I knew everything would slow down now. In addition to the Ramadan delay, I understood that Jaabri was angry with Ghazi, so Ghazi was very reluctant to see him. Jaabri was not someone you wanted to be angry at you.

Our back and forth was beginning to resemble an absurdist play – *Waiting for Mr. J.*

Chapter 15

Instability as Opportunity

It didn't matter that Ghazi and I – with some help from our respective governments – had finally put progress within reach. Hamas wanted the final deal to be inked in Egypt, perhaps as a show of not recognizing or dealing with the "enemy." David Meidan said he understood that Jaabri would not move forward without the talks moving to Cairo. Israel was reluctant to allow that. Although Egypt had played an important role in the past, well, that was then. Now, there was great apprehension about the situation emerging in Egypt after the fall of Mubarak. Amid the chaos, the Muslim Brotherhood had arisen as the people's choice for stability – and the Brotherhood was not keen on the peace deal Anwar Sadat has signed with Israel. Israel's longtime ally, Omar Suleiman, was no longer in charge. Murad Muwafi was the new head of Egyptian intelligence.

It happens David knew him well. And with my old friend General Nader El-A'aser now head of the Israel and Palestine desk within Egyptian intelligence, David decided to approach Muwafi and discuss the possibility of holding proximity talks in Cairo with Egyptian intelligence mediating between the sides.

The timing couldn't have been more propitious for Hamas to soften its hard lines: Its comfy redoubt in Damascus was crumbling.

The uprising in Syria was gaining strength, and President Bashar al-Assad was responding with a violence that shocked former regional allies. Prominent Islamic politicians such as Turkey's Recep Tayyip Erdoğan – who, to Israel's chagrin, had been showing a sympathetic face to Hamas – had condemned Assad's attacks on his own people and demanded the Syrian president step down. Even the Arab League was wringing its hands over the bloodbath, making Egypt's turmoil look like child's play. By mid-July, with Syria more and more isolated in the Middle East, the Hamas leadership had decided to begin removing its offices and operations from Damascus. Egyptian officials were signaling that some of the Hamas leadership could come to Cairo. I don't know whether Israel was aware of the full scope of the dynamics unfolding within Hamas, and its relations with Egypt. Just as David Meidan had instinctively advanced the secret channel I had opened, he decided to bring the Egyptians in at this moment to help close the deal, hoping they would use their newfound leverage to apply the appropriate pressure on Jaabri when needed.

Ghazi called and told me my old friend General Nader El-A'aser – head of the Israel and Palestine desk within Egyptian intelligence – would be leading the Egyptian team in negotiations to close the deal. That sounded good to me.

August 8, 2011

Ghazi,

I am convinced there will be a decision to hold the talks in Cairo. David received the green light from Netanyahu to hold the talks based on the July 14 document. If they decide to go to Cairo, the talks can be intensive and concluded in a matter of days. You and I must preserve our role and make sure they take us along. It is easier for Hamas to bring you along because you're an official. If they bring you, I can make the case to bring me as well. Our role can remain central and crucial. Talk to me later.

Gershon

Ghazi and I chatted the following morning, August 9:

>*Ghazi: Boker tov.*[1]

>*Gershon: Sabah al kheir.*[2] *How are you?*

>*Ghazi: Fine.*

>*Gershon: Good. Did you manage to speak to Mashal or anyone else?*

>*Ghazi: I tried to call him, but you know the network in Syria is very, very bad. But I talked to some friends here in Gaza, and they support me.*

>*Gershon: Will you see J. today?*

>*Ghazi: I will see the Hamas figure responsible for this file.*

>*Gershon: Who's that?*

>*Ghazi: Secret.*

>*Gershon: Osama Mazini?*[3]

>*Ghazi: No, he has no connection.*

>*Gershon: Okay, what will it take to get J. to sign the document of principles for the negotiations?*

>*Ghazi: I met the guy in charge in Gaza two weeks ago, and he supported the document. J. accepts it too. I suggest that we go to the Egyptians, because J. wants them to lead the negotiations.*

1. "Good morning" in Hebrew.
2. "Good morning" in Arabic.
3. Someone who always appeared on Hamas TV talking about Schalit.

Gershon: David is willing to go to Cairo for the negotiations. It's not nearly as good as having the Egyptians come here, but he's willing to show flexibility.

Ghazi: J. prefers not to allow anyone else to negotiate on his behalf. In spite of this, he trusts me, and I have good contact with him.[4]

Gershon: Jaabri wants to lead the negotiation or someone else?

Ghazi: There is a team from the political and military wings, from inside and outside.

Gershon: And is Jaabri the head of the team? We need to make sure you and I are part of the negotiation teams.

Ghazi: Right. I will discuss it with J. I hope to see him today.

Gershon: GOOD. So much time has been wasted and lost.

Ghazi: Right. I am really sorry for that wasted time.

Gershon: Me too.

Ghazi: I wanted to finish in our track, but J. wants the Egyptians to intervene.

Gershon: It's okay. We need the Egyptians to finish the deal, and we couldn't complete it without them. But we also need to make sure we are there in Cairo and able to have direct contact on the sidelines. There will always be misunderstandings, and they will always need creative ideas to help close the deal again. If the Egyptians came here, it would be better. Ramadan kareem umubarak.

---

4. Ghazi had apparently made peace with Jaabri.

In the next forty-eight hours, it became clear to me that what Ghazi and I had in mind was not unfolding, if the Egyptians had anything to do with it. Jaabri had gone to Cairo with his team, and David Meidan was on his way there.

The Egyptians had insisted that Ghazi and I not be there – they were afraid that a parallel channel would somehow undermine their efforts. I wrote to David and implored him not to leave Ghazi and me out at this late stage in the game. I reminded David that even my Egyptian contact, Nader El-A'aser, had said that the need for people on both sides who can speak directly to each other was crucial. Moreover, I told David, while the Egyptians could help, they were ultimately stakeholders with interests of their own.

This wasn't a power trip of trying to secure my role or Ghazi's. They were moving to the "proximity talks" model, which meant no face-to-face contact for Israelis and Palestinians. But I believed, as I do now, that a direct channel was the key not only to reaching a deal, but to building some modicum of trust in the process. And in my thirty years of experience with the Palestinians, I was more convinced than ever that everything begins and ends with basic trust between people. I wished David luck, but I was sure this round of negotiations would not be the last.

I wanted to propose an Israeli initiative that would, I believed, enable the negotiations to get off to a good start and conclude quickly. I had sent a detailed proposal to David with some new ideas, the most important of which was to put a full Israeli proposal on the table from the outset, so we wouldn't have to wait for Jaabri all the time. The initiative would be Israel's and could speed things up.

David thanked me for the proposal and said he was studying it and consulting with the decision makers involved. He contacted me to say that the talks had gotten off to a good start. He noted especially that Nader El-A'aser was in charge of the talks and that he and David had wonderful chemistry. This was a very encouraging sign. David was born in Egypt in 1955 and came to Israel with his parents two years later. Before Hebraicizing his name to Meidan, he was David Mosseri – related to Masr, the Arabic name for Egypt. David speaks Egyptian Arabic, and there is no doubt that the resulting closeness – as well as the camaraderie of sharing the same profession, intelligence – was a good beginning to a very important relationship.

David explained the importance that the Israeli side attached to the July 14 document – the breakthrough guidelines that were to serve as the basis for the deal. David told Nader that Jaabri was apparently trying to back away from it. Still, Israel's intelligence information showed that the Hamas political leadership supported the document. The Egyptians were already applying heavy pressure on Jaabri to stick to the document's principles so a deal could be closed. David also told me to continue pressuring Ghazi to get Jaabri behind the document.

It was clear to the Egyptians that Hamas' upper echelon supported reaching an agreement on the basis of the July 14 document. It was less clear that Jaabri was going to cooperate.

We expected delays and stalling tactics. But the last thing we expected was a cross-border terror attack. On August 18, gunmen opened fire on Egged bus 392, traveling on Highway 12 between Eilat and Mitzpe Ramon. The terrorists had infiltrated from Egypt. More striking, they wore military vests and were armed with assault rifles, roadside bombs, and suicide bomb belts. Several minutes later, a bomb was detonated next to an Israeli army patrol along Israel's border with Egypt. And then, in a third attack, an antitank missile hit a private vehicle, killing four Israeli civilians. In the wake of an hour and a half of attacks, seven Israelis lay dead – six of them civilians – and another ten passengers were wounded. An eighth Israeli, a police sniper from a special commando unit, was killed later that day after an Israeli patrol was fired on near the Egyptian border. In the ensuing gun battles, the Egyptian military killed some of the militants, and lost five of its soldiers in circumstances that remained in dispute when the bloody day was over. Israel said it avoided shooting at the Egyptian military, but Egyptians blamed Israel. There was a massive protest outside the Israeli Embassy in Cairo the following day. (In October, Israel sent a letter of apology for the deaths of the Egyptian soldiers, the *New York Times* reported.)

After feeling closer to an agreement than ever, it was hard to imagine a more disastrous chain of events. And it wasn't just about the Egyptian-Israeli diplomatic fallout. Defense Minister Ehud Barak said that the attackers had originated in the Gaza Strip and that the military would respond "forcefully and decisively." Acting on intelligence provided by the ISA, the Israeli Air Force attacked in the southern Gaza Strip, killing six Palestinians, including the head of the Popular Resistance Committees (PRC) and several other senior operatives.

According to one report, Israel had killed six leading militants in the PRC, one of the groups responsible for Schalit's abduction. I knew immediately that there would be retaliation and we would now witness several days of intensive escalation. More than two million people on both sides of the Gaza border would be living the next few days in constant fear. Not only was I afraid for the innocent people who would pay with their lives, be wounded, or lose property, but I feared that all the progress made in the Schalit negotiations would be derailed. I had to work to encourage my Hamas contacts to scale down retaliation from Gaza, and to see that Israel would contain its response as much as possible. We had to get back to a cease-fire soon, and Hamas had to take control of the events on the ground in Gaza.

The following is a sampling of text communication with the explicit goal of reaching a cease-fire. These texts were interspersed with phone calls to various players. In Israel, I was texting mostly with David Meidan, who forwarded my messages directly to Major General Benny Gantz, chief of staff of the Israeli army. On the Hamas side, I was texting mostly with Ghazi Hamad. I also texted and spoke directly with Nader El-A'aser in Egypt.

As events unfolded I also communicated with the staff of Ambassador Robert Serry, the special representative of the UN secretary general who had gone to Cairo to try to close the deal on the cease-fire. In one month I sent 1,450 text messages.

Immediately after the announcement of the Israeli retaliation in Gaza, I called Ghazi. He was angry and confused. He insisted that the attack against the Israeli bus had not come from Gaza. The PRC was denying its role, and Israel's targeted killings would make it impossible for Hamas to prevent a response. He also thought Islamic Jihad would join in. He assured me that Hamas was not involved and would do everything possible to stop the rocket fire into Israel. Hamas was not interested in escalation and wanted to maintain the cease-fire.

> *August 18, 2011, 5:50 p.m.* [SMS]

> *From: Ghazi*
> *Prime Minister Haniyeh assures that the government is doing its best to keep Gaza calm. J. surely supports the government position.*

> *August 18, 2011, 5:51 p.m.* [SMS]

> *To: Ghazi*
> *Ghazi – You know that people in Israel don't think the PM is really in control. The strong man is J., and he's the one with the power.*

> *August 18, 2011, 8:54 p.m.* [SMS]

> *From: Ghazi*
> *Israel started targeting Gaza and killing people before knowing who was behind the attack. Why do they always accuse Gaza even though we do everything to keep it calm? Israel is doing wrong and punishing in a way that leads to escalation.*

> *August 18, 2011, 8:56 p.m.* [SMS]

> *To: Ghazi*
> *Ghazi – They identified the Popular Resistance Committees from the attackers and then targeted the leaders who the ISA knew sent them to attack. If there is no escalation now from Gaza, and if Hamas takes real action to prevent rockets, this can be contained beyond all the killing that has already happened.*

I spoke with David and told him Ghazi had said that the attack hadn't come from Gaza, and that Hamas wasn't interested in escalation. I asked him to use his influence to get the Israeli side to contain its response.

August 18, 2011, 10:04 p.m. [sms]

From: David
If Hamas is the sovereign in Gaza, then it is responsible for what happens there. There is no partial sovereign and no partial responsibility. They can't be sovereign only when it suits them.

Throughout these nights, there was rocket fire into Israel. Israel attacked Gaza from the air, mostly targeting cells firing rockets.

August 19, 2011, 09:10 a.m. [sms]

To: Ghazi
Good morning, Ghazi. I would be happy to speak to you this morning to hear about the atmosphere in Gaza. It seems we have entered the gate of escalation – too many rockets fired on Israeli cities will bring the Israeli response to Gaza, and we both know more people will be killed. We both know that in a few days or a week or two, God willing, we will return to the cease-fire. How many people will have paid with their lives by then? It can be avoided. You know it too. If Hamas rules in Gaza, it must take control and stop the rocket fire, unless it also supports the rocket fire, and then Israel will go after the leaders of Hamas as well.

There may come a time, as I've said, when the prime minister of Israel will decide that a single captive soldier in Gaza cannot be the reason to grant immunity to the enemy leaders who hold him. I am afraid of this scenario, but it could happen. Jaabri may think he has an insurance policy because he holds Schalit, but I believe the insurance policy has a time limit. He risks losing everything. Today he can get his thousand prisoners. Soon, who knows, maybe nothing.

I spoke to Ghazi on the phone throughout the morning, trying to make sure we had a channel of open communication. Each time I heard about rocket fire in the south and Israeli retaliation, I felt as though Ghazi and I were the only people in the world who were actively trying to prevent a war between Israel and Hamas.

August 19, 2011, 11:25 a.m. [SMS]

To: Ghazi
Ghazi, let's not lose hope. We have to continue to convince the leaders on both sides to prevent the situation from getting out of control. I am afraid for every person who may lose his life. This kind of situation will only create more hatred. We have to stop this madness. We also have to make sure the prisoner negotiations continue. We can't let these events make our progress disappear.

August 19, 2011, 11:29 a.m. [SMS]

From: Ghazi
Gershon, u r good friend but i'm very sad and upset & sometimes feeling have no words to say.

August 19, 2011, 11:34 a.m. [SMS]

To: Ghazi
I understand and feel the same. Please try to speak to Dr. Mousa [Abu Marzouk] so we can know what happened in Cairo and what we have to do to help move forward. We have to succeed and can't let the setbacks hold us back.

August 19, 2011, 11:48 a.m. [SMS]

To: Ghazi
David is asking if you spoke to Dr. Mousa yet. I guess the answer is no, not yet.

August 19, 2011, 1:15 p.m. [SMS]

From: Ghazi
Dr. Mousa and everyone are concerned with what is happening in Gaza. They don't want escalation. They want Israel to stop killing people. Hamas is committed to the cease-fire and is doing everything

to stop the rockets. Dr. Mousa says, how can we continue to negotiate the prisoners with all the Israeli killing?

I spoke with Ghazi. I wanted us to continue to focus on the Schalit negotiations while also talking about cease-fire. I didn't want to allow Hamas to wriggle out of committing to the breakthrough document. Jaabri had to be locked in. I understood that the higher leadership had not yet imposed discipline on him. He was running the show. It seemed to me that Ghazi was not speaking directly to Jaabri anymore, that his relationship with Jaabri had soured. Only later did I learn that this was because he had put all Jaabri's cards on the table in the July 14 document, and was now even afraid to speak to him.

August 19, 2011, 2:43 p.m. [SMS]

To: Ghazi

For most of the past five years, I have held Israel responsible for the failure to reach an agreement with Hamas and bring Schalit home. Now that is no longer the truth. David and Netanyahu have demonstrated amazing flexibility. Your side simply does not want a deal – maybe it is not your whole side. It is Mr. Jaabri. Let's face it, Hamas is controlled by one man with a militia, and everyone bows down to him. I don't know why he doesn't want a deal – maybe because he thinks holding onto Schalit is what keeps him alive. Maybe he doesn't want the same fate as Yassin, Rantisi,[5] etc.

I don't understand why one thousand Palestinian families – mothers and fathers – allow this one man with a militia to make their sons stay in prison. I don't know why your leaders show such a lack of courage and leadership. If I am correct, then there is no point in even trying to negotiate – Jaabri is not interested in reaching an agreement. If so, don't expect Israel to simply accept this. Hamas has done a great job of humiliating Israel. How much longer do you expect Israel

---

5. Sheikh Ahmed Yassin, founder of Hamas, and Dr. Abd Aziz al-Rantisi – two Hamas leaders assassinated by Israel.

to tolerate this humiliation? I hope you share this message with Mashal and Abu Marzouk and others.

August 20, 2011, 1:01 p.m. [SMS]

From: Ghazi
Gershon, I assure you Hamas wants to complete the deal for the prisoners. We do not want escalation, and the prime minister has met with all the faction leaders and instructed them to stop shooting rockets. Hamas will do everything possible to stop the fire. We need Israel to stop also so we can make the ground quiet. Please tell the Israelis we are doing our best to stop the rockets.

August 20, 2011, 1:09 p.m. [SMS]

To: Ghazi
Ghazi, your message about cease-fire and your willingness to take it upon yourself to inform all the forces and commanders in Gaza has been brought to the attention of Amos Gilad, Bibi, and Barak.[6] I think you should inform Nader that the Egyptians should set the time for a full cease-fire and then get formal agreement from both sides.

August 20, 2011, 3:22 p.m. [SMS]

From: Ghazi
I spoke with Nader and others. He said they're very close to having an agreement for a cease-fire very soon.

August 20, 2011, 3:46 p.m. [SMS]

To: Ghazi
Ghazi – In your talks with Nader could you ask about renewing the negotiations on the prisoner exchange? Are the Egyptians waiting for

6. General Amos Gilad heads the Political Security Department in the Ministry of Defense; Bibi is Prime Minister Benjamin Netanyahu.

your side to say something about the lists of names? I think we can use the cease-fire to return to negotiations.

August 20, 2011, 10:54 p.m. [SMS]

To: David
Ghazi just came from a discussion with Haniyeh. They spoke to the heads of all the organizations, including Islamic Jihad and the Popular Resistance Committees – everyone agrees to enter into a cease-fire. They are waiting for the Egyptians to set the exact time. They want the cease-fire to come into effect and then raise the issue of the attack in the south, because they claim they had nothing to do with it. There have been retaliation attacks in Gaza – now it's enough.

August 20, 2011, 11:08 p.m. [SMS]

To: Ghazi
This is my proposal: If you tell Ambassador Serry that Hamas would agree to a midnight cease-fire, he will pass it on to Israel. David is forwarding my messages to Gantz exactly as I send them. I proposed the midnight deadline.

August 20, 2011, 11:21 p.m. [SMS]

From: David
What about the military wing? We don't hear them. Is Jaabri again sending the moderates to the fore while he plays with fire from behind?

August 20, 2011, 11:33 p.m. [SMS]

To: David
As opposed to what our Arab affairs experts on television are telling us, in my assessment, Hamas has no feeling of victory or of being on top. It fears losing control. The balance of blood (what a horrible concept) is still in Israel's favor, for the time being.

August 21, 2011, 2:03 a.m. [SMS]

To: David
It's 2 a.m. and I am seriously disappointed that there was no official announcement of a cease-fire. Wisdom must prevail. Enough innocent people have lost their lives in recent days. Hamas is a bitter enemy and there is no forgiving its hatred, but the government of Israel must restore calm now, when there is a clear opportunity to do so.

August 21, 2011, 2:05 a.m. [SMS]

To: Ghazi
Ghazi – I am really sorry there has not yet been any announcement of a cease-fire. There is too much hatred in the land, and our leaders don't always use their wisdom. I hope the situation can be controlled. Too many innocent people have already been killed in recent days. I hope God has mercy on us all.

Here I was, an avowed secularist, hoping God would get us out of this mess. But the rockets from Gaza kept slamming into Israeli towns, one of them injuring a nine-month-old. A thirteen-year-old Palestinian boy was killed when a militant cell's Grad rocket fell short and landed in Gaza instead of Israel. The list of tragic victims was growing once again. More rockets came, and Israel ordered its air force to hit Gaza harder.

August 21, 2011, 8:58 a.m. [SMS]

To: Ghazi
Ghazi, good morning. It seems the government will make a decision this morning about how hard to hit Gaza and Hamas – this is what I know from the media only. I am still pushing for the cease-fire.

August 21, 2011, 10:19 a.m. [SMS]

To: David
I spoke to Minister Mickey Eitan[7] about a cease-fire. He told me there's no cabinet meeting today. So I assume the whole matter is in the hands of the prime minister and the minister of defense. I am trying to encourage restraint on the other side, but I wouldn't count on it with continued Israeli retaliations.

August 21, 2011, 1:18 p.m. [SMS]

To: David
The air force just attacked Beit Lahia.[8] Now is the time to declare victory and stop the fire. It is now becoming a game with fire that will cost the lives of more people. Enough flexing of muscles.

August 21, 2011, 1:23 p.m. [SMS]

To: Yoni Koren, Chief of Staff of Ehud Barak, Minister of Defense
Shalom, Yoni, I am Gershon Baskin, and this is a message for Ehud Barak. During the past twenty-four hours I have sent messages to the chief of staff by way of David Meidan. Hamas wants a cease-fire. Its people are prepared to enforce it on their side in all the factions. The more Israel attacks, the more dangerous this game becomes. Stop playing with people's lives.

---

7. Likud Minister Michael Eitan, an old acquaintance who once asked me to coach him on the Palestinian issue. Immediately after Meidan's appointment, I asked that Eitan speak to him and put in a good word for me. Eitan was the only person outside the official inner circle who knew about the secret back channel. I had met with him twice, at his request and with Meidan's authorization, during the months of the channel. I gave him very little information. He wanted to share some of his own ideas on how to move the negotiations forward.
8. In the northern part of Gaza.

August 21, 2011, 2:32 p.m. [SMS]

To: Ghazi
Hi, Ghazi – I am still trying to get Israel to accept the cease-fire. The Israelis attacked in Beit Lahia – have there been other attacks? Have you been able to control the Jihad and PRC?

August 21, 2011, 3:16 p.m. [SMS]

To: Ehud Barak
Very big efforts are being made by Hamas, including Jaabri, to keep the calm. All the factions have agreed, and now it depends on Israel. Ghazi Hamad has notified Nader El-A'aser in Cairo and Ambassador Robert Serry of the agreement of all the forces in Gaza. They are requesting that Israel allow them to calm the area and then enter into an agreed-upon cease-fire. The proposal is that the agreement will begin officially at 9 p.m., and then everyone will judge the seriousness of the other and the ability to enforce the cease-fire. Israel should also cease all fire from then on.

August 21, 2011, 3:44 p.m. [SMS]

To: David
I am on the phone now with Ghazi, and there is another round of attack by the air force in northern Gaza. Who on our side is interested in more rocket fire from Gaza? Now every single Israeli attack will draw retaliation. What are we doing?!

August 21, 2011, 3:50 p.m. [SMS]

To: Yoram Cohen, head of the ISA
Shalom, Yoram, this is Gershon Baskin. Over the past thirty-five hours I have been in constant contact with the heads of Hamas regarding a cease-fire. There is agreement in Gaza among all the

factions – including Islamic Jihad, including Jaabri – to enforce it. They have notified the Egyptians and Robert Serry that they are making real efforts to keep the quiet. The Egyptians have requested that by 9 p.m. Israel should examine the seriousness of Hamas' actions and its ability to enforce the cease-fire. Hamas has requested that Israel hold its fire. Five minutes ago I had a call from Ghazi Hamad, and there was another air force attack in northern Gaza. This is too dangerous already. There is a readiness for a cease-fire.

August 21, 2011, 4:07 p.m. [SMS]

To: Robert Serry
I have spoken with ministers in the Israeli government, sent messages to Yoram Cohen and to Barak. Mickey Eitan will now speak to the prime minister. There was just an Israeli Air Force attack in northern Gaza – fortunately no casualties. As you know, Hamas is ready to impose a full cease-fire. It's time to put the pressure on Israel. I suggest that you enlist the Egyptian intelligence minister to send a message directly to the prime minister. He can also send it via David Meidan. Every minute is important now. We can't allow the situation to snowball. Thanks. Gershon Baskin

August 21, 2011, 4:24 p.m. [SMS]

To: David
David, please tell the chief of staff – Hamas wants to deploy its troops in the areas where rockets are being launched. The Hamas people are serious and need IDF cooperation to allow them to take control of the field.

August 21, 2011, 5:30 p.m. [SMS]

To: Minister Mickey Eitan
Mickey, please tell Bibi that the UN has come up with a plan for a cease-fire at 9 p.m. tonight. Hamas has agreed, but there is still no

answer from Israel. Hamas wants to deploy its troops now to prevent more rocket fire. I hope the IDF won't attack them.

By 5:10 p.m. everything was in place. It seemed both sides had had enough for this round, but neither side would announce a cease-fire. I received notification from the Egyptians, the UN, Hamas, and Israel that a cease-fire at 9 p.m. was acceptable, but no one would admit it in public. I feared that without a public announcement, there would be no cease-fire. The UN didn't want to risk making announcements on behalf of the parties. After hearing from Ghazi that Hamas was fully committed to enforcing the cease-fire, I spoke with one of Ambassador Serry's staffers and told him that I understood from all my conversations on the Israeli side that the 9 p.m. ceasefire was acceptable.

At 5:15 p.m. I began sending text messages to all the Arab affairs correspondents on Israeli television and radio. At 5:20 Ehud Yaari, the leading Arab affairs expert on Channel 2 news, announced – following the wording of my text message – that the parties had reached an agreement for a 9 p.m. cease-fire. By 7 p.m. all the Israeli media were announcing the cease-fire. At 7:30 Al Jazeera also announced the cease-fire.

Weeks later I met one of Ambassadors Serry's staffers and told her about how I'd gotten the Israeli media to issue the announcement. She told me she'd been in Cairo with Ambassador Serry at the time, and they were bewildered by how the Israeli media had gotten the message to make the announcement. In all my years of working to bring about a prisoner exchange, I always maintained the level of secrecy I promised to various Israeli and Palestinian officials. But this was one time when a little leak to the press could only help.

At 9:15 p.m. Mickey Eitan called me. "Four grad rockets just landed in Ofakim," he said heatedly. "Where's the cease-fire?!" I immediately called Ghazi and, without masking the anger in my voice, asked him what was happening. He told me he was in the prime minister's office with the heads of all the factions and the heads of Ezzedin al Qassam, including Jaabri. They were prepared to send out forces to stop the rockets, but they'd received no assurances from Israel that the IDF wouldn't shoot at them.

I immediately told David what Ghazi had said. David asked me to text it to him so he could forward it to Chief of Staff Gantz. I did, and then Jaabri sent out the forces.

Ten minutes later, I texted Ghazi again.

August 21, 2011, 9:25 p.m. [SMS]

To: Ghazi
Ghazi – If it holds, and if Israel observes the cease-fire too, it's the right time for you to renew direct contact with Mr. J. and for us to get the prisoner talks back on track.

August 22, 2011, 8:27 a.m. [SMS]

To: Ghazi and David
Good morning, Ghazi. About fifteen mortars and rockets during the night. A lot more work to do on your side. Israel is demonstrating restraint, and I think our messages have had an impact. Now we have to get to a full cease-fire on both sides. I also firmly believe that renewing the prisoner talks would be a good sign as well. See if you can talk to Mashal about this. I'm sure the Egyptians would be happy to invite both sides back. While you're speaking with Mashal, see if you can get clear Hamas backing for the basis of the talks – our July 14 document. Thanks. Speak to me this morning. I am also online in my office.

That morning, I sat down and wrote a letter to Khaled Mashal and Mousa Abu Marzouk.

August 22, 2011

Mr. Khaled Mashal
Dr. Mousa Abu Marzouk

Dear Mr. Mashal and Dr. Mousa,

You may not know this, but Ghazi Hamad and I have played an instrumental role in achieving a cease-fire over the past forty-eight hours. *Ghazi Hamad has played an extraordinary role in advancing Palestinian interests and welfare during this period. It is now time to use this opportunity to return to the negotiations in Cairo and complete the deal for the prisoner exchange.*

David Meidan has received authorization from Netanyahu to negotiate and reach an agreement on the basis of the July 14 document. This document is to be the cornerstone of the agreement. It was written and delivered by Ghazi Hamad to me based on hours of discussions with Ahmed Jaabri and you two. If this document is the basis for the negotiations, I am authorized to tell you that it will be possible to reach a final agreement on the prisoner exchange within several days of intensive negotiations. This document must be the basis, and the lists in question should be those that have been dealt with until now – not new ones.

The main thing is that Jaabri should be instructed to use this document as the basis for the negotiations. The Egyptians should invite both parties to return to Cairo very soon to complete the agreement. It is time to close this chapter now.

Regards,
Gershon Baskin

Later that day, Islamic Jihad announced that it would fully adhere to the cease-fire. As long as Israel didn't attack anymore, Islamic Jihad would also refrain from all rocket fire. I told Ghazi what I'd heard from David Meidan: Israel was very much ready to move on based on the July 14 document. The lists of the prisoners' names were from Jaabri, after all. Israel was willing to tweak the list, adding or subtracting a few names, but would not go back to square one.

There were still violations of the cease-fire, and it wasn't at all clear that it would continue to hold. Before we knew it, Ramadan had only one week left. Afterward would come Eid al-Fitr, the festival that concludes the month of fasting. Khaled Mashal and friends had gone to Mecca – and were likely to be out of touch until after the holiday. In a week, the Islamic month of Ramadan, the Hebrew month of Av, and the Gregorian month of August would all be over. Gilad's birthday would have come and gone, and he wouldn't be back in his parents' arms. Nor would hundreds of Palestinians be holding homecoming celebrations. But at the very least, the Egyptians had invited the parties back to negotiations in Cairo. I had to believe we were inching closer to an agreement.

Chapter 16

Sealing the Deal

The Egyptians had invited the parties to Cairo to continue the negotiations. They were held on a military base. The Hamas delegation was headed by Jaabri and included his deputy, Marwan Issa; Salah Arouri, an exiled Ezzedin al Qassam leader from the West Bank, then living in Damascus; and Nizar Awadallah, a Hamas official from Gaza. The Israeli side comprised David Meidan, A. from military intelligence, and Y. from the ISA. Nader was in charge of the negotiations along with two colleagues. The Egyptians had assurances from the Hamas political leadership that it accepted the July 14 document as the framework. The principles were set, and now the participants had to work on the list of names and the categories they belonged to.

As usual, and probably as expected, Jaabri became the spoiler. He accepted the July 14 document – not necessarily by choice – but now he sprang a new list of VIP names on the Israelis. Instead of the fifty names from the German proposal, Jaabri pulled out 153. The Israeli side decided Jaabri had to be forced to stick to the original list or there would be no negotiations. General Nader tried to get the Israelis to compromise. The Egyptians wanted David's team to at least look at Jaabri's list and consider adding some names.

David's group returned to Israel. One member of the team leaked to the media that there was a crisis in the talks with Hamas, although there had never been any announcement of negotiations in the first place.

During this period, almost everything written in the media about the negotiations was incorrect. In fact, much of what the media reported during the entire five years was fabricated or only partially based on fact. There was one exception: a woman journalist writing for *Al-Hayat*, whose name, I believe, was Hanan Shafey. Her articles had no byline, but it seems she was the only woman working in Cairo at the time for the London-based newspaper. Her reporting was precise and more accurate than any other journalist's. I gathered she was close to someone on the Hamas side. The Israeli media hungrily reiterated whatever *Al-Hayat* published on the subject. Israel never formally confirmed whether the reports were true. Noam Schalit was often the only address in Israel, and he usually responded that the media reported many things that weren't true.

On September 9, 2011, I flew to Cairo. I was invited to a conference organized by the Middle East Citizen's Assembly. There were supposed to be other Israelis attending the conference. The situation in Cairo was very tense, and Israelis were being warned by the Israeli government not to go to Egypt. The Israeli Embassy in Cairo had been repeatedly attacked by mobs setting out from Tahrir Square. There was a definite lack of law and order on the streets of the Egyptian capital. All my Israeli colleagues dropped out of the conference.

I decided to go anyway. I would be traveling with my good friend Walid Salem from East Jerusalem, and I wanted to be in Cairo to meet with Nader. That was much more important to me than the conference.

The conference was held in a hotel in Zamalek, an island in the middle of the Nile. Zamalek is home to many embassies, and most of Cairo's diplomatic community lives there, along with some of the wealthiest Egyptians. Given the affluence and status of many of Zamalek's residents, there are far more police deployed there than in the average Cairo neighborhood, and security is tight. My hotel was less than third of a mile from the Israeli Embassy.

On the second evening of the conference, I heard gunshots while in my hotel room. I thought it was a wedding – at Arab weddings celebratory gunshots are often fired in the air. The next morning I learned that the Israeli Embassy had been attacked. Egyptian commandos had rescued the Israeli security guards inside, who were apparently close to being set upon by an out-of-control street mob. Nearly all Israelis left Egypt early that morning on an air force plane. I was probably the last one left, except for the deputy ambassador. The participants at my conference were from all over the Arab world – and they were concerned. They all wanted me to feel safe and know I was among friends.

I met Nader that day. He came to my hotel, and we had a very good and productive conversation. Nader wanted to know my assessment regarding the possibility of adding to the lists of names. I assured him that this was a deal breaker. The Israeli security services had spent months going over every name and estimating the danger each person could pose in the future. David had given assessments to Netanyahu together with the input of Yoram Cohen, the head of the ISA. Israel would not change the list. The Israelis also perceived Jaabri's new demands as his way of preventing an agreement. It was essential for the Egyptians to understand how Israel saw Jaabri's behavior, and to realize this wasn't the first time Jaabri had pulled the same trick.

I suggested to Nader that the Egyptians put a comprehensive Egyptian proposal on the table, one that would be as detailed as possible. Rather than allowing the Israeli and the Hamas negotiators to ping-pong their points back and forth for weeks, the Egyptians should present a proposal that would become the focus of the negotiations and enable them to control the talks and to reach a quick agreement. Nader liked the idea and said they would work on it before the next round of talks. He asked me to continue coming up with ideas of how to break the deadlock, and encouraged me to speak to him anytime I thought necessary.

I felt that my four-day trip to Cairo had been worth all the risks. I told Nader that Walid and I were planning to travel back to Israel by land across the Sinai. I asked if he thought it was safe enough. Nader offered to contact Egyptian security officials in Sinai so they would know we were coming. He said he just wanted to be sure we wouldn't encounter problems at various checkpoints. I packed my bags.

A few hours later, Nader called me. "Gershon," he said, "fly back home. It's much safer." Needless to say, we took his advice.

When I got back to my room that afternoon, I called David and reported to him about my meeting with Nader. I also sent Ghazi an update:

September 11, 2011

Hi, Ghazi – I had a good meeting with Nader. He thanked both of us for opening up the process and for making progress when no one else was able to.

Now the key to the deal is Jaabri. There is agreement with what David told me: If Jaabri agrees to the lists from the German document, it will be easy to reach an agreement.

The Egyptians are working on putting a full agreement on the table at the next meeting. They're working on Jaabri to get him to agree, but I still think the most important thing is to get Mashal and Dr. Mousa to understand that they have to instruct Jaabri to agree. Israel is not the obstacle now. There has never been more Israeli flexibility. You have to work on Mashal and Mousa Abu Marzouk. If you succeed, we'll have an agreement.

Gershon

I then wrote Nader to summarize our meeting:

September 12, 2011

Dear Nader,

Thanks for coming to see me yesterday.

The most important thing right now is to put a deal on the table that both sides can agree to, with all the names and all the conditions. The final deal, not too complicated – names, categories and where they go. This is what I have been pushing the Israeli team to do for the past month. If it comes from you, I think there's a good chance of completing the deal.

I spoke with Ghazi and emphasized how important it is for him to push Mashal and Abu Marzouk. The essential pressure can come from the Hamas leadership in Syria and now in Cairo. I believe they would also listen carefully if the message came from the Egyptian side.

Gershon

The negotiations had reached a critical stage. The Egyptians placed massive pressure on Jaabri. They also worked on softening him. They dined him and took him for a jeep tour in the desert. They even arranged for laser surgery for him, so he could get rid of his glasses. Jaabri was a simple man, a religious Muslim without money or property. The Egyptians worked on getting him to appreciate life beyond the cause. Ghazi managed to get Mashal and Abu Marzouk and others in the political leadership to understand that this was the critical moment to make the decisions. They would never get a better deal.

David was optimistic but also nervous because of the lack of faith in Jaabri's ability to see an opportunity. He was apprehensive about my direct contact with Nader. The Egyptians were doing a great job, and he wanted the process to be very controlled now. He was afraid of new initiatives or anything that would enable Jaabri to withdraw. He asked me not to make direct contact with Nader during this period.

I assured him that I wouldn't do anything that would damage the negotiations in any way.

He wrote back to me:

September 16, 2011 2:02 p.m. [SMS]

From: David
I have no fear whatsoever that you would damage the negotiations. Quite the opposite. No one knows better than I how much you have contributed and how dedicated you are to this issue. I have full confidence in you and in your motives – complete trust. The issue is your

> *direct contact with Nader and the potential problematics concerning*
> *the negotiations. Don't forget what his position is [head of the Israeli*
> *and Palestinian desk in Egyptian intelligence].*

The official negotiations intensified. I could do little except monitor and see if there were misunderstandings that needed to be dealt with. Ghazi was in contact with the political people, but not much with Jaabri. We both knew progress was being made – Nader confirmed that much for me. David and his team were going back and forth to Cairo for a few more rounds of talks.

On the eve of Rosh HaShana, David called me and told me to halt all communications: "Don't speak to Ghazi or to anyone else. We're waiting for the pressure on Jaabri to have its effect. We're waiting for the Egyptians to close the understandings with the Hamas leadership. There is good reason to be optimistic, but we don't want new initiatives now."

During the next week I kept myself very busy. Rosh HaShana was September 29, 2011. I remembered that first Rosh HaShana of Gilad's captivity, when I read Noam and Aviva's letter to him at my family dinner table. Five years since that night, there seemed to be hope that Gilad would not spend another Jewish New Year in captivity in Gaza.

On October 3, Ghazi called and asked if I'd heard anything. I told him no. I said we were all waiting for his side to respond to the proposal on the table. Israel had agreed, and now it was in the hands of the Hamas leadership. Ghazi said he would look into it with Mashal and others.

When no answer came from Cairo or from Gaza, I began getting nervous. I contacted David, Nader, and Ghazi. I said maybe we weren't getting an answer because Jaabri couldn't give one – perhaps Gilad was no longer alive? I was despondent – more so than at any other time in the past five years. If Gilad was dead, that would explain Jaabri's refusal to provide a sign of life. Negotiations resumed only with Jaabri's assurance to Nader that Gilad was indeed alive and well.

Nader, David, and Ghazi all assured me that Gilad was alive and in good health. They weren't concerned about this question. I felt better, but still very tense. I accepted an invitation to attend a conference in Barcelona sponsored by EuroMeSCo, the network of European-Mediterranean strategic think tanks, of which IPCRI was a member. I considered canceling my participation in the three-day conference, which was to begin October 5. I had already backed out of two other conferences in recent months because of the negotiations. Instead, I decided to go. I needed the distraction, and I couldn't change anything by staying in Jerusalem.

I sat through the conference staring at my phone, waiting for a call or text message. I spoke to Ghazi and David several times to find out if there was any progress.

On October 7, the eve of Yom Kippur, the holiest day on the Jewish calendar, David informed Noam and Aviva that he had received the green light from the Egyptians – Jaabri was ready to close the deal, and it was time to come back to Cairo. Israel and Hamas were now in the final stages of the negotiations, though both sides hid that from nearly everyone. In fact, David had also sent me a text message on the eve of Yom Kippur, asking me to meet him in Tel Aviv on October 11. I agreed. He didn't mention that in the meantime, on the evening after Yom Kippur, he and his team – including A., Y., and Yoram Cohen – were returning to Cairo. Noam and Aviva drove down to David's home in Hod HaSharon to see him before he left.

Over the next seventy-two hours, intensive negotiations took place, with the negotiators going over every single name to compile the final list of 450. The Egyptians went back and forth between the sides and finally produced a list acceptable to both sides. Unbeknownst to the rest of the world, a deal had been sealed. Sworn enemies had managed to meet in the middle.

On the morning of October 11, I texted David to find out where and when we would meet. He didn't answer. That was strange, because he always replied immediately, unless he was meeting with the prime minister or in Cairo (where, for security reasons, he preferred not to communicate).

I thought he must be meeting with Netanyahu, so I went to Tel Aviv. I had filled my day with meetings, and in the evening the One Voice organization (where I'm on the board of directors) was holding a "public democracy" event with roundtables headed by pro-peace politicians. There was also a table there to promote the public campaign for Gilad Schalit. I walked around and heard some of the debate. A few politicians asked me to co-chair their discussions, but I had no patience for political debates. I sat quietly at the Schalit table, where people were talking about how to convince the government to free him. Then, at 7:30 p.m., Ynet – the website of *Yedioth Ahronoth,* an Israeli daily – reported that Netanyahu had convened his cabinet to vote on a deal to bring Gilad Schalit home. Now I understood why I couldn't reach David all day.

I called David. His phone was off. I texted him. He responded that he would be in the cabinet meeting for the next few hours. He was confident that the deal would be approved.

I drove directly to the Prime Minister's Office in Jerusalem. Aside from Netanyahu, Barak, and Mickey Eitan, no one in the government knew of my involvement. David was in the room with the cabinet, along with Yoram Cohen, the chief of staff, and the prime minister's military attaché. They alone knew about the secret back channel that had led to the agreement.

David described the channel that had created the breakthrough in mid-July. He didn't mention my name, he later told me. He didn't want details of the channel to be publicized, lest some Hamas leaders disapprove of the direct contact and sabotage the deal.

I waited for David to come out. At 10:30 p.m. he texted me that he'd slipped out of a back door in order to avoid the press and was now driving home to Hod HaSharon. He hadn't slept for three days. He said the deal would be approved by an overwhelming majority. The heads of the ISA, the Mossad, and IDF all backed the deal, as did the prime minister. David said it wouldn't have happened without me.

At around 2 a.m. the government voted twenty-six in favor, three against. Gilad would be back in Israel in seven to ten days. I was elated!

Government Press Office

The government votes

My wife and I stayed up to watch the news. The television crews were covering the Schalit family tent outside the prime minister's residence. Hundreds of people were there. Aviva Schalit smiled for the first time in more than five years. But she said she was still anxious. She said that it was "time for Gilad to become my son once again, not the son of the nation." After the Sukkot holiday, the government had to publish the names of the prisoners to be released. Then the public would have two days to appeal to the Supreme Court to prevent the release of those who had maimed or killed their loved ones.

I spoke to David the next morning, reminding him of my one request: to be there when Gilad crossed the border. David said he would do everything possible to make sure I was there.

Throughout Sukkot, the entire country was focused on the Schalits, who'd folded up the tent in front of the prime minister's house and headed back to Mitzpe Hila to prepare for Gilad's homecoming. Meanwhile, the Ministry of Justice, the police, the ISA, and other security organizations were preparing the list of prisoners for publication on the website of the Israel Prison Service.

David was trying to catch up on missed sleep, but the excitement kept his adrenaline high. During the holiday he called several times. I was so glad our mission had been accomplished, but he stressed that everything still had to go according to plan. The mission wouldn't actually be accomplished until Gilad was home.

Early in the morning on October 14, four days before Gilad's homecoming, I received a call from Gal Berger, the Palestinian affairs correspondent for the Voice of Israel radio station. Berger had heard about the back channel and wanted to interview me. He had already spoken to Ghazi Hamad, who'd told him he should speak to me. I called David and asked if it was alright to be interviewed. David said that it was, and that he'd known the story of the people behind the scenes would break soon. He told me two things I shouldn't say, but everything else was okay to report.

Then I called Ghazi and asked if it was alright to mention his name and the role he'd played. I also congratulated him and thanked him for everything he'd done.

"Gershon, you did it all," he said.

"Ghazi, this would not have succeeded without your commitment and engagement, without the role *you* played. We did this together!"

I could feel him smiling at the other end of the phone. We both felt enormous relief.

I met Gal Berger in my office in Jerusalem and gave him the highlights of our story. I knew that as soon as it broke, I would be getting calls from all over the world and from everyone in the media. I had meetings in Hebron later that morning and was glad to be away from the office and in areas without phone reception. At 10 a.m. the story broke on the Voice of Israel. I didn't hear it.

When I returned to Jerusalem, the calls started pouring in. I was interviewed for two days, then decided I didn't feel comfortable speaking further until Gilad was back in Israel.

Ronit Nuriel, widow of my wife's cousin Sasson, also called. She was very angry and was crying. Four of the six people responsible for killing her husband were to be released. My wife spent almost an hour with her on the phone. Ronit was in deep pain. After less than six years in prison, the man who had butchered her husband with his own hands was about to go free. As I saw it, nothing in the world was going to bring Sasson back to the people who loved him, regardless of whether his killer was in prison. But from her point of view, no one cared about her anguish or that of her children.

I called Ronit back and listened with empathy. I really did feel her pain. I told her that if she wanted to write a letter to Netanyahu, I would make sure he received it. She said it wouldn't matter. Throughout the call I was thinking: *I couldn't save Sasson, God knows I wanted to, but Gilad is coming home alive. We should all celebrate that.* But I didn't say it, because I knew it wouldn't console Ronit.

Ronit and her children were among those who appealed to the Supreme Court to block the prisoner exchange. The court ruled that this was not a legal issue but a political-military one, and the government had the right to make the deal.

Gilad Schalit was coming home – five years and four months after his capture in Gaza.

Chapter 17

A Surreal Homecoming

Tuesday, October 18, 2011. All of Israel seemed to wake up early, waiting with excitement and trepidation to see what had become of our missing soldier. Was he really going to be released as promised? Would he be emotionally and physically destroyed, a shell of his former self? Would he suffer from Stockholm Syndrome, sympathizing with his captors as hostages sometimes do? Maybe he had become a Hamas ideologue, and fluent in Arabic to boot. Or maybe he would barely be able to hold a conversation.

We soon found out that quite the contrary, Gilad very much had his wits about him. He had been neither broken nor brainwashed.

Early that morning, I heard from David. He had done everything he could to honor my request to come see Gilad arrive home safe on Israeli soil. But the higher-ups had decided his welcoming committee would be minimal. When he was transported by Jaabri from Gaza into Egypt, I got a text from Ghazi telling me that Gilad was now out of Gaza. Already getting phone calls from various media outlets, I agreed to an interview at Al Jazeera's offices in Jerusalem. From there, I watched the live coverage of Gilad's arrival in Egypt.

Israelis – and others around the world, I imagine – were glued to their TVs. We watched Gilad being paraded before Egyptian intelligence officers. Nader El-A'aser was at his side, holding his arm. Ahmed Jaabri and Hamas gunmen were seen behind him, smiling. He wore an ill-fitting black-and-white Oxford shirt that looked like it had been purchased that morning from a Gaza flea market. It seemed his captors had gone out of their way to make him look presentable. But Gilad was ghostly white and painfully thin – only a few pounds away from a concentration-camp survivor. He looked like, well, like someone who hadn't seen the light of day in half a decade.

The next thing we knew, Gilad had been sat down for an interview on Egyptian television. Contrary to everything Israeli intelligence and Gilad's own family wanted, he was forced to answer questions before the whole world when he wasn't even yet on safe ground or reunited with his loved ones. Most Israelis watched this interview with horror. Gilad was obviously uncomfortable and uncertain, shifting in his seat and sometimes struggling to catch his breath. Yet he handled the difficult questions amazingly well. He seemed stronger than anyone could have imagined: aware, alert, coherent, healthy, and in control. What a relief! Shortly afterward, it became clear that Jaabri and several Hamas gunmen had been standing behind Schalit the whole time, exposing the sham of this "interview."

Then, on Al Jazeera, I watched David, A., and Y. talking with Nader. I so wanted to be there! I saw David escort Gilad to the Israeli side. A few minutes later I got a text from David: "Gilad is with us in Israel!"

Gilad disappeared from the cameras while the commentary rolled. He soon reemerged, dressed in an IDF uniform that seemed to accentuate how emaciated he was. Yet there he was, walking, smiling, shaking hands, and saluting the prime minister who had made the tough decision to free him.

Only later did I learn that when Gilad got to the Israeli side, he'd fainted. The army doctors gave him a quick infusion of glucose and then sent him back out. He was malnourished and overwhelmed. Who knew what he'd been through? But we knew he was home.

David sent another text. "I'm very moved. I'm the first Israeli who spoke with him. This kid has melted my heart."

Government Press Office

Gilad Schalit comes home

Government Press Office

Noam and Gilad Schalit, Benjamin Netanyahu, and Ehud Barak

Chapter 18:

Ghazi Hamad, the Man Who Made It Happen

Gilad Schalit would not have come home if Ghazi Hamad had not taken personal responsibility for keeping a channel of communication open between Israel and Hamas. At the time of Gilad's abduction, Hamad was the spokesperson for the Hamas government and its prime minister, Ismail Haniyeh. Haniyeh's office instructed Ghazi to make contact with me six days after Schalit's abduction. No one appointed him to maintain contact with me for years, however, or to communicate with other Israelis and foreigners concerned with negotiating an end to this long and bitter saga.

In mid-2007, Ghazi Hamad resigned as spokesperson for the government. Some claim he was forced to step down after drafting a critical article in the Hamas newspaper *Al-Risalah* in late August 2006. His bold op-ed was titled "Have Mercy on Gaza."

> *After the withdrawal from Gaza, we hoped for a bright future. We thought that this year we would reap the fruits of our sacrifices. But*

I ask myself today – why did the occupation return to Gaza? The occupation – wise men and commentators will say – is responsible. I am not defending the occupation, but I want to stop and examine our mistakes, which we are accustomed to blame on others.

Anarchy, wanton killing, land stealing, thuggery... is the occupation responsible for all this? Palestinians should stop espousing conspiracy theories that "limit our thinking." Let's admit we've erred. We didn't succeed in preserving the victory of liberating Gaza. Five hundred people have died in the Strip since the withdrawal, as opposed to three or four Israelis killed by rockets. The reality in Gaza today is one of neglect, sadness, and failure. When someone errs, we are afraid to criticize him, lest we be accused of opposing the resistance. When efforts are made to open the Rafah border crossing in order to ease the humanitarian crisis, someone always fires a rocket on the crossing. When we speak about a truce, someone always fires another rocket...

The land is full of anarchy, corruption, thuggery, and gang killings. Isn't building the homeland part of the resistance? Let's admit our mistakes; let's do some soul searching and place the interest of our people before us. Let us say honestly: We were right here and we erred there. Only then will we see the face of Gaza and of the homeland change.

The article also criticized the kidnapping of foreigners in Gaza, which was becoming a worrisome trend and scaring away international media and diplomatic staff.

In February 2012, fascinated with Ghazi and his ability to go where few Palestinians had gone in publicly calling for Hamas to do some soul searching, I asked if I could interview him. Ghazi agreed.

*   *   *

Q: Who is Ghazi Hamad?
A: I was born in Rafah, in the southern Gaza Strip, in 1964. My parents were born in Yibne [Arabic], which is now called Yavne [Hebrew]; it's near Tel Aviv. My father died when I was seven years old. He spent

about eight months in an Israeli prison. He suffered from leukemia. I was orphaned at a young age.

I studied at the UNRWA[1] elementary and secondary school. After that, I went to Sudan and studied to be a veterinarian. I finished in 1987. Then I returned from Sudan and participated in the First Intifada. I engaged in various activities, such as distributing leaflets, and I took part in demonstrations against Israel.

I joined the Muslim Brotherhood in 1982. When Hamas was established in 1987, I joined the organization and became active in protests against the occupation. I wrote slogans on the wall and participated in other activities. I was arrested by Israel in 1989 and sentenced to five years in prison. I was charged with membership in Hamas and activities like participating in demonstrations, writing slogans, distribution of leaflets, and punishment of drug dealers and collaborators.[2] I served part of my jail sentence in Gaza and in Shata Prison, in the north. I was released in 1994.

Q: Had you met Israelis before?
A: No, never.

Q: In prison, did you meet Israelis? Prison guards?
A: Yes. In prison I became the spokesman for prisoners. I had discussions with the guards. We discussed many issues related to the political situation outside and the situation inside the prison. I think it was then that I started to get more experience with negotiating with Israel. We had some very difficult times in the prison, especially when we declared hunger strikes in order to improve our situation. It was a positive experience, negotiating with Israeli officials.

In prison, I read many books and learned Hebrew and English. I studied politics and learned a lot more about the history of the conflict.

---

1. The United Nations Relief and Works Agency for Palestinian Refugees in the Near East.
2. During the First Intifada, Palestinian combatants from Hamas and Fatah killed drug dealers and other "collaborators with the Israelis." Ghazi Hamad didn't kill anyone.

Q: So it was a good university?

A: I think so, yes. In terms of education it was very good, because inside the prison we had a good program and lots of time. People read the Koran and many books about the history of Palestine. The prisoners taught each other, everyone helped everyone else. I think it was most interesting that we had good contacts with other organizations, like Fatah, Islamic Jihad, and people from the Democratic and Popular Fronts.[3] We met in our cells and had good political discussions. It was very good for establishing positive connections with them. We felt we could work together. I think it was very, very interesting and an example of coexistence between all the Palestinian factions. We created a model for being a state, because we dealt with all kinds of important issues and relationships between the groups.

Q: In 1993, after the Oslo agreement was signed, you were opposed to it, right?

A: Hamas was against the Oslo agreement. We felt this agreement did not answer the demands of the Palestinian people, because it excluded most of the important issues, like refugees, settlements, borders, Jerusalem. Oslo focused on interim issues and on the establishment of the Palestinian Authority.

Q: What happened when you were released from prison, after the beginning of Oslo?

A: I worked for six months as a veterinarian. I had a private clinic. But then I was invited by some of my friends inside Hamas to be the chief editor of the first Hamas newspaper, *Al-Watan*. It was established in 1994 and it was published until 1995. After that I was moved to be the chief editor of *Al-Risalah*, between 1997 until 2006.

Q: In 2006, Hamas won the elections, and you became the spokesperson for the government.

---

3. The Democratic Front for the Liberation of Palestine (DFLP) and the Popular Front for the Liberation of Palestine (PFLP), members of the "rejectionist" camp of the PLO, on the Palestinian political left.

A: Yes. I started working in the Prime Minister's Office. I attended all the cabinet meetings. I attended the meetings between President Abbas and Prime Minister Ismail Haniyeh. I was also the prime minister's special envoy to the Palestinian factions, dealing with the internal issues and conflicts regarding how to control the situation that was erupting between the different Palestinian political movements. This also added to my experience as a negotiator.

Q: On June 23, 2006, Gilad Schalit was abducted from Israel. Six days later, you and I spoke for the first time. You got very involved in the Schalit issue, but it wasn't your job. It wasn't your position. It wasn't your responsibility. Why did you go to such lengths?

A: I heard in the news that a soldier had been kidnapped. The prime minister asked me to convene a press conference. I spoke in three languages – Arabic, English, and Hebrew – and in the name of the Hamas government. I called on the kidnappers to deal with him gently, not to harm him, and to protect him. The Hamas government did not have direct control over these people. They had not informed us of their plan to attack the Kerem Shalom military base. We also called on Israel to behave rationally and try to listen to the captors; to deal positively with their demands. I felt this issue was very, very important. Soon after that, Israel began bombing Gaza. The situation grew harsh, and we needed to find a solution quickly. I heard from the Egyptian delegation in Gaza[4] that it was interested in helping to find a solution. I talked to some contacts in Hamas and told them that we have to start negotiations, but you know Hamas has a policy of not negotiating with Israel directly.

Q: What amazed me, during that first conversation, was that you spoke to me in Hebrew. Do you remember that?

A: Yes, I remember. We worked together to get a letter from Gilad Schalit.

Q: But before the letter, I asked you to get me a video of Gilad, and you

---

4. The Egyptian government opened a representative office in Gaza when the Palestinian Authority was created and Israel withdrew from the populated areas. The office was headed by military personnel led by General Mohammed Ibrahim.

told me that Hamas then demanded that all the women prisoners and minors be released in exchange.

A: Yes, I remember; but Olmert refused.

Q: He declared that Israel wouldn't pay for information on the soldier's condition. After failing to convince Olmert to be flexible on the issue of "payment" for the sign of life, I came to Gaza to meet you for the first time.

A: Yes, yes, I remember. You came to my office in the prime minister's building, and later I met you again in a restaurant.

Q: It was at that meeting in the morning that I suggested a letter, instead of a videotape.

A: Yes. I thought it was a good idea and maybe we could break the deadlock and begin negotiations.

Q: The next day, you called and told me that the letter was on its way and would be delivered to the Egyptian representative office in Gaza, but the letter didn't come. I asked Noam Schalit to write to Khaled Mashal, father to father. His letter was translated into Arabic and sent just before Ramadan 2006. Two days later, you called to say that Gilad's letter had been received by the Egyptians.

A: Yes, that's right.

Q: That was the first letter.

A: That's right. This letter was sent from Gilad, via the Egyptians in Gaza, to his parents.

Q: Did you have contact at that time with Ahmed Jaabri and the Ezzedin al Qassam fighters?

A: No, no. At this point I had contact with some Hamas members connected to the military wing. I talked to them many times, saying that to start serious negotiations we had to do something to send a signal that Schalit was still alive. I heard from you that Israel needed something in order to begin negotiations.

Q: Right.

A: Finally, after a number of weeks, I convinced people to release a letter from Gilad Schalit. After the letter arrived, we started serious negotiations between the Egyptians and the Israeli side.

Q: Right, but before the Egyptian negotiations began, you sent me a list of Hamas demands for Schalit's release. I kept trying to convince Olmert, through his daughter, that negotiations should open through you and me as a secret back channel. Olmert wouldn't go for it. He was still convinced that Schalit could be rescued in a military operation. Soon the Egyptian representatives in Gaza took over and said they would negotiate a deal. But my feeling was that the Mubarak regime didn't really want an agreement. Do you agree?

A: Yes. I think many times the Egyptians said they were ready to help… but sometimes they felt that Hamas' demands were very difficult. They tried to make a breakthrough, but I think at that time the situation did not allow them to make one. Israel did not wish to start negotiations, thinking it could bring the soldier back by a military operation. I think Hamas was also suspicious of the Israeli position. Later Hamas became clearer and more pragmatic.

Q: Why did your side take so long to come up with a list of names?[5]

A: The Hamas leaders wanted to understand the negotiation principles. Israel rejected any talk about the release of prisoners. In the beginning, it was very hard to talk about the demands and the list of names. Israel was always demanding a sign of life, and giving instructions on what we have to do. I think Hamas also rejected all Israel's demands and conditions. I think Israel started to be more flexible and tried to move very, very slowly. Maybe this is what made the process very long, because as I said, at that time Israel asked many times for a sign of life. The Egyptians did not get a clear position or answer from Israel about whether or not it even agreed to conduct negotiations, or about how to find a mechanism

---

5. Hamas sent its first list, 350 names, to the Egyptians only three months after Schalit was abducted.

to make a kind of exchange. I had good contacts with the Egyptians, but at that time I had no direct connection with the military wing of Hamas. It was very hard to get the real information, or to know what the military people in Hamas wanted. You know this was a very secret file.

Q: You and I spoke at least five times during the Olmert period about a secret direct back channel. You seemed to believe that if Olmert agreed to that, you could convince people on your side to agree to it, too. Do you think that's true? Could we have done it then? I remember, in December 2008, I called you after Ofer Dekel had asked me to check whether my friends in Hamas were ready for a secret back channel. You looked into it and said no, they weren't ready.

A: Yes. The policy of Hamas was not to have direct contact with the Israelis. I thought I could convince the leadership for you and me to have contact, because you were not an official. After the events of 2007,[6] I left my position, because I was not satisfied. The fighting between the factions in Gaza was a catastrophe. I was hoping the national unity government[7] would continue to work as normal. I was shocked – all my dreams at that time collapsed, because there was division, confrontation, victims, and many people were killed. I told the prime minister I didn't want to continue as government spokesman, and he accepted this. I worked for him for a while after that.

Later I moved to the other positions in general security in the prime minister's cabinet. Before that, I wrote an article describing the confrontation between Hamas and Fatah in Gaza. It was a horrible situation. I thought that after Israel withdrew from Gaza, we could create a good model of government. I thought we could create coexistence among all the Palestinians of Gaza, and make a good future for our people. I tried to contact all the Palestinian factions in order to find some way to start with deep discussions and dialogue. I wanted Hamas to give

---

6. The Hamas military takeover of Gaza in June 2007.
7. From March 17 to June 17, 2007, the Palestinian factions established a national unity government following the assistance of the Saudis in negotiating the "Mecca Agreement for National Unity." Following the Hamas *coup d'état* in mid-June 2007, President Mahmoud Abbas officially disbanded the unity government.

a new picture for the Palestinians, away from the violence and internal confrontation. But the situation was very bad. It is very hard to create change inside Palestinian society.

Q: So you got a new position in general security, and were in charge of the crossings.
A: Yes, after that I was appointed by the prime minister to head the crossings. I started before the war in Gaza and was responsible for the three crossings, Erez, Kerem Shalom, and Rafah.[8] I spent about two and a half years as head of the crossings.

Q: During this period, did you get to know Ahmed Jaabri?
A: At that time, no, I had no connection with him. I had a connection with him after January 2010, when the German mediator failed in his mission and stopped mediating. Jaabri knew who I was, of course. I tried to contact him in order to convince him to renew the negotiations. From January 2010, there were no continuous talks or negotiations.

You and I spoke many times about how we might resume the negotiations. Hagai Hadas was not serious, and I know you suffered a lot from his refusal to answer you. So at that time I did not succeed in convincing people here that there was any good intention on the Israeli side, that Israel was interested in a compromise.

Q: When David Meidan got the job in April 2011, I contacted him and then you. You started talking to Jaabri. David would give me messages to transfer to you. Israeli security, I know now, was listening to us, tracing both the messages that I sent to you, and that you sent to Jaabri, and those that came back – through you – to me.
A: Yes. Jaabri was interested in reaching an agreement, and he supported me in trying to explore possibilities for moving forward.

---

8. The Erez crossing between Israel and Gaza is used mostly for the movement of people. After Hamas won the elections in 2006, the Erez crossing became quite dormant. Kerem Shalom, where Schalit was abducted, became the primary zone for the transport of goods from Israel into Gaza. The Rafah crossing is the international border and crossing point between Israel and Egypt, and between Gaza and Egypt.

Q: Israeli officials discovered there was a direct line of communication between you and me that was leading to Jaabri on one end and Meidan on the other. Then Netanyahu gave Meidan the green light to make our channel the official one for advancing the negotiations.
A: Yes. Jaabri also gave his green light and encouraged me to continue.

Q: What kind of response were you getting on your side?
A: Look, first of all, people here were very suspicious and doubtful about the seriousness of the Israeli side. But I did not give up, and I started to talk to the people here in Gaza and in Damascus many times. Everything was blocked. There were no talks or negotiations, and time was passing and nothing moved. So when you and I discussed that we could do something, I talked to Jaabri about it. I think at that time he was very, very flexible, and he really encouraged me to continue and understand the Israelis and what they sought. He wanted to understand.

I told him that there was something new, that we could convey messages from one side to the other. I understood that with David Meidan the Israeli side was willing to listen to you, which was totally different from how it was with Ofer Dekel and Hagai Hadas. I felt David was really interested in making a breakthrough. I conveyed these feelings to Jaabri, and told him there was a good opportunity to move forward.

Then we started to talk about principles. I understood that Jaabri was very interested in making a deal, especially after we got some positive signals from your side, especially about sensitive issues like prisoners from Jerusalem, and from 1948,[9] and deportees.[10] I began to have an exchange of ideas with Jaabri. I sat with him many times for many hours, sometimes in the middle of the night. I visited him in many different places.

Q: But he wouldn't agree to negotiations directly through you and me. We proposed that you and I meet, that we go to Turkey, to Egypt, that we would even negotiate via Skype.
A: Jaabri was against direct contact of any kind.

---

9. Referring to Palestinian citizens of Israel in Israeli prisons.
10. Israel insisted that most of the released prisoners be deported abroad or at least to Gaza.

Q: But he gave you a green light to continue talking to me.

A: He knew there was an exchange of ideas, and he agreed because I said you were not an official in the government. But in general he said he was against any direct contacts with Israeli officials.

Q: So you and I started working on a document. It went through many versions, and on July 14 you sent me your version, containing Hamas' conditions for sealing a deal. David took that paper to Netanyahu and got a green light for it. Did you realize then that paper was the breakthrough?

A: I sent you this document following intensive discussions with the people here. From my conversations with the military people – especially Jaabri – I had details about women, about Jerusalem, and 1948, the deportees, and the VIPs. Jaabri made some changes here and there. I told him we were on the verge of a breakthrough, and he really listened to me. I think he was extremely cooperative. He is a strongman, but he is open-minded. He made up his mind that he was on a "holy mission" to release the prisoners. It's not easy to get concessions from him.

Q: The Israelis, too, thought that the document was a breakthrough, because it showed willingness on Hamas' part to compromise, and because, at the top, it bore the word "Final." This was the first time the Israelis thought it was possible to reach an agreement.

A: There is a part of the story that you don't know, and I can't really tell you about.

Q: After I sent the document to the Israeli side, David asked me to have you bring it signed on Hamas stationery. You asked me in reciprocity to bring an official paper saying I was working through an official channel.

A: David wanted to be sure the situation was approved by both sides. You sent me this letter in Hebrew, signed by David. But on my side, as I explained to you, it was very difficult for Hamas to send an official letter to the Israeli side. Jaabri would not sign such a letter; neither would Mashal or any of the other political leaders. I was in a difficult situation, because I had asked you to give me an official letter and you did, but I could not do the same. I had some problems with Jaabri after that.

Q: I know. But what Israel wanted to know was that Jaabri stood behind the content of the letter and would not deny its contents after that. David wanted to agree to enter into intensive, non-stop negotiations in order to conclude the deal. That was the agreement he'd received from Netanyahu. But you had difficulty with Jaabri after that.
A: (*Laughing*) Yes.

Q: He got very angry with you. Why?
A: As I mentioned, from many long discussions for many days and many weeks, I understood what was on Jaabri's mind. I knew what his vision was for the whole deal. I knew what he was willing to accept, all the details. Based on that, I wrote the document. I know it reflected the position of our people. But you know sometimes, maybe because this is part of negotiations, you should not put all the cards on the table. This is what Jaabri thought. I believe in a different philosophy of negotiations, that we have to approach the other side with new cards. You have to begin. I exerted more pressure on people. I talked to some people, big figures, and political leaders of Hamas.

Q: The Israelis, I know, knew that the political leadership of Hamas was behind this paper. They expected problems with Jaabri because, according to Israeli intelligence assessment, he didn't actually want an agreement. The Israeli evaluation was that one of Jaabri's sources of power was holding Gilad, and that to give him up Gilad was, for him, a big risk of loss of power.
A: No, no, no. Jaabri has power. He was highly respected within Hamas before and after Gilad. He had no intention of keeping Gilad forever in order to have power. He believed that when he made this deal, he would succeed in releasing prisoners. Now he has become a real hero in the eyes of Hamas and the Palestinian people, because he succeeded in his mission. He did something big for his people. So he really was interested in a compromise.

Q: But Jaabri didn't like this paper.
A: I can say 99 percent of the document was not rejected by the people in charge.

Q: The political side supported it. But Jaabri had problems with it, and then you had a problem with Jaabri.
A: Jaabri didn't want to send such a document to the other side.

Q: But that's what made the breakthrough. That's what made the negotiations possible.
A: Yes, I know.

Q: Before we started composing the document, I wrote to you that you and I had to see ourselves as a team working together to solve the problems. The Israelis and the Hamas side would negotiate, but our job was to come up with solutions, to – as you said – put all the cards on the table and work together.
A: Yes. I agreed with that. I think we had a great role. We had patience and tried to find creative solutions, especially on the hard issues. I think we succeeded in making progress from time to time because we really tried not to deal with these issues as black or white. We tried to find points in the middle, and to find creative solutions, to continue talking day and night. I think this was the key to the whole process – to have initiatives, and the will to work day and night. It was, for me, really a very, very good experience.

Q: Hamas and Israel have no trust between them, but you and I succeeded because we had trust.
A: Yes. I think that when we tried to convey messages, we understood each other. Both of us believed we had to work on this issue until we reached a positive result. And I think we did it.

Q: My sense was that you and I were not competing in the negotiations; we were cooperating to find the solutions that would enable the two sides to reach an agreement. When, for example, I explained to you the limitations of the Israeli positions, it wasn't as if I was trying to negotiate with you, but rather that I was being honest and explaining to you what was possible.
A: Yes, yes. That's right.

Q: So when it finally happened, and it succeeded, and people knew about your role, what was their response? What did they say to you?

A: While we were working together I had contacts with only one or two leaders, no more than that. At that time most people did not know anything about my role.

Q: But Khaled Mashal knew and Abu Marzouk knew, and of course Jaabri knew as well.
A: Yes, about three people knew about my role. Maybe after the deal, more people started to understand my role in it. I think many people appreciated my role. They spoke in very beautiful words in some high-level meetings. They were very grateful.

I spent five years in prison, so I know what it means to be released. It's a new life, a new future. You get out of the grave to the light and the sun and see the world. The entire time I was dreaming of contributing to this. I feel I did something for the prisoners. It was my duty to help these people. Some were my friends in prison. I know them. I spent a lot of time with them. So I think it is a success story.

Q: I knew that for you the most important thing was to free the Palestinian prisoners, but I always had a sense that you really cared about Gilad. It was more than just the prisoners; there was something human about your concern for him too.
A: Well, Gershon, to be honest, you know, first of all I am Palestinian. I looked at the Israeli soldiers as the enemy for all Palestinians. They came and took my homeland and killed my people and so on. Gilad was a soldier. I talked to Gilad's father, and he told me, "I am a father," and I told him many times, "Okay, I have no problem that your son will be released," but we had at that time about ten thousand Palestinians in the prisons. I said to him that if his son spends five years in captivity, we have some people that spent twenty years, twenty-five years. I felt, honestly, the pain and suffering of my people, because I think it was bigger than my shoulders. I felt I did something for them. As I said, in the eyes of my people, Gilad is a soldier; he's coming here to fight against Palestinians and kill Palestinians. So maybe these are the feelings.

Q: But I'm trying to understand if for you it was something more than just freeing Palestinian prisoners. I'm not denying that you're a

Palestinian nationalist, and that you care deeply about your people, but you got very involved in this, and you didn't have to. You were involved in this emotionally. And my sense was that you also cared about Gilad – not as a soldier, but as a person.

A: Maybe sometimes. I cannot explain to you that. Maybe in the current situation it's not easy to care, because you know now what's going on between the Israelis and Palestinians. It's a hate-filled, continuous confrontation.

Q: I'm talking at the level of you as an individual, as a person. I know you're part of a struggle.

A: But, Gershon, it's not easy for me to separate myself from the whole feelings here, especially after the war in Gaza.

Q: I know, but every person who knows you as an individual says this about you – and it doesn't make you less of a Palestinian nationalist or a loyal member of Hamas – but everyone says there is this human side to Ghazi Hamad that goes beyond politics.

A: Yes. Look, I know I am a human being. I believe it's not easy to keep someone in prison, it's not easy…. Because of this I insisted on participating, and I started to talk to people about how we needed a new policy, a new vision and a new proposal. I had just a very, very small part…because you know some people before that, like Dr. Mahmoud al-Zahar, spent a very long time with the German mediator, and other people spent a very, very long time, and I appreciate their roles.

Q: But you played a very big role, Ghazi, even bigger than al-Zahar, with all due respect.

A: Yeah, I know I did something, that's right, but as I said, it's a kind of accumulation.

Q: You know, one thing I don't understand – maybe you can explain to me: Your people, your side, Hamas, Gaza, paid a very heavy price for Schalit. You got 1,027 prisoners released, but more than three thousand people were killed in the five years Gilad Schalit was in Gaza. Do people talk about that at all, about the heavy price that was paid?

A: Look, I think this issue was discussed many times from different angles here and there. Some people blamed Hamas. Some people appreciated that Hamas held the soldier for such a long time and kept him away from the eyes of Israeli intelligence. Some people appreciated Hamas because it was fighting for such a holy issue, which is very, very important for all Palestinians. Yes, we know – we paid a heavy price. Most Palestinians in the West Bank and Gaza appreciate Hamas for releasing more than one thousand people from prison. This was really a success story. The attacks from Israel, the siege, blockade, victims, demolition, and destroying of government buildings were very hard for us. Really, it was a very heavy price, that's right, but we were sure that what we did was right and we have to continue to do this until we release the prisoners.

Q: So even now, if you can, you will kidnap more soldiers?
A: The question is not like that. It is very painful for the Palestinians to see that there are still six thousand prisoners. You know this is the most painful issue, that a woman is waiting for her husband – or son – for twenty years.

Q: So you know what I say, Ghazi: Make peace, and all the prisoners will be freed.
A: According to our experience, I think Israel until now is not interested in this. If the Israelis really want to make peace, to avoid confrontation, and to have a kind of stability in this region, for me I think it is very easy, not very complicated. We, the Palestinians, we have some dream to build our state, this small state in the West Bank and Gaza and Jerusalem. But, as you know, Fatah and Israel spent about twenty years in negotiations, and the situation became very complicated. We are still under occupation, we have no borders, we have no sovereignty, and we have nothing. I think Israel has to end the occupation over us and get out. After that you can talk about peace. You can talk about peace initiatives, but every day Israel is making more checkpoints, more settlements, more pressure against our people, and this will not create peace.

Q: Did the positive outcome of the prisoner-exchange negotiations open the door to more contacts, to positive movement between Israel and Hamas? Do you think there is a chance for something?

A: According to my knowledge, Hamas is still far from this. The Hamas leaders still believe that negotiation with Israel will lead to nothing. They still believe Israel is interested in keeping the land and imposing its power over the Palestinian people. I think there is no trust, no confidence. I think the situation on the ground makes it more complicated and worse.

*   *   *

I have known Ghazi Hamad for seven years. We have spoken so many times. We are still in contact. I really wanted Ghazi to say something from his heart, sincere and genuine, regarding his feelings for Gilad Schalit, who was all of nineteen when he was captured. I tried to get Ghazi to say it in this interview; I knew it would be difficult for him to express it, knowing it would be widely publicized. Ghazi Hamad is, after all, a political personality in Hamas.

I am quite sure that if Ghazi were a much more senior leader in Hamas, he would move toward eventually recognizing Israel and peace. He remains quite critical of his own movement, but has learned from the past not to go public with all his criticisms. He has political ambitions, yet when I asked him about them all he said was, "It is all in the hands of Allah."

I do hope Ghazi will advance and continue to gain more public support and authority. Without him, Gilad Schalit would never have been released. In my opinion, the State of Israel and the Schalit family owe him a debt of gratitude and recognition. Unfortunately, they have not found a way to thank him. From these pages I am doing it in their name. Thank you, Ghazi.

Chapter 19:

Looking Forward, Lessons Learned

On October 19, 2011, the day after Gilad came home very early in the morning, David called to ask how I felt.

"Mission accomplished," I said. I told him I appreciated the role he played and his confidence in me.

I considered adding something about the wasted years. About how this could have been done a long time ago, and five years of a young man's life need not have gone to waste. During these past many months, however, David had kept saying we needed to look forward, so I didn't bring it up. But he did.

"The establishment should have listened to you years ago," he said.

It felt so good to hear those words. It was exactly what I had been dragging around with me for years. This deal could have been completed a long time ago. It distresses me to think about that, to contemplate all the time that Gilad had wasted away underground in Gaza. The long years of suffering that he, his family, and the entire nation had endured could have been reduced. I remain convinced that the same deal could have been reached just six months after his abduction, and maybe even earlier. What was lacking was the leadership necessary to make a bold decision. Perhaps the powers that be were initially focused on the military options. Had there been a military option with minimal risks, that would have been the best possibility of bringing Gilad home. It would have enabled the soldier to be rescued without negotiating with terrorists or giving in to their blackmail. But this was not possible. While considering a military option, sincere efforts should have been made to explore the negotiating option, as well. This wasn't done during the first months of Schalit's captivity.

The deal was eventually made possible by a fortuitous alignment of conditions that eventually created a moment of irresistible opportunity. The Arab Spring that began in Tunisia and spread to Egypt and then to the rest of the region changed the conditions on the ground. The most significant of these were, on the one hand, the fall of the Mubarak regime in Egypt, and, on the other, the Assad regime's do-or-die reaction to the uprising in Syria, sparking a bloody civil war between the Alawite elite and the Sunni majority, of which Palestinian refugees are a part. The revolution in Egypt enabled the emerging leadership there to offer Hamas refuge from an increasingly insecure Syria. This provided the Egyptians with a great deal of leverage in dealing with Hamas. They understood that the first prerequisite for any move toward normalcy in Gaza was ending the Schalit saga. They now had new tools and the political will to use them.

On the Israeli side, the social justice uprising in the summer of 2011 put considerable pressure on Netanyahu to restore public support. While not a primary element of the prime minister's decision to complete the deal with Hamas (he had already given Meidan the mandate to free Schalit in April of that year), the assessment that bringing Schalit home would increase his popularity was, I believe, a relevant factor. That said, the anticipated public support for the Schalit deal couldn't have been *that* central to the prime minister's decision making because, as David Meidan told me, it far exceeded Netanyahu's expectations.

In the past, Israel's security community had voiced strong reservations about any deal with Hamas that would free one thousand Palestinian prisoners. The recent replacement of all three security chiefs – the IDF chief of staff, the head of the Mossad, and the head of the ISA – enabled the defense establishment to re-evaluate the positions held by their predecessors, which might have sounded good on paper but could only interfere with reaching a deal.

The Schalit family campaign successfully rallied public opinion behind a prisoner exchange. Everything had an impact: the tent in front of the prime minister's house, the demonstrations around the country, the bumper stickers, the yellow ribbons, the posters and Facebook profiles bearing the image of our captured soldier. Daily radio and television programs sometimes closed with the number of days Gilad had spent in captivity. Major Israeli singers dedicated songs to Schalit, such as Shlomo Artzi's "King of the World" or Aviv Geffen's "The Son of Us All." Gilad's face had become a specter haunting the country. His enduring captivity in hostile territory, just a ninety-minute drive from Israel's nerve center, shamed the country's leadership.

Sara Netanyahu, the prime minister's wife, was also influenced by the campaign. Gilad's last Passover in captivity was marked by a large public Seder at the Schalit tent, making it very uncomfortable for the Netanyahu family, a few yards away in the official residence, to hold its own Seder. On Gilad's birthday, August 28, the Schalits chained themselves to a fence in front of the prime minister's home, shocking the nation. There was growing concern among decision makers that the window of opportunity to bring Gilad home could close, as it had with Ron Arad in 1982. Enough key people feared Schalit could become another Arad, whose disappearance is viewed as a state failure.

Prime Minister Netanyahu deserves praise for bringing Schalit home. Against his principles of not negotiating with terrorists or freeing prisoners in a deal like this one, he weighed the significance of a single soldier. Netanyahu had written the book on terrorism, exhorting leaders and civilians worldwide not to capitulate to it. But there was a conflicting value on the other side of the scale: the unwritten covenant between the State of Israel and its soldiers that nobody is left behind. The prime minister decided against his personal principles in order to bring Gilad home. This was true leadership. Two days before Gilad's release, I sent him the following letter:

October 16, 2011

Dear Prime Minister Netanyahu,

I want to praise you for the demonstration of courage and leadership that you showed in your decision to support the secret back channel that I ran with Hamas people. In my first conversation with David Meidan, he told me he agreed to take the job when he heard from you that despite your principled objection to a prisoner exchange, to negotiations with terrorists, and to releasing murderers, you said there was no other way to bring Gilad home and the time had come to do so. Real leadership is measured by coping with situations in which there is an obligation to weigh opposing values and decide between them, making the hardest decisions. Mr. Prime Minister, you have proven your leadership.

You must know I am not among your political supporters, yet I very much appreciate the support you gave David Meidan and his team, and of course the trust you placed in me during these past months.

May we never be forced to deal with situations like this in the future. Now we must dedicate all our efforts to advancing real peace with our neighbors.

Once again, I praise you and the government of Israel for the holiday joy you have brought to all the people of Israel this Sukkot.

Sincerely,
Gershon Baskin

Netanyahu sent me a brief letter of thanks. Its brevity, I think, indicates the difficulty of the establishment in admitting that an outsider had accomplished what its officials could not.

October 26, 2011

Dear Gershon,

I would like to once again thank you for taking part and helping the negotiating team free the soldier Gilad Schalit. Very few people know of your role and contribution to advancing the deal. In the name of the government of Israel, and in my name, I thank you for the time and effort you devoted to this important cause.

    I wish you success in the future.

Sincerely,
Benjamin Netanyahu

Letter of thanks from Prime Minister Benjamin Netanyahu

Perhaps the people of Israel would not have accepted the deal had Gilad's captivity not dragged on for more than five years. Some 80 percent of Israelis supported the government decision to exchange 1,027 Palestinian prisoners (twenty-seven women prisoners, mistakenly omitted from the list, were added in the final round of negotiations) for one soldier. Perhaps the nation needed that time to accept a deal that was so painful for so many Israeli families, like the Nuriels. There is no knowing.

It was quite significant that the heads of the military and security branches were all in favor of the deal. Once they were on board, most government ministers backed the deal, as did the public. The security question was paramount in the negotiations; the deal took the risks into account and minimized them to what the security heads thought could be contained. Those Palestinian prisoners deemed most dangerous were deported abroad and placed under the watchful eye of the local intelligence services, to which they must report regularly. The second most dangerous group of prisoners was sent to Gaza instead of back home to the West Bank, where the chances of their mobilizing and attacking Israel are limited. The remaining prisoners, sent to their homes in the West Bank, are required to check in regularly at local Palestinian police stations. There is full cooperation between the Israeli and the Palestinian security forces on this and other matters.

Between October 2011 and April 2013, fourteen prisoners were re-imprisoned by Israel, all for violating their parole obligations, including not reporting to Palestinian police stations or leaving their designated areas.

The main question that remains regarding the prisoner exchange is why it took so long. The primary problem seemed to have been that Hamas wouldn't significantly reduce their demands, and that the Israeli prime ministers wouldn't accept them. Only once the Israeli prime minister decided the time had come to bring Gilad home, was the deal made possible.

During the five years and four months, the public largely remained passive – save the popular activism to free Gilad that grew toward the end. There appeared to be no demand from the public, the media, or the politicians for accountability. Everyone seemed to accept the conventional wisdom that discussing the issue would only raise the price of Schalit's freedom.

It might be worth mentioning, as a matter of historical record, that this was ultimately not the case. The initial price tag I received some time after the abduction was 1,500 prisoners (though there were indications that Hamas was prepared to accept roughly 1,000); the final deal was 1,027.[1]

Israel has a very aggressive press, which is typically a good watch-dog against corruption and government abuses. On the issue of Schalit, however, the media behaved more like a puppy, wagging its tail in agreement with government policy.

If, God forbid, we ever face a similar situation, I hope that things will be different. The public should insist on government action. The appointed mediators must be more accountable to the government. The media must ask hard questions – and demand answers.

Is there anyone to speak to on the other side? I'm often asked this question, and my answer is complicated. Hamas still refuses to have direct contact or dialogue with Israeli officials or even NGO representatives. It doesn't accept the Quartet conditions[2] of recognizing Israel, adhering to the Oslo agreements, and renouncing violence. Yet changes are taking place within the Hamas movement, and these should be recognized.

Key Hamas leaders have stated that their political goal is to establish a Palestinian state within the 1967 borders, rather than what the Hamas charter demands: a Palestinian state from the Jordan River to the Mediterranean – i.e., in place of Israel. They do not, however, speak about peace with Israel, nor do they recognize the state that will exist on the other side of their borders, should they achieve their goals. To some, this sounds like a more pragmatic Hamas; to others, it's simply a plan to liberate Palestine in stages. Khaled Mashal is a good example of such

---

1. One could correctly argue that the price is not solely a matter of how many prisoners are released. It also involves *who* is released, and what happens to him afterward.
2. Conditions set out by the UN, EU, USA, and Russia for the recognition of a Palestinian government.

a leader. He generally speaks about a Palestinian state within the 1967 borders, yet when he visited Gaza for the first time, in December 2012, he told a sea of supporters at an open-air rally, the highlight of his three-day stay in Gaza, "Palestine is ours from the river to the sea and from the south to the north. There will be no concession on an inch of the land." The same Hamas leaders have spoken about focusing on non-violent popular resistance even though, when probed, they don't renounce violence, and state that armed struggle remains part of their legitimate means. Nonetheless, the emphasis today is on non-violent resistance. Some Hamas leaders have clearly weighed the steep price they have paid for launching rockets against Israel and the consequent pressure by Palestinian President Abbas on them to put down their arms. Hamas, in Gaza, has occasionally enforced cease-fire understandings and has even established a special force aimed at preventing rocket fire against Israel by other militias. This is not insignificant.

In April 2013, Mashal was re-elected head of the Hamas politburo. He has demanded Hamas' integration into the Palestine Liberation Organization. If this were to happen, Hamas would find itself in the position of having to accept both past agreements which the PLO has signed with Israel, and the organization's right to conduct future negotiations with the Jewish state – unless, that is, Hamas plans a complete takeover of the PLO (just as it had taken over Gaza).

In February 2012, less than four months after the completion of the deal, Hamas – through me – requested Israel's assistance in providing emergency medical care for the brother-in-law of Hamas Prime Minister Ismail Haniyeh. Haniyeh's wife's brother was dying of advanced cancer and couldn't receive the necessary care in Gaza. Ghazi Hamad asked me to see if he could be treated in an Israeli hospital. I immediately spoke with David Meidan, who contacted General Eitan Dangot, coordinator of Israeli government affairs in the territories. It took thirty hours, but Israel agreed. Unfortunately, half an hour before receiving the go-ahead to come to Israel for treatment, the patient died. This incident, while without a happy end, demonstrates change on both sides.

Has the release of 1,027 Palestinian prisoners increased the determination of Hamas and other Palestinian groups to abduct more Israeli soldiers? The festivities surrounding the prisoner exchange in Gaza

and the West Bank raised support for Hamas throu
ian community. The joyous homecoming of the first
broadcast live on Arabic satellite stations around
leaders, especially those directly connected to the
the heroes of Palestine. Green Hamas flags flew high
welcome home the prisoners. The speeches accompanying the release
emphasized that Hamas would abduct more Israeli soldiers until the
last Palestinian prisoner was released.

In the five years and four months that Gilad Schalit was captive
in Gaza, some three thousand Palestinians there lost their lives. The
Gazan economy was destroyed. The city was under siege, its infrastructure demolished. The international community strengthened its resolve
not to deal with Hamas directly until Schalit was free. The price paid for
Schalit's captivity was extremely high. Perhaps this is why, despite declarations that Hamas will continue abducting Israeli soldiers, instructions
have been issued not to do so.

Schalit was kidnapped by rogue organizations that at the last
moment brought Ahmed Jaabri and Ezzedin al Qassam into the picture.
There had been no official decision of Hamas leadership or the Shura
Council to abduct an Israeli soldier or even to attack the Kerem Shalom army base. Despite the attempts of some leaders – such as Prime
Minister Haniyeh – to separate themselves from the abductors, Hamas'
political leadership had to bear responsibility for the actions of these
rogue militias. Ultimately, powerbrokers and poor Gazans alike paid a
very high price for an abduction not of their choosing. This point has
not been emphasized enough by Palestinians, Israelis, or other parties.

Trust, trust, and more trust. For five years, I heard from both
sides that no trust existed, which makes negotiations virtually impossible. When trust is absent, there is little reason to compromise, the
basic premise being that the other side will accept the concession and
demand more without giving up anything of its own.

The key to the secret back channel was the trust that had developed between Ghazi Hamad and myself, based on hundreds of hours of
communications focused on the prisoner exchange. During those years,
we had ample opportunity to demonstrate our humanity and fellow feeling. I detected quite early that Ghazi truly cared about Schalit's welfare,

...at his sincerity transcended politics and conflict. While I expressed genuine empathy with the suffering of the Palestinian people, more than once Ghazi expressed sorrow over the killing of innocent Israelis. Several times he simply said, "Gershon, you are a good friend." Our many conversations over the years – about family, values, life – allowed us to get past the natural suspicion between enemies.

The bridges of human contact built in inhuman circumstances, the humanity expressed in the face of blind hatred, were the foundations of trust that enabled us to become a model of "co-mediation," or "binational stakeholder mediation." Rather than representing our respective sides, we were joint problem-solvers, capable of understanding the difficulties and limitations of the other side. We went beyond being negotiators.

When the breakthrough was finally made in mid-July 2011, Ghazi came under attack from Ahmed Jaabri. Ghazi had disclosed Jaabri's negotiating cards, and had made him angry. For weeks, Jaabri refused to speak to Ghazi. I didn't envy him. In the end, Ghazi's decision to show the cards and stand behind the July 14 document enabled the closing of the deal. Jaabri became a hero to the Palestinian people, and ended up thanking Ghazi for his role, as did the entire Hamas leadership.

The deal would not have been made without Israel's key negotiator having the confidence, knowledge, and ability to make tough decisions. David Meidan opened the door for negotiations because he identified the opportunity I had laid at his doorstep, and had the confidence to seize it. He had the experience to know that if the opportunity proved useful, he could convince the decision makers to let him move forward. He had the strength and reputation to stand up to skeptics within the security establishment, who told him not to waste his time with a "leftist peacenik" as a go-between with Hamas. He understood that a direct link to Hamas, though against Israeli government doctrine, was the fastest and most efficient route to conducting these difficult negotiations.

Over the years, David said, it had taken weeks, even months, to get responses from Hamas. "From the beginning of our contact, I was suddenly getting answers from Jaabri within an hour. When we checked the information, we understood that we had a direct line of contact with the people holding Schalit," he told me. David's ability to think outside the box, and to stay the course against the tide of senior officials from his own security community, is a credit to his foresight.

When the final round of negotiations took place in Cairo, David and another member of the team clashed over how many prisoners should be allowed to return to the West Bank. Part of the security establishment had come up with a maximum number, a "red line." In the end, the negotiations hinged on crossing that line and adding fifteen people. Jaabri wouldn't budge; he wouldn't make further concessions. At this point, the negotiations could have failed, and Schalit might very well have remained in captivity for many more months or years. In the moment of truth, David took responsibility and agreed to Jaabri's demands.

David said that there were two calculations behind his bold decision: One, that the security situation at the time was calm, with high-level coordination and cooperation between the Israeli security apparatus and the Palestinian Authority. Moreover, he recognized the fact that Hamas was capable of enforcing a cease-fire in Gaza. This context was quite different from the prisoner exchange negotiated with Ahmed Jibril's Popular Front for the Liberation of Palestine in 1985, which helped launch the First Intifada. Two, that if the release of fifteen additional Palestinian prisoners in the West Bank threatened Israel's security, then the State of Israel was in such bad shape that their release wouldn't make a difference. David understood that the West Bank security forces were quite effective in preventing terrorism, and that cooperation between the PA and Israel would enable all released prisoners to be monitored. On this basis, Meidan took responsibility.

As long as there are Palestinians in Israeli prisons and the conflict continues to breed hatred, there will be Palestinians who believe that the only way to free those prisoners is by abducting Israelis – civilians or soldiers. The incentives still exist. Most Palestinians perceive that Israel is not generous about releasing prisoners. Since the beginning of the Oslo peace process in 1993, President Abbas has been asking Israel to release over one hundred veteran prisoners. When Israel did release some as a confidence-building measure, they were either nearing the end of their sentences or were common criminals – not political or security prisoners.

It would be wise for Israel to announce that when it does reach a real and comprehensive peace agreement with the Palestinians, Israel all Palestinians in its jails. That is what's done when peace [this] release will be part of a reconciliation process that will [...]edly be painful, but necessary to ensure that the peace be more th[...] agreement on paper.

And how is Gilad?

I visited the Schalits almost one month after Gilad's release. He was pale, weak, unresponsive, and definitely looked like he was suffering from post-traumatic stress. He had gained some weight but remained in a bad physical state. He hadn't seen the light of day for nearly two thousand days. The most dramatic effect of lack of exposure to the sun is vitamin D deficiency, which can be the cause of clinical depression. Imagine the effect of more than five years of this deficiency. Gilad's depression caused a loss of appetite. He apparently didn't eat very much in his last two months in captivity. His captors tried to force him to eat, without much success. Someone on the Hamas side said that, had he been in captivity another two months, he probably would have died. His captors must have been aware of his situation, which may have influenced them to conclude the deal. He was worth a lot more alive than dead.

In April 2012, having heard from David that Gilad was feeling much better, I invited him to join me for lunch. When I had seen him in November 2011, he'd known nothing about me or my role. Even his parents were not fully aware of my involvement in bringing him home. By April, however, David had fully briefed him about my activities, at least during his last six months of captivity.

Gilad, my wife, and I went to an outdoor restaurant in Tel Aviv. Gilad is now one of the most famous people in Israel, so he wore sunglasses and looked down to avoid recognition. Reserved by nature, Gilad is very modest and uncomfortable with his newfound fame.

We chose a table at the edge of the restaurant's garden and had Gilad sit with his back to the crowd. But his sunglasses scarcely obscured his identity. Passersby waved to him, thrilled to see him. Several approached to say hello. Two people took his picture, and one Knesset member came by to talk to him. It was a pleasure to see him eat, although it was difficult for him to decide what he wanted. We ordered one dessert for the three of us. What a delight to see him enjoy the cake!

I felt a special joy throughout the meal, as well as the satisfaction of having had something to do with the fact that Gilad was alive and eating lunch in Tel Aviv. I remain grateful that life afforded me the opportunity to help bring him home.

Gilad told us a little about his captivity, and we didn't probe much. What I know comes from him, his parents, and David.

Gilad spent most of the time in three different locations, although he was moved around for shorter periods. He was underground the whole time and mostly treated well. He had ample food – fresh fruits and vegetables as well as meat. He ate many meals with his captors. There was always someone who spoke either English or Hebrew. He didn't really learn to speak Arabic, but he understands it. For at least the last three and a half years, he had a television and radio. On TV he watched primarily Arab sports programs with his captors. It was a way of passing the time without fear of entering into political arguments that could too easily anger them. On the radio, he listened to at least two Hebrew-speaking channels. He knew of the efforts being made on his behalf. He heard the daily count of how many days he had been in captivity. He heard his parents interviewed. He knew about the public campaign, the tent in front of the prime minister's house, and the demonstrations. This information was encouraging but also depressing, because nothing seemed to come of it.

Gilad's captors gave him five books – four on mathematics and physics, and one (in English) about Islam. They told him that if he became a Muslim, he could marry a girl from Gaza and go free.

About ten days before his release, Gilad was informed that serious negotiations were taking place and that the parties were on the verge of an agreement. Once the deal was made, he was informed that he would be going home in a week.

When Gilad was transported to the Rafah crossing between Gaza and Egypt, Hamas deployed a convoy of fifty identical vehicles, so the IDF wouldn't be able to swoop down and pull him out without implementing the prisoner exchange. Gilad actually wasn't in any of those vehicles. He was brought to Rafah by Ahmed Jaabri himself via a different route.

Today, Gilad doesn't seem bitter, depressed, or hateful. He is taking advantage of his freedom and doing what he enjoys – playing and watching sports, spending time with family and friends, traveling, hiking, and bike riding. He joined Facebook but has a private profile – featuring pictures of everything from the world's top sporting events to the beautiful scenery of New Zealand – so he can add friends but cannot be directly approached. He now has a smart phone filled with applications and has caught up on the latest technology.

It's unclear where he stands politically or whether he thinks about political matters relevant to his own story. I offered to take him around East Jerusalem. He thought that for now it wouldn't be a good idea to walk around Palestinian areas. He was probably right.

We remain in contact – phoning, texting, occasionally visiting. We're also Facebook friends and continuously "like" statuses on each other's pages. It's a miracle that after five years and four months in captivity he is so strong, so genuinely positive.

Gilad has a passion for athletics and is building a career for himself as a sportswriter. He's gone to the US to cover the NBA (the National Basketball Association). He has also toured the globe and been hosted throughout the Jewish world. It's almost as if he were seeking to sit in all those empty chairs designated for him in Jewish homes during his captivity. Gilad recently returned from two months on the road in Australia and New Zealand. He was back in Israel for a short time, then off again.

For all intents and purposes, Gilad Schalit is catching up on life.

Epilogue

Everyone who meets Gilad Schalit is overwhelmed by how healthy he is in body and spirit. "Simply amazing" is the response I've heard from so many people who've spent time with him. One might expect that after so many years in captivity he would be filled with rage. He's not. He's really focused on looking forward, enjoying life, and making up for lost time.

Gilad has been instructed by the army and by psychologists not to talk about what he went through, not to give interviews, write a book, or spend time recalling those years. The psychologists and other former military prisoners have advised him that he'll have time for that in a few years. Now it's important for his sanity and well-being to focus on the present and future, not on the past. Just live, they told him.

Nonetheless, pieces of information come out in conversation, and he has shared some of his experiences with me. I've also gleaned interesting details from Israeli officials and Hamas people. Much of what Gilad went through remains unknown, and I assume someday he'll feel more comfortable talking about it. I would never think of asking him the many questions I have. Some information I won't share; it's private.

Gilad's good state of mind suggests that he wasn't mistreated in captivity. His captors knew his value and kept him relatively healthy, feeding him as much as he was willing and able to eat. He did spend a lot of time alone and had to occupy himself during many long hours. Gilad developed a strict regimen of daily physical and mental exercise. He worked on math problems, played with numbers, recalled past experiences. He drew a map of his village, Mitzpe Hila, and added details to each home, such as the names of those living there. He didn't sleep during the day, in order to sleep through the night.

For much of the time, Gilad was behind bars in underground rooms fitted to serve as a prison. I had thought it curious when he said in his audio and videotaped messages that he was "in jail," not "in captivity." I didn't give it much thought then, but it turns out he really was in a kind of jail. He used the bars for exercising.

Food seems to have been an issue. Apparently Gilad has never been a big eater. The few times I've eaten with him, he has stuck to the same limited menu. His captors provided fresh fruits and vegetables, meat, and other cooked foods, but much of the time he preferred canned goods and other products. He ate a lot of humus made in Israel. From time to time, usually during Muslim holidays, the captors received food from Gaza hotels, which they shared with Gilad. Nonetheless, he came home severely malnourished. He didn't eat much in his last four to six weeks in captivity.

Interestingly, Gilad's captors were also "prisoners." The youngest, about his age, was underground with him for more than four years. His family didn't know what happened to him. They thought he'd been killed. Tight security had to be maintained at all times, so Gilad and his fellow captors had no contact with the outside world, excepting the few Hamas commanders who were their direct superiors. I understand that Jaabri, whose forces were behind the abduction, visited occasionally. Gilad didn't know who Jaabri was and doesn't recall ever speaking to him. The captors themselves, I was told by somebody who had met one, were afraid of Jaabri. They were under extremely strict discipline and constantly under his watchful eye. Because of the tight security, once they took the assignment, there was no way out. They were held captive as long as Gilad himself.

When Gilad was freed, he wasn't allowed to take with him the papers on which he'd drawn (including his picture of Mitzpe Hila) or done math problems. I kept asking Ghazi to get those papers from Jaabri. I once even called him with Gilad in my car and told him that Gilad was with me and wanted his papers back. Ghazi promised to try. A few days before Israel assassinated Jaabri, Ghazi told me that the Hamas commander had agreed to give the papers back. That never happened.

About a month after the first phase of the prisoner exchange was completed, Ghazi and I began discussing a long-term cease-fire. He said the Hamas leadership was interested in a long-term arrangement that would prevent escalation. We began speaking about the principles for such an agreement.

I informed several Israeli officials in very senior positions that my talks with Hamas were now focused on a cease-fire deal. I was encouraged to continue and, when I had something concrete, I was requested to present it. I regularly reported to Israeli officials.

Israel and Gaza had entered into a dangerous pattern of periods of calm followed by days of rocket fire. When the cease-fire, or *tahdiyah*, broke down, it was generally because Israel took preemptive action – based on intelligence information – against cells organizing in Gaza to attack the country. These preemptive strikes usually killed combatants from Palestinian-Islamic militias other than Hamas, which would then shoot rockets and mortars into Israel, with the larger Popular Resistance Committees and Islamic Jihad using their firepower to intensify the situation. Hamas, for the most part, neither joined the fighting nor prevented it, until the number of casualties in the Israeli Air Force attacks increased. Then Ghazi would ask me to inform Israeli officials that Hamas wasn't interested in an escalation and wanted a cease-fire. This was the cycle in the months following Schalit's release.

I drafted a proposal for a long-term cease-fire. Actually, I drafted two agreements, one between Israel and Egypt and another between Hamas and Egypt. The agreements were parallel and set the same terms for the cease-fire, with fail-safe clauses in case of time-bomb situations or violations. Another clause included a mechanism for Israel to relay information – via Egyptian intelligence – to Hamas, which would be required to act on it in order to prevent attacks against Israel. If no action was taken within a designated time-frame, Israel would be permitted to neutralize the security threat without being considered in breach of the agreement.

My proposal went through four drafts, each incorporating minor changes based on consultations with Ghazi on one side and Israeli officials on the other. I presented the drafts to senior UN officials and senior Egyptian intelligence officers. I also met with President Abbas to ask him if an Israeli-Hamas cease-fire was in his interest as the president of the Palestinian Authority and chairman of the PLO. Abbas responded that it definitely served his interests, because he couldn't negotiate with Israel on behalf of the Palestinian people if Gaza was constantly under Israeli attack. The best way to prevent that was a formal cease-fire arrangement.

On May 1, 2012, I presented Israeli Defense Minister Ehud Barak with the proposed agreements. Barak was skeptical about Hamas' upholding a cease-fire. Nonetheless, he formed a study committee composed of officers from the IDF planning department, the Southern Command (responsible for Gaza), and military intelligence. There were also representatives of the Prime Minister's Office, the Foreign Ministry, and the ISA.

About two months later, Israel decided against formal arrangements with Hamas. Three main opinions were voiced by the committee:

One opinion was that Israel would eventually have to go into Gaza and bring down Hamas by force. This option was militarily feasible, but the cost would be Israel's reoccupation of Gaza. Israel would once again be responsible for 1.6 million Gazans, who refuse to live under Israeli occupation.

Another opinion stated what I myself believe; that there were significant pragmatic elements in Hamas whose power was on the rise and who must be strengthened. Among these elements were Khaled Mashal, Ismail Haniyeh, Ghazi Hamad, and Ahmed Jaabri (the latter clearly supported a long-term cease-fire with Israel). I believed these officials should at least be given a chance to prove their ability and political will to honor a long-term cease-fire.

The majority opinion contended that Israel shouldn't strike deals with Hamas, because doing so only strengthened it. Israel should do one thing only: build deterrence. Hamas had to be made so afraid of attacking Israel that it would think twice before launching rockets, and would use all its power and control to prevent others from doing so.

My response to this is that deterrence is a very nice concept, but not an exact science. How many people have to be killed to build deterrence? How many homes destroyed? How much infrastructure must be demolished?

Without a positive Israeli response to the cease-fire proposal, Ghazi couldn't push forward on his side, despite the initial support he was receiving.

By October, Israel and Gaza had been through repeated rounds of violence. The periods between cease-fires were getting shorter, and the intensity of the rocket fire increased. Hamas could no longer sit on the sidelines. It joined the fire in the last rounds.

Lest the situation get out of hand once again, I phoned Ghazi and suggested that we renew our efforts to achieve a long-term arrangement. He agreed. In each previous round of violence, Ghazi and I spent hours on the phone transmitting messages between the sides, trying to prevent further escalation and loss of life. This time, Ghazi proposed that he draft a text based on our many conversations, and present it to the people in Gaza and the Hamas leadership in Cairo and the Persian Gulf. I reported on his progress to senior officials in the IDF, the Prime Minister's Office, and the Foreign Ministry.

I also met with General Nader El-A'aser in Cairo about our cease-fire proposal. (I had been in constant contact with Nader, who played a key role in renewing the calm after each round of violence.) I returned to Israel on the morning of November 12, when a rocket from Gaza hit Israel. I immediately spoke with Ghazi and Nader, who said that Hamas was taking care of the situation on the ground in an attempt to prevent escalation.

On November 14, Ghazi informed me that Mashal, Abu Marzouk, and other leaders in and out of Gaza had approved the cease-fire agreement. He told me he would see Jaabri that morning. He knew Jaabri supported it as well. He said he would send me the draft after seeing Jaabri.

I called and texted senior officials in the IDF, the Prime Minister's Office, the foreign minister, and defense minister, saying I would receive

Hamas' proposal for a long-term cease-fire later in the day. That after-noon, while I was participating in a conference of the Israeli-Palestinian Peace NGO Forum at the Intercontinental Hotel in Jericho, the Israeli Air Force assassinated Ahmed Jaabri. That was the beginning of Opera-tion Pillar of Defense, Israel's war on Gaza in 2012.

I am convinced that the assassination of Jaabri was a strategic error. It reflects precisely the thinking of the majority opinion in the committee: If Israel takes out the most powerful man in Gaza, the head of Hamas' army, everyone will know that no one has impunity; Israel can get anyone, anytime, and this – together with blowing up warehouses of longer-range rockets – will create deterrence. The problem is that after eight days of aerial bombardment, with more than 1,500 sorties dropping hundreds of tons of explosives on Gaza, the leaders of Hamas and Islamic Jihad came out of their bunkers virtually unscathed and declared victory.

I do not believe Israel was successful in creating deterrence. Time will tell if this assertion is correct. I believe Hamas stopped shooting and is adhering to a cease-fire for the time being because it perceives it in its interests to do so (as it did even before Pillar of Defense). But the pragmatic camp within Hamas was temporarily weakened by Jaabri's assassination, and my relationship with Ghazi was damaged.

Hamas has completed its politburo elections. Key pragmatic per-sonalities like Mashal came out on top, while more extreme leaders such as Mahmoud al-Zahar were pushed out. Perhaps this is a positive sign.

Egyptian intelligence, backed by President Mohammed Morsi, played a key role in working out cease-fire arrangements after Pillar of Defense. The Egyptian role in negotiations has been strengthened, as Egypt continues to try and end the remaining vestiges of the Israeli siege on Gaza. Egypt is also sealing the tunnels into Gaza and trying to cope with the huge weapons smuggling business that has developed in Sinai and endangers its own security.

There are no direct talks between Israel and Hamas, as of now. The Egyptian negotiations are between Egypt and Israel, and between Hamas and Egypt – the very model I had proposed.

Major gaps remain between the two Palestinian movements, and no real unity seems to be on the horizon. Following President Barack Obama's visit to Israel and Palestine in March 2013, there have been renewed efforts to launch Israeli-Palestinian negotiations. Few people think they'll succeed.

I remain optimistic. I believe Israeli-Palestinian peace is possible. This conflict is solvable. I also believe negotiations can succeed only via a secret direct back channel.

So I continue my efforts.

Timeline

2006

— June 25   Gilad Schalit abducted.
— June 28   Israeli forces launch operation "Summer Rains" in Gaza.
— July 1   Back channel between Israel and Hamas opens: first phone call between Gershon Baskin and Ghazi Hamad.
— July 12   Hezbollah attacks northern border; Udi Goldwasser and Eldad Regev abducted, Second Lebanon War begins.
— Aug. 14   Ehud Olmert appoints Ofer Dekel to the case of the abducted soldiers.
— Sept. 9   Hamas releases first proof that Schalit is alive, a handwritten letter.

2007

— Jan. 7   Fighting erupts between Fatah and Hamas in Gaza.
— June 7   Hamas takes over Gaza.
— June 15   Mahmoud Abbas declares Hamas government illegal; Israel declares Gaza enemy territory.
— June 25   Exactly one year after the abduction, Hamas releases an audio tape of Schalit.
— Nov. 27   Annapolis peace conference is convened.

2008

— May 14   Grad rocket fired from Gaza hits Ashkelon; the situation escalates.

— June 18   Israel and Hamas agree upon an Egyptian-brokered cease-fire.

— July 16   Hezbollah returns the bodies of Goldwasser and Regev in exchange for Israel releasing five terrorists and 199 bodies.

— Sept. 21 Olmert submits resignation after being indicted on charges of corruption.

— Nov. 4   Fighting flares up between Hamas and Israel; Israeli forces enter Gaza for the first time since mid-June.

— Dec. 18   Hamas officially announces end of cease-fire, launches over two hundred rockets into Israel.

— Dec. 27   IDF launches Operation Cast Lead.

2009

— Feb. 10   Benjamin Netanyahu wins government elections.

— March 31 Olmert leaves Prime Minister's Office; Netanyahu enters.

— April 21 Dekel resigns.

— May 31   Netanyahu appoints Hagai Hadas as special envoy for the Schalit case.

— Oct. 2   Eve of Sukkot, Hamas releases video of Schalit.

— Nov.   First draft of agreement is submitted by Gerhard Conrad and rejected by Ahmed Jaabri.

— Dec.   Conrad submits second draft and is thrown out of Gaza. Jaabri fires Mahmoud al-Zahar from negotiating team; Israel accepts, waits for Hamas' formal response to the proposal.

2010

— July 6   Schalit family begins march to Jerusalem and public campaign for the release of Gilad.

2011

— Feb. 11   Following Arab Spring riots, Hosni Mubarak steps down as Prime Minister of Egypt.

— April 13   Hadas resigns.

— April 18   David Meidan appointed.

— July 14   Breakthrough document received and approved by Netanyahu.

— Sep.   Marathon negotiations held between Israeli and Hamas delegations in Cairo.

— Oct. 11   Meidan returns from Cairo with a deal; Israeli government votes in approval.

— Oct. 18   Gilad Schalit comes home.

The fonts used in this book are from the Arno family

The *Toby Press publishes fine writing*
on subjects of Israel and Jewish interest.
For more information, visit www.tobypress.com.